THE
BOOK OF
MYTHS

THE
BOOK OF
MYTHS

AMY CRUSE

ILLUSTRATED

GRAMERCY BOOKS
New York · Avenel

This 1993 edition is published by
Gramercy Books,
distributed by Outlet Book Company, Inc.,
a Random House Company,
40 Engelhard Avenue,
Avenel, New Jersey 07001

Printed and bound in the United States of America

Library of Congress Cataloging-in-Publication Data

Cruse, Amy, 1870–
The book of myths / by Amy Cruse.
p. cm.
Summary: Presents traditional tales from Greek, Roman, Norse,
American Indian, Asian, and other mythologies.
ISBN 0-517-09335-9
1. Mythology—Juvenile literature. [1. Mythology.] I. Title.
BL311.C78 1993
291.1'3—dc20

93–17341
CIP
AC

8 7 6 5 4 3 2 1

CONTENTS

Contents

Contents

LIST OF COLOR ILLUSTRATIONS

Section following page 128

Phoebus Apollo

Artemis and Her Nymphs

The Ride of the Valkyrs

The Old Gods Vanquished

The Chest of Set

Toth and the Chief Magician

Hanuman Sets Fire to Lanka

Jizo, the Children's God

FOREWORD

THE WORLD is comprised of many distinct peoples or cultures and every culture has its myths. Myths are nothing more than stories that people long ago made up to answer the questions that arose in their minds as they tried to make sense of the mysterious and often frightening world in which they lived. Today, every child eventually asks the same questions as those early human beings: What is the sun? How did the stars get into the sky? Where do clouds come from? What is thunder? The list is endless.

Today we have astronomers, geologists, physicists, and sophisticated scientific research to give us the answers to these questions. Early men and women did not. And so, over time, they came up with what were to them logical explanations for the existence and behavior of the natural phenomena around them. Because they themselves were human, they gave human qualities to many of these things—trees, flowers, streams. But they knew these natural phenomena were more than human, and some—the sun, for example—were so wondrous that they really *had* to be more than human. Thus arose the idea of the gods and goddesses, who were far more powerful than mere humans and whose qualities, both good and bad, were responsible for what took place in the natural world.

The gods and goddesses most familiar to the cultures of Western civilization are those of the Greeks and Romans (which are essentially the same gods with different names, the Romans having taken over the Greek gods and added them to their own

Foreword

pantheon) and the Norse gods, whose province is the area now known as Scandinavia.

It is interesting to note that very different cultures that developed geographically far apart sometimes have similar myths. The Greco-Roman story of creation (Chapter 1), for example, is very like that in the Bible, and the Norse story of creation has many parallels to both of these; another example is the Egyptian tale of Isis (Chapter 5), which is remarkably like the Greek tale of Demeter (Chapter 1). Some scholars believe that this is proof that all people had common ancestors. Others discount this theory, citing another that says these separate and distinct groups of early peoples all inhabited the same world with the same natural elements and, therefore, asked the same questions and came up with the same answers.

And so the various cultures explained how the world was created; how humankind came to be; where fire came from; why summer turns to winter; why drought follows a rainy season; how weaving developed; where corn, olive trees, horses, spiders, and tools came from. Myths were created to explain almost everything, and these myths have come to us over the course of history; they have endured because they are, when all is said and done, great and wonderful stories about gods and men and the triumphs and failures common to both.

The language and imagery of myths are with us today. One need only look to our everyday language to see that the gods are still among us: all the planets of our solar system are named for gods and goddesses; cars, missiles, and sneakers are named for them (Mercury, Titan, Nike, Thor); the symbols of the American Medical Association, FTD Florists, and at least one global oil company come from mythology; and the list goes on and on.

Aside from the three major mythologies mentioned above, you will find collected here a rich sampling of myths from many cultures, including the Native American Indian, the Aztec of Mexico, the Aboriginal natives of Australia, and the Japanese, Chinese, Hindu, Egyptian, Babylonian, and more.

Foreword

You will find parallels and distinctions, some familiar stories and others that will be new to you. But, above all, you will find enduring and astonishing proof that it is human nature not only to wonder about the world but also to create a rich and satisfying way to be comfortable in it.

NAOMI KLEINBERG

Pomona, New York
1993

THE
BOOK OF
MYTHS

CHAPTER I

MYTHS OF THE GREEKS AND THE ROMANS

With airs and lineaments divine.
ADDISON

THE Greeks who made these myths lived in a sunny land in southern Europe. Their country was full of beauty; the blue waters of the lovely and peaceful Mediterranean Sea washed their shores. Their climate was warm and delightful and they knew little of the hardships of winter. Their soil was fertile, producing such food as was sufficient for their wants in return for short and easy labour. They had time to enjoy the beauty that lay all around them; and they became a beauty-loving, almost a beauty-worshipping people. Their ambition and delight was to create and increase beauty. They were naturally a finely formed and well-proportioned race, and they set themselves to attain bodily perfection by every means in their power, and especially by regular and carefully planned exercise, so that the standard of grace and beauty among them rose to a height such as no other nation has ever reached. The powers of their minds as well as of their bodies were set toward the attainment of beauty; so that, as the ages went on, they produced works of art—poetry, drama, sculpture, architecture—which are still among the world's greatest treasures.

The gods of such a race would naturally be, before all things, physically beautiful. " As beautiful as a Greek god " is a phrase which is still used among us. They were largely conceived, and given an air of majesty and power which makes them stand in the imagination as beings great and noble in spite of the fact that they did not always act in a noble fashion. For the Greeks, like all the early peoples, did not imagine a god to be a being

The Book of Myths

all-righteous and all-powerful. He was, they thought, in many ways like themselves, sharing their weaknesses and desires, and feeling their temptations; it did not seem to them, as it would seem to us, an unnatural and even an impossible thing for a god to be sometimes cruel or selfish or untruthful. Cunning was with them a quality to be admired, and vengeance an act befitting a deity.

But in spite of these things the spirit of Greek mythology is high and splendid. When we have read its stories the things we remember most clearly are not the fickleness of Zeus, the jealousy of Hera, the cunning of Hermes and the riotousness of Dionysius; we think, rather, of the great and noble qualities such as make Prometheus, Demeter, Apollo, Orpheus, and many other of its heroes the embodiment of that beauty which the Greeks so dearly loved.

Roman mythology is substantially the same as that of the Greeks, for the Romans took over the whole company of the Greek deities, with their myths belonging to them, and added only a small number of their own.

Prometheus and his Gift to Man

There had been ten long years of war between the gods who dwelt on high Olympus and the giant Titans who had rebelled against their rule. At last the war was over, and the triumphant gods, serene and unmolested once more, took up the work of creation which this strife had interrupted. The earth which they had made lay before them, green and fresh and lovely, though in places cruelly torn by the mighty Titans, who had hurled rocks from their places and piled mountain upon mountain in their mad efforts to reach the stronghold of their foes. Above the earth spread the blue sky, with the lights that the gods had made set in it to mark the day and the night; and the river Oceanus flowed round its shores, as they had bidden it do. They had created also the trees and herbs and flowers which covered it and the wild animals that roamed over it, seeking their food from the plenty spread before them.

Prometheus and his Gift to Man

So far all was good; but the work was not finished. The animals were simply living creatures, with no marked qualities and very little to distinguish them from each other. They were stupid and dull, certainly not fitted to make the best of the beautiful world that had been given them to live in. Some further gifts must be bestowed upon them, and a new race of beings must be created, of a higher intelligence, fitted to worship and serve the gods in a manner pleasing to their greatness.

Looking round to see who was fittest to help him in completing this work of creation, Zeus, king of the gods, chose two of the conquered Titans—brothers, named Prometheus and Epimetheus. He put a great store of gifts at their disposal, and Epimetheus at once set to work to allot these to the different animals, while Prometheus overlooked and directed his work. The animals were endowed first with such bodily organs as would enable them to get their food and to defend themselves in the position in which they had been placed, some being given wings, some claws, some scales, some teeth, or beaks, or tusks. Afterward they were given the qualities which would help them to make use of these things—strength, courage, sagacity, patience, fidelity. Epimetheus gave so generously that soon the store entrusted to him by Zeus, great as it was, was exhausted; and the higher beings designed by the god had not yet been created.

Prometheus and Epimetheus consulted very earnestly together before they began this work of creation. "We will make this new being," said Prometheus, "in the likeness of the gods themselves. He shall not bend his face to the earth, but shall stand erect and turn his eyes heavenward." So he took a handful of the dust of the earth, and mixed it with water, and kneaded it into clay; then he shaped of it a figure in the likeness of the gods, which he called man. Next, he appealed to Eros, the god who had first brought life upon the earth, to breathe into this image that it might live; and to Athene he appealed also, begging that the great daughter of Zeus, the goddess of wisdom, would grant to mortal man an immortal, indwelling soul. Eros and Athene, greatly interested in this new work of creation, willingly consented; so now upon

19

the earth appeared a race of beings who, because they had souls as well as bodies, could love and worship as well as serve.

Prometheus, the wise and tender, looked proudly upon man as he walked the earth with his face turned to the stars. The heart of the creator yearned over the being he had created, and longed to give to him more and greater gifts; to light up the soul within him that it might glow with a noble ardour; to make him lord over the lower creation; to lead him from height to height of wisdom and knowledge and power. He thought long of what he could do to bring these things to pass, and at last a great and terrible idea came into his mind. " In the dwelling of the gods," he thought, " is the divine fire which helps to make them all-powerful; it is by means of this fire that the thunderbolts of Zeus are forged. On the earth no fire exists; if I could obtain some and bestow it upon men, all that I desire might be accomplished. But Zeus would never consent to give to man a portion of the sacred fire. I must not dream that such a thing could be."

Yet Prometheus could not drive the idea from his mind. By day and by night he brooded over it, debating how the fire could be obtained. " Could he steal it from the abode of the gods ? " The very thought brought terror. " Swift and merciless would be the vengeance of Zeus on such a thief, more fearful would be his agonies than those already inflicted upon the rebellious Titans. Yet, the fire once given to man, even Zeus could not take it back. Man would be raised for ever above the beasts, and could go on from achievement to achievement, from glory to glory. What, if this could be done, would it matter though Prometheus should suffer the worst tortures the angry god could inflict ? Would not the thought of the godlike race he had nurtured comfort him in his pain, so that he would triumph still ? "

For many days Prometheus brooded over his great plan, until he quite lost sight of his own certain punishment in the splendid vision that rose before him of man inspired and ennobled by the divine fire; and at last he determined to undertake the great adventure. He chose a night when heavy clouds were

Prometheus and his Gift to Man

hung across the sky, so that not a glimpse of the moon goddess's bright chariot could be seen upon the earth. In the thick darkness he set out, going softly and stealthily across the plains lest any should meet and question him. At the foot of Olympus he paused and looked upward to where he knew the shining city of the gods stood on the summit that pierced the heavens.

PROMETHEUS BRINGING FIRE FROM OLYMPUS

Then with dogged courage up and up he went, climbing steadily until he passed through the dark, enfolding clouds and stood in the clear and lovely light that shone upon the dwelling-place of the gods. Twelve fair palaces he saw, their walls like burnished gold ; in their midst the palace of Zeus, highest and most glorious of all. Trees and flowers grew around, so wonderful and so beautiful that Prometheus longed to step aside to touch and smell them ; but he remembered the peril and the greatness of his errand, and he wasted not another instant in gazing on the glories of that heavenly realm. Everything was quiet, and he could see no watchmen on the shining walls. Treading quickly and lightly for all his great stature, he passed into the city which none except the gods might enter, on pain of death.

In a moment he was out again, carrying a reed which he had lighted at the fire of the immortals. The great deed was done.

Back by the way he had come went Prometheus, guarding with fearful care that wavering, sacred flame. If any watchers from heaven or earth had seen that small point of light travelling through the night's blackness there would have been great marvel and questioning, for no light save that of the sun and the moon and the stars had ever shone on the earth. But none saw him, and he returned safely with the divine flame.

Yet Prometheus knew that he had not escaped, and that his punishment was certain. It could not be very long before Zeus would discover that there was fire upon the earth, and to find the thief would be easy for the god of all the world; then, swift and terrible, his bolt would fall. The assurance of this did not frighten Prometheus or lead him to extinguish the sacred flame. He had counted the cost beforehand, and was prepared to pay it to the uttermost. Now he only felt a great desire to spread the fire through all the world, to kindle hopes and aspirations in man and set him in the way of attaining them.

So he began, and laboured without ceasing. He revealed to man the divine fire, and showed him how it would help him in his labours; how it would burn wood and melt metals and fashion tools; how it would cook food and make life bearable in the frozen days of winter; how it would give light in darkness so that men might labour and travel in the night-time as well as by day. He taught them how to dig the fields and grow corn and herbs, how to build houses and cover their roofs with thatch, how to tame the beasts of the forest and make them minister to their master's needs.

And the sacred flame did also a greater work than all these. It gave inspiration and enthusiasm, and urged men on to gain ever higher and greater things. Marvellously the work progressed. Men seized on each art that the teacher introduced

Prometheus and his Gift to Man

to them with a wonderful ardour and energy; no difficulties daunted them and no toil depressed their eager spirits. The whole earth thrilled with their activities, and in the midst moved Prometheus, teaching, guiding, opening out before men's delighted eyes fresh fields for effort and attainment.

Zeus, being occupied with other things, looked but little upon the earth at that time, but there came a day when the points of light scattered over its surface caught his attention, and with a shock of terrible anger he realized that daring hands had stolen heaven's fire. In a voice that sent echoing thunders throughout all creation great Zeus made his accusation, and heaven and earth trembled. Poseidon, ruler of the Ocean, and Pluto, ruler of the Underworld, from their kingdoms thought it well to appear and assure their brother of their innocence; and the other gods and goddesses made haste to protest that they knew nothing of the theft. Yet Zeus was certain that no mortal could have put his foot over the shining threshold of the gods, and very soon his suspicions rested on the mighty Titan, the creator of man. Prometheus was summoned and appeared before him. "Who is it that has stolen fire from heaven?" thundered Zeus; and the Titan calmly answered, "It is I."

Then the anger of Zeus turned to fury, and he seized a thunderbolt to destroy the daring thief; but Prometheus stood so calmly, holding his head high, and looking at death with such fearless eyes, that the father of the gods dropped his bolt and asked in wonder, "Why did you do this thing?"

"Because," answered Prometheus, "I loved man, whom with the help of the gods I had created; I longed to give him some gift that would raise him high above the brute creation and bring him nearer to the gods. I knew of nought that could do this save fire from heaven, and to ask the boon from you, O Zeus, would have been to ask in vain. So I scaled the walls of your city and lit my reed at the flame, and now all over the earth fires are kindled; and in men's hearts too has arisen the flame of a pure and high ambition. Not all your power, O ruler of heaven and earth, can put out those fires, or bring men back to the easy content which marks the beasts of the field."

The Book of Myths

As Zeus listened to these proud words his fury died, and there came in its place a cold and bitter hatred of the being who had thus defied his power; so that he no longer thought of hurling a thunderbolt, deeming that would bring a death too easy for the deserving of such a rebel. He wished to see Prometheus suffer slow and awful and unending tortures, that would not only wring his body, but would seize on his proud spirit and lay it low in agony. So he called to his son, Hephæstus, the god of the forge, who had marvellous skill in the working of metals.

"Take this Titan, this Prometheus, and stretch him upon a rock in the mountains of Caucasus, and fasten him to it with chains that cannot be broken. There shall he lie through endless ages, and none shall succour him. Also I will send an eagle who each day shall devour his liver, causing him fearful torments; and each night the liver shall grow again, so that in the morning his suffering may be renewed."

The gods of Olympus were used to Zeus's fits of passion, and to the terrible punishments that he ordered for those who resisted his will; but at this sentence, which condemned Prometheus to unending agony, even they were aghast. But the Titan himself stood calm and proud, never flinching as he heard the dreadful words.

"Let it be so, O tyrant," he said; "because you are strong you are merciless. My theft has done you no harm; there is still fire and to spare on Olympus. In your selfishness you will not share a privilege though it be to advance the whole race of mankind. Chain me to the rock and leave me to my cruel fate. It may be that not for long you will sit in the high seat of the gods. The word has been spoken, and the fate of Zeus is in the balance."

By this time Hephæstus, ugly and deformed and covered with soot from his forge beneath Mount Etna, had come with his dusky servants, the Cyclopes, to carry out his father's will. Prometheus did not resist, but allowed the god, misshapen yet of tremendous strength, to bear him to his place of punishment. There they fastened him to the rock with chains that could not be broken, and left him to lie without shelter from the sun

Prometheus and his Gift to Man

or the rain, and with none to succour him, through countless ages.

But Zeus, though he had worked his will on his enemy, was troubled. He could not forget the words of Prometheus that threatened him with some vague, dark evil to come. What could harm the lord of heaven and earth? and how had the Titan learnt what was hidden from the gods themselves? He did not guess that the saying of Prometheus concerned a certain nymph [1] named Thetis, whom Zeus had set his heart on marrying. An oracle had declared that the son of this nymph should be greater than his father; if therefore that father were Zeus, the king of the gods would be overthrown by his son. Prometheus had heard of the oracle's prediction, while as yet it had not reached the ears of Zeus, and so he had uttered his warning.

At last his unrest and foreboding determined Zeus to go to the Caucasus and speak with Prometheus once more. There lay the Titan, his great body stretched helpless on the rock, and showing already cruel marks where the sun had burnt and the wind had scourged it. There was the great eagle with horrid beak thrust through the torn flesh devouring the liver within, while the victim writhed in anguish. Yet when he saw Zeus he made no sign of submission, and when the god spoke to him offering him release from torture if he would explain his dark sayings Prometheus refused.

"I suffer," he said, "for the whim of a jealous tyrant. Unjustly I suffer, and I submit because the strength of my oppressor is greater than my own. But I will not acknowledge his power or do his bidding; and I will not accept release as an act of favour rather than of justice."

In vain Zeus bowed his pride, entreating Prometheus to tell him of the dark and terrible danger that threatened his power. The Titan always gave the same answer, and at last Zeus left him and went back to Olympus. Again and again, tormented by the fear which Prometheus had implanted, he returned and

[1] A nymph was a female deity who possessed a lower form of divinity than the gods of Olympus.

25

tried to wring the secret from the tortured giant, but in vain. So through countless ages Prometheus remained chained to the rock, until at last a hero came and released him, as will be told in a later story. And all the while men blessed him as their friend, and the sacred fire still burned and worked among them.

The Apple of Discord

One day when the ocean nymphs were sporting in the water they saw a beautiful little girl baby lying in the hollow of a great wave as happily as if she were in her cradle. In high delight they carried her down to their coral caves at the bottom of the sea, and there they tended and taught her with loving care. They called her Aphrodite, from a Greek word that means ' foam,' and they said that she was a goddess, born of the sea-waves.

Aphrodite, or Venus as she is more often called, grew into the loveliest maiden that had ever been seen by gods or by men. All the ocean deities loved her, and wished her to stay with them always, but the nymphs decided that the time had come for her to know something of the world above the sea. They took her to the surface and very tenderly laid her down again on a great blue wave; and then they called Zephyrus, the gentle south wind, and prayed him to take care of her and bear her safely to land.

With his soft breath Zephyrus carried her toward the island of Cyprus, where a group of fair nymphs stood on the shore ready to receive her. Zephyrus laid her gently down upon the golden sand, and the maidens gathered round in wonder. Beautiful as they were, they saw that she was far more beautiful, and they bent before her, doing homage to her as their queen. They combed out her golden hair and dressed her in shining robes; and then they took her to Mount Olympus and presented her before the high gods.

A throne had been prepared for her and the gods assembled to see this beauty of whom such wonderful accounts had reached Olympus. They did not quite believe all they had been told,

The Apple of Discord

and they were eager to see for themselves how much was true. When she came they freely owned that her loveliness was greater than could be described. The whole company was enraptured. Each one of the gods desired her for his wife. Even Zeus, in defiance of jealous Hera, wooed her openly. But dainty Venus would have none of them, and turned up her bewitching nose even at the great king of the gods himself.

Then Zeus in great anger declared that she should marry the one whom he, whose will all must obey, should choose. He called his son, Hephæstus, from his workshop and commanded the proud beauty to take this man—misshapen and sooty from the forge—as her husband. It was useless to rebel, and with a very bad grace Venus consented.

The marriage took place, but she refused to live in her husband's underground home, and had very little to do with him. She spent most of her time in befriending true lovers upon earth, and the youths and maidens were her devoted worshippers, and raised many temples in her honour.

It happened very often that Venus and Athene were opposed to one another in the affairs of men with which they concerned themselves. Venus nearly always sympathized with the young and beautiful, while Athene had more regard to thoughtfulness and nobility of character. So a sort of rivalry in power grew up between them, and at last they came to an open quarrel.

It happened that a great feast was made at the marriage of Thetis, a beautiful sea-nymph, with King Peleus. Zeus, with all the gods of Olympus, was present. He brought his splendid train to the coral caves under the sea where the wedding was to take place, and the banquet was begun with much rejoicing. In the midst of the merriment there walked into the hall an uninvited guest. It was Ate, the goddess of discord. She had not been asked with the other deities because she was so sour and bad-tempered that wherever she went merriment and good-fellowship were changed into bitter strife. She was very angry at having been slighted and was bent on revenge. Her venomous looks made everybody feel uncomfortable, and when, after a few minutes, she went rudely away, she left discord behind her ;

27

for she threw upon the table a golden apple upon which was written, " To the fairest."

At once many voices claimed the apple, for there were maidens and nymphs and goddesses present at the feast whose title to be considered beautiful none could dispute; but after a time all save Hera, Athene, and Venus withdrew from the contest. Hera claimed the apple as the right of the acknowledged queen of Olympus; Athene urged that there was no beauty so precious as the beauty of mind and spirit; while Venus lifted up her fair face, surprised that there should be any question, for was she not, by the consent of all, queen of beauty?

Bitter words were said and angry looks exchanged. Each claimant called on one after another of the guests to give judgment in the matter, but all shrank from offering an opinion, for to please one must mean that the other two would be offended. At last Zeus, to end the dispute, bade his messenger, Hermes, take the three goddesses to Mount Ida, in Asia Minor, and call upon the shepherd whom they should find there to decide the question. The shepherd was really Paris, son of Priam, King of Troy. At his birth an oracle had predicted that he would bring great misfortune to his family and his native city, and to avoid this he had been taken to Mount Ida and left there to die. But a shepherd had found him and had taken him home and brought him up as his son. When Paris grew to be a man he also became a shepherd. He was a very beautiful youth and all three goddesses were at once charmed with him.

Athene spoke first. She promised him wisdom and glory in the eyes of gods and men if he would award the apple to her. Hera followed and promised wealth and power if she were chosen. Then came Venus. She looked sweetly at the shepherd and for a moment did not speak. Then, when she had given the young man time to realize her marvellous loveliness, she stepped softly up to him and whispered, " Give me the apple, shepherd, and you shall win a bride as beautiful as I am."

Paris could not resist this appeal. Venus's face made him forget wisdom and glory and riches and power and think only of love. Here was the fairest. He would give her the apple.

Pallas Athene and Arachne

So Paris gave judgment in favour of Venus, and henceforward Hera and Athene hated their successful rival and hated Paris too. The decision which he made that day brought about the fulfilment of the oracle's prophecy that he should bring great woe upon his family and his native city, as you will see when some day you read the famous story of the siege of Troy.

Pallas Athene and Arachne

Pallas Athene was, next to Hera, the greatest among the ancient Greek goddesses. She was the goddess of wisdom, and she watched over everything that had to do with the safety and prosperity of the state. She loved peace, but she helped the people to fight when their country was attacked ; and though she bore no weapons, she went armoured in helmet and breastplate, and over her shoulders hung a goatskin to which was fastened a broad and shining shield. This was the ægis, and any person over whom it was cast was safe from all hurt or danger. Athene also taught the people many useful arts—how to till the ground and rear cattle. She invented the rake and the plough, and the bridle by means of which the people might tame the wild horses to their service. To the women she taught the arts of spinning, weaving, embroidering, and all kinds of needlework ; so that as time went on the women of Greece became famed for the beautiful work that they produced.

There was one maiden, named Arachne, whose skill was greater than that of any other woman in the land. People would gather to watch her as she sat at her spinning-wheel and spun the soft, many-coloured wools into fine, even threads, and then wove them on her loom into a web enchanting both to the sight and to the touch. Most marvellous of all it was to see her take her needle and cover the web with pictures such as glow on the canvas of a great painter. Her lovely, smiling face, her white arms and slender, graceful body were as pleasant to look upon as the pictures she created. Nymphs stole from the streams and the woods, and stood on tiptoe looking over the shoulders of the mortals, marvelling at Arachne's wonderful skill.

The Book of Myths

"Athene herself must have taught her!" exclaimed an admiring onlooker one day.

Arachne turned round quickly. Her face was not so beautiful now, there was such an ugly look of pride and scorn upon it.

"Athene teach me, indeed! My skill is equal to hers, and that I would prove if she would match herself against me."

The hearers cried out in astonishment and alarm that a mortal should speak in such terms of the great goddess. But Arachne held to what she had said, and repeated it again and again to other listeners, until all through the land it was known that the boastful maiden had challenged Athene to a contest. Soon the goddess herself heard of it, and though she was very much displeased, she resolved to warn the girl and give her a chance to escape the punishment she deserved.

So, taking the form of an old woman, Athene joined the group assembled to watch Arachne at work. Quietly she made her way to the girl's side.

"Is it true that you have said that your skill is equal to Athene's?" she asked.

"Indeed it is," answered the girl proudly, "and I only wish she could hear me. If she should beat me in the trial I should be quite willing to pay the penalty."

"Maiden," said the old woman kindly, "listen to the words of one who has lived long in the world and seen much. Boast if you will that no mortal can excel you, but do not match yourself against the high gods. Rather, ask pardon of Athene for your presumptuous words. She will forgive you if your repentance is sincere."

Arachne was very angry, and spoke rudely to the old woman. "Keep your advice for those who ask it," she said; "as for me, I repeat that my greatest wish is that Athene should come and let me show what I can do."

"Athene is here," said the old woman, in tones that startled the graceless girl. She turned and saw a tall and gracious figure with noble brow, and deep grey eyes that looked sternly upon her. For a moment she was overawed, but quickly recovered herself and spoke boldly.

30

Pallas Athene and Arachne

"Then I say once more that I am ready for the contest."

The looms were set up and the goddess and the maiden began their work. The bystanders bent in awe before Athene, then watched silently as the deft fingers of the two weavers moved swiftly among wools of rare and brilliant dyes. Soon the pictures began to grow before them. Arachne's showed a sunlit stretch of sea where swelling waves tumbled and splashed so that the onlookers almost felt the salt spray in their faces. Swimming among the waves was a magnificent white bull, his golden horns, round which were twined a careless garland of meadow flowers, glinting in the sun. On his back, holding to one of his horns, lay a girl. Her eyes were wide with fear, but it seemed that the cry of terror coming from her parted lips was arrested as she bent her head to listen to the words of the lordly bull, while a faint flush was creeping back into her whitened cheeks. The girl was Europa and the bull was Zeus himself, who had taken that form because he wished to woo the maiden unnoted by Hera's jealous eye.

Arachne knew, even before she heard the delighted and astonished cries of those who watched, that this was the best piece of work she had ever done. She turned triumphantly and looked at the web of Athene. Then her heart sank, for, conceited as she was, she was yet a true artist, and she recognized that here was work beyond anything that she could accomplish.

Athene had chosen as the subject of her picture the contest that she had held, in the presence of Zeus and all the dwellers on Olympus, with Poseidon, god of the sea. Zeus had decreed that a new and beautiful city, lately founded in Greece, should bear the name of whichever deity could produce the gift most useful to man, and Athene and Poseidon met in rivalry for the honour which both coveted.

Poseidon struck the ground with his trident, and a horse, finely formed, noble and spirited, sprang up. The assembled gods shouted in delight, and declared that nothing Athene could produce could surpass this wonderful animal. When Athene, in her turn, caused an olive-tree to spring up, there were cries of derision and scornful laughter. The goddess,

31

unmoved, proceeded to explain the manifold uses of the tree; and when she had finished, the assembled gods agreed that it was far more valuable than the horse of Poseidon. The city was therefore called Athens.

All this Athene had shown upon her web, with the details as lovely and as lifelike as in the picture of Arachne; but here was a radiance and a glory which clearly showed that the work was done by no mortal hand. The onlookers had admired the web of Arachne; they were awed and enraptured by that of Athene.

No need to ask who was the victor. Arachne knew only too well. She felt she could not live to bear the humiliation she had brought upon herself. A rope was hanging from a beam above her head; she seized it and drew a noose about her neck, intending to hang herself.

But Athene would not allow her thus to perish. "Live," commanded the goddess, "that you may be a warning for all time to those who bear themselves proudly toward the high gods. Live, and spin and weave without ceasing; not as you will, but in the way that the gods have chosen."

She raised her hand and sprinkled upon the girl a few drops of the juice of aconite. At once the lovely colours died out of the maiden's face and hair and hands, and they became a dingy grey. Her head, limbs, and body shrank until only a tiny grey mass was left; her fingers grew threadlike and stood out round this grey mass raising and supporting it. Arachne had become a spider.

Artemis and Orion

Artemis, or Diana, the moon-goddess, was the sister of Apollo, and, like him, loved all woodland pastimes, so that she became also the goddess of hunting. She was tall and straight and strong and very beautiful, and she had many suitors; but she would not marry, declaring that she loved best to be free and live with her nymphs in the forest. Her nymphs also vowed to remain unmarried.

It was a fair sight to see the train of lovely maidens who,

Artemis and Orion

dressed in short green tunics and carrying each a bow and sheaf of arrows, ranged gaily through the forest glades. Artemis went in front, a shining crescent on her head to mark her out as moon-goddess and leader of the band.

One day seven of the nymphs—the daughters of Atlas, and known as the Pleiades—had left the others and were walking by themselves through the shady woodland, when they heard a shout, and saw coming toward them a gigantic youth, comely and handsome in his hunter's dress. This was Orion, son of Poseidon, and he was followed by his dog, Sirius. The Pleiades turned quickly and ran away in the opposite direction, for the nymphs of Artemis were vowed to shun the society of man. The hunter caught only a glimpse of their faces before they turned from him, but in that one glimpse he saw that they were young and beautiful, that their eyes sparkled and their lips smiled. He followed quickly, calling to them to stop, but they only fled the faster. They were strong and lithe and trained to running, so that Orion found it very difficult to catch up to them. On and on they ran, speeding down forest paths and across open glades, and still Orion followed, until at length the strength of the nymphs began to fail, and they called upon Artemis to help them.

Orion saw them flag and came on triumphantly ; but the goddess heard the prayer of her followers, and when Orion put out his hand, thinking to touch the fair form of a maiden, a white pigeon fluttered from his grasp and flew swiftly, with six companions like itself, toward the heavens. Orion watched them in amazement as they mounted higher and higher until they became seven white dots against the blue sky. Then, to his astonishment, the white dots turned to points of light, and there, shining in the heavens above him, he saw a group of seven stars.

Orion turned away in great vexation, but he soon forgot his disappointment and went off on other adventures. Some time after he met Artemis herself, and the two became great friends. Both loved hunting, and were daring and fearless in their favourite sport. Artemis found all her pastimes far more

33

enjoyable when they were shared with this mighty hunter than when her more timid nymphs were her only companions.

Apollo looked with great disfavour upon his sister's friendship with Orion. He feared that she was about to forget her vows as a maiden-goddess, and marry this son of Poseidon who had just the qualities to win her love. He laid his plans very carefully, resolving to put an end to the friendship. He knew that Poseidon had given his son the power of wading or walking through the waves, and that Orion might often be seen far out at sea. He waited for one of these occasions, and then he went to his sister, and talking pleasantly to her, drew her toward the seashore. Then he began to talk of the wonderful marksmanship of himself and his companions, and Artemis, jealous for the honour of her maiden-band, told in her turn of the feats that they had performed.

"All very well!" said Apollo, pretending doubt, "but show me what you can do. Can you hit that black spot far out at sea?" and he pointed to Orion's head, which showed dark above the waters.

Eager to prove her skill, Artemis at once took her bow and shot with such exactness of aim that the black spot disappeared beneath the waves. The goddess turned triumphantly to her brother, who praised her warmly, being delighted that his scheme had succeeded so well.

But the waves lifted the body of Orion and bore it toward the shore, where they laid it gently down in the sight of Artemis; and there, piercing the dark head, was her own arrow.

Artemis wept bitterly, reproaching her brother, and reproaching herself also that she had fallen so readily into his trap. But she could not bring Orion back to life. So she placed him among the stars, and there he shines to this day, with his dog Sirius following and the Pleiades flying before him.

Demeter and Persephone

When the good Prometheus, who had loved men and suffered in their cause, was taken from them men did not forget the arts

Demeter and Persephone

that he had taught them. Year by year the earth grew more fruitful as men diligently dug and ploughed and sowed, so that when the time of harvest came they gathered in bounteous supplies of corn and fruit. Demeter, the sister of Zeus, took the crops under her charge and helped man in all his efforts to turn barren lands into golden cornfields and gardens fair with flowers. She helped him, too, to leave off his rough ways and uncouth customs, and to become gentler and more courteous; to love beauty and find it everywhere—in earth and sea and sky.

Demeter was a tall and stately woman with hair the colour of the ripe corn and kind, smiling, blue eyes. She had tender, motherly ways, and she and her daughter Persephone loved one another dearly. Persephone was like her mother, except that she was slighter and fairer, and her hair made one think of spring daffodils rather than of autumn corn. The two led a busy, happy life, going to and fro in the beautiful valleys and shining uplands of Greece, caring for the crops, blessing man's efforts, and encouraging him to go on to still greater things. Wherever they went soft airs and sweet scents followed them; and shining tracks gay with green grass and rosy blossom showed where they had been working.

Persephone loved especially the flowers. She loved to tend a sunny glade until bright patches broke through the dark earth and spread and glowed and the whole place became a glory of colour and fragrance. There was a vale in the island of Sicily in which her blithe spirit particularly delighted. In that vale it was always spring; the flowers of spring bloomed all through the year—flowers such as Shakespeare has described for us:

> Daffodils
> That come before the swallow dares, and take
> The winds of March with beauty; violets dim,
> But sweeter than the lids of Juno's eyes
> Or Cytherea's breath; pale primroses,
> That die unmarried, ere they can behold
> Bright Phœbus in his strength. . . .
> Bold oxlips, and
> The crown imperial; lilies of all kinds,
> The flower-de-luce being one.

35

The Book of Myths

This valley was Persephone's favourite playground, and on the days when her mother said to her, " Go, my darling, take a holiday to-day and play among the flowers ; it is not good for girls like you to work through all the sunny hours," she would dance gaily off to find her playmates, beautiful, happy maidens like herself ; and they would all go merrily to the valley and laugh and dance and sing and weave bright garlands through the long glad hours.

The world was very fair to Persephone, and she knew nothing of things ugly or sad. She had no idea that far down below the earth lay a region where the sun never shone ; where everything was dark and gloomy. She had seen some of the bright deities who were akin to her mother, but she had never seen dread Pluto, the god of the underworld ; she had never even imagined a being so stern and dark and terrible. But there came a day when she was to see him and to see the kingdom which he ruled.

It was seldom that Pluto appeared on the upper earth, but now and then he came, casting a dark shadow over the fair day. On one of these excursions he came to Sicily and passed by the vale of Enna where Persephone and her friends were playing. When he heard the sound of merry voices he stopped the four coal-black horses that drew his chariot of jet and listened. The happy laughter of light-hearted girls was never heard in his dark kingdom, and it sounded pleasantly in his ear. He left his chariot and walked softly over the springing grass ; then, standing hidden behind a fragrant, blossoming hawthorn, he looked out.

The girls had tired now of their play and were scattered about the lovely valley picking flowers, searching out the sweet violets, filling their hands with yellow daffodils. As they picked they called to one another, and now and then one laughed out gaily ; or some one started a snatch of happy song and the others joined in, clear and full-throated like the birds.

The whole scene made Pluto feel how dark and bare and joyless his own life was ; and then suddenly he saw Persephone, most beautiful amid all the beauty about her, and at once he loved her, and made up his mind to carry her away that she

Demeter and Persephone

might live with him for ever. He crept nearer and nearer to her behind the sheltering hawthorn bushes, then stood still, waiting. Persephone looked up from her flower picking and saw a dark, beautiful face, its great, shining, awful eyes looking at her with an eagerness that seemed like fierceness to the startled girl; but before she could cry out the strong arms of the god had seized her, and were bearing her swiftly to where the four noble horses tossed their impatient heads.

Then indeed she cried out—such piteous, heart-moving cries that her companions raised themselves from their flowers and listened with whitening faces; then rushed toward the place whence the cries came. But by that time Pluto had climbed into his chariot, and still holding Persephone in his arms had taken up the reins and urged his horses forward. The terrified girls saw nothing but a dark object fast vanishing in the distance, heard nothing but the far-away beat of horses' hoofs. Persephone was gone. There lay a trail of crushed and broken flowers that she had dropped, but nowhere was there any trace of her captor. Weeping and trembling the maidens stood, while the bright day waned and the cool breeze of evening sprang up; and when the sky began to redden in the west they saw Demeter coming toward them over the grassy slopes, moving serene and stately, happy in the thought of her day's work well done and the coming meeting with her daughter.

She drew near, and one look at the little group showed her that Persephone was not there; a second look showed her tearful eyes and white, anxious faces, so that even before the frightened girls began to pour out their story she knew that some harm had befallen her darling. She listened and questioned, then quietly turned away, her mind set on the recovery of her sweet daughter. Swiftly she travelled over the island, searching fields and glades, rocks and caverns; and when the darkness came she lit a great torch at the flaming summit of Mount Etna and continued her search.

Morning dawned, and Aurora, the rosy goddess of the day, saw the poor mother, haggard and miserable, still searching for her lost child. Of every one she met, of the winds, the rivers, and the trees, Demeter asked the same question, "Have you seen my daughter Persephone? O tell me where she is gone." But there was no trace of the lost girl to be found through all the sunlit land. It seemed as if the earth must have opened and received her, then closed again, holding her fast.

This, in truth, was what had actually happened. Pluto, driving furiously, in fear lest Demeter should follow him and force him to give back her daughter, saw before him a river, flowing quietly between its flower-strewn banks, so that it seemed to him an easy thing to cross it in his smooth-running chariot. But as the foremost of his horses touched its edge, the river rose as if a great wind had stirred it, and swirled and raged and foamed in such fierce strength that Pluto knew the crossing would be long and dangerous. He did not shrink from danger, but he feared delay ; and so raising the great two-pronged fork that he always carried he struck with it a mighty blow on the earth. Instantly a great chasm opened, and Pluto turned his horses toward it.

A sick horror seized Persephone. What dark and dreadful region was she now to enter ? A moment before she had felt a faint hope rise within her, for she had seen by the raging of the waters that the nymph of the stream was trying to help her, and even now in her uttermost terror she held this hope in her heart. With a swift movement of her deft fingers she unclasped her girdle and flung it far out on the stream, bidding the nymph carry it to her mother ; but she could not see what happened to it, for at that instant the horses leapt into the dark gulf. Down, down, and the earth closed above them, shutting out the little strip of blue sky on which, to the last, poor Persephone had fixed her despairing gaze. Down through steep, dark, narrow passages raced the black horses, until at last their feet stayed upon level ground, and the maid, whose home had been always in the freest, loveliest places of the bright earth, looked round upon the sad and sunless kingdom of Pluto.

Black-robed, stern-faced attendants lifted her from the chariot and brought her into a dark and splendid room in the palace of the king. Servants bearing rich jewelled robes came to wait

Demeter and Persephone

upon her, and others in haste prepared a banquet of rare and costly dishes. King Pluto himself bowed before her, promising if she would be his queen all the riches of his kingdom should be hers. He told her that he was very lonely here in this sad place, but that if she would live with him its gloom would be turned to brightness. His dark face looked kind and sad, and for a moment she pitied and longed to comfort him, but then she thought of her gentle, beautiful mother now heart-broken at her daughter's loss, and she hid her face again and hated the cruelty which had dragged her to this unhappy place. She would not look at the rich robes, she would not taste the wonderful dishes, she did not wish to be the bride of a great king; she only wanted to be with her mother again in her happy home among the flowers.

Poor Demeter was heart-broken indeed when day after day passed and she could find no trace of her daughter. All her time was spent in searching. She neglected the work in which she had delighted, and the corn drooped, the flowers languished, the earth brought forth weeds and thistles. She left Sicily and wandered over Italy and Greece, taking the form of a poor old woman that she might pursue her search without being suspected by those who had taken away her daughter. At last she came to the city of Eleusis, which stands on the seashore near to Athens. Tired and despairing she sat down by the wayside, not heeding the wind or the rain, not caring whether it was night or day, never looking up either at the burning sun or the silver moon; and thus she sat for nine days and nine nights. Then it happened that the daughters of the king of that country passed by and were sorry for this old, forlorn woman, whose aspect was so noble and whose face was so pitiful in its sadness. They spoke gently to her. " Mother," they said, using the word as a title of respect, " why do you sit here all alone ? Come with us, and in our father's palace you shall rest and be comforted."

Demeter looked at the fair young princesses, and they reminded her of her own daughter; and so she went with them, though she did not hope for comfort. At the palace she was kindly received, and her noble, stately bearing made the king and queen feel that here was no common servant, but one who could be trusted with the highest work in their household.

The princesses had a baby brother, named Triptolemus, who was so delicate and sickly that his parents feared he would never grow up to inherit his father's kingdom. The charge of this baby was offered to Demeter, and she accepted it willingly,

DEMETER AND THE BABE OF METANEIRA

for as soon as she saw his little white face and heard his wailing cry her loving heart longed to do something to help him. She took him in her arms and kissed him, and at once his crying ceased, and it seemed to the anxious parents that his face looked less wan and his eyes brighter. Day by day under Demeter's care he grew rosier and stronger. Demeter soon loved him dearly and determined to give him the gift of immortality. One night she took him from his bed, anointed his limbs with nectar, and gently laid him on the red-hot embers of the fire, murmuring over him powerful charms. But his mother had never been

40

Demeter and Persephone

quite easy at leaving her darling son in the charge of a stranger, and from time to time she came to watch over him and see that all was well. It happened that just as Demeter laid Triptolemus on the fire she opened the door, and screaming with terror at her child's danger, she rushed in and snatched him from the flames. Then she turned in anger on the nurse, but her words died unspoken when she saw, not the humble woman whom she had befriended, but a radiant goddess robed in splendour.

"Had you trusted me," said Demeter gently, "I would have given your son the greatest gift that the gods can bestow upon man. But now I must leave him, and he will grow up mortal, as his fathers. Yet I will watch over him, and some day I will return." [1]

Then she left the queen, swiftly and silently, and they saw her no more. Once again she took up her search, wandering from Greece to Italy and back again to her own island of Sicily. One day she came to the banks of the river Cyane, and the nymph of the river saw and recognized her. Taking the girdle of Persephone, which she had carefully guarded, she cast it gently at the mother's feet. Demeter knew it at once as her daughter's, the first trace she had found in all her wanderings, and she looked eagerly round, longing to know more. But the nymph dared not speak, for fear of Pluto, and Demeter walked on, intent on finding some further token, until she came to a beautiful crystal fountain. By its side she sat down to think, and as she sat the murmur of the fountain gradually formed itself into words.

"I have seen your daughter," said the voice, "and I can tell you where she is and how she fares; but first I must tell you my own story. I was once a woodland nymph in Elis, following in the train of the goddess Diana, and I was called Arethusa. One hot day I went to bathe in the river Alphæus, and while the cool water gently lapped my limbs I was happy, deeming myself seen of none. But suddenly the waters were ruffled so that I could no longer see the golden sand below, and there came a sighing sound that turned to a voice calling my name—

---

[1] See the story of Isis and the babe of Queen Astarte, page 198.

41

The Book of Myths

Arethusa! Arethusa!' I sprang from the water in affright, but the voice went on: 'I am Alphæus, the god of the stream I love you. Do not flee from me.' Fast I ran, but the fleet god came behind. Over hill and valley, forest and glade, I fled until my strength was almost spent, and still I heard his voice calling to me, and his footsteps close behind. 'Diana, great goddess, help your poor servant!' I cried; and Diana heard, and sent a mist that hid me from sight. Yet through it I still heard the voice of Alphæus calling. Cold terror took hold of me, cold drops fell from my body. Faster and faster they fell, until my body turned into crystal drops, and I became a fountain. Then I thought I was safe, but a soft wind came from Zephyrus and blew away the mist, and at once Alphæus saw and recognized me. Swiftly he changed himself into a stream, and came hurrying to mingle his waters with mine; but I sprang from my place and rushed over the rocky ground until Diana, pitying me, opened a crevice in the rocks, and into it I plunged. Then for a long time I flowed in silence and darkness within the earth, and I came to the realm of Pluto; and there I saw Persephone sitting on the throne by the side of the dread king. Sad she looked, but queenly, and older than when she played on the sunny fields of earth. I longed to ask how she came to that place, but I feared to stay, and so I flowed on and on until at last I came out once more into the blessed sunlight, in the fair land of Sicily."

Demeter listened eagerly to the tale, and when at length she heard where her daughter was she stood for a while stupefied with amazement; then, recovering, she called aloud for her chariot. Her cry was heard by the nymphs of the field, who hastened to do her will, and in a few moments Demeter was driving with all speed toward Olympus. She did not stay until she was in the presence of Zeus himself; then, alighting, she bowed before him, and said, "Great Zeus, my daughter is a captive in the dark land of Pluto, dragged thither against her will. Send your command therefore to this king of the underworld that he release Persephone and send her back to me, her mother."

Demeter and Persephone

Zeus heard and was troubled. He was unwilling to arouse the anger of Pluto, and would give no assurance to the grief-torn mother. Then Demeter in anger vowed that until her daughter was restored to her the earth should bring forth no fruits, but should lie bare and hard, so that man's labour should fail to bring him food. So the crops, which all this time had been languishing for lack of Demeter's care, now blackened and died, the leaves fell from the trees, the flowers disappeared; everywhere the earth lay bare and hard, and men starved for want of its kindly fruits. Then the people joined their prayers to the prayers of Demeter that Zeus would release Persephone; and at last the great god consented.

" You shall receive your daughter again," he said, " if she has not tasted food while she has been in the kingdom of Pluto; but if she has eaten, the Fates forbid that she should be released."

Full of hope Demeter made haste along the dark way that led to the underworld. There seated on the throne she saw her daughter, no longer the happy maid who had tended the bright flowers by her mother's side, but sad and queenly as Arethusa had said. But when she saw her mother, Persephone sprang toward her with the old love and delight; and Demeter clasped her closely, calling her by the tender, familiar names she had known on earth.

" Who is this that intrudes unbidden into my realm ? " demanded a stern voice. Demeter turned and saw the dark face of Pluto, awful in its anger.

" It is I, Demeter," she replied, undaunted. " I come from high Olympus bearing the command of Zeus that you give me back my daughter."

" That will I not," said Pluto; and Demeter, brave as she was, shrank at the terrible voice. " Tell me, what message did the great Zeus send to me, his brother ? "

" That it was his will that Persephone should return if, while she stayed in your realm, she had not eaten of your food," replied Persephone.

Pluto frowned, for he knew well that Persephone had refused all food that had been set before her, though she had been tempted with many rich and delicious dishes. But at that moment one of his subjects stepped forward.

"This morning," he declared, "I brought to the queen a ripe pomegranate, and of that she ate six seeds. Is it not true, Queen Persephone?"

It was true indeed, and Persephone could only bow her head, weeping bitterly, when she heard the fated words. Pluto laid his hand upon her arm, and drew her back to her place beside him.

PERSEPHONE RETURNS TO THE UNDERWORLD

But the brave Demeter would not give up her attempt to regain her daughter. Once more she made her way to Olympus and appealed to Zeus; and Zeus decreed that for every seed Persephone had eaten she must remain for one month of the year in the underworld, the rest of the year she might spend with her mother. Persephone, though she longed for the brightness of her old home, felt a little glad that she was not to leave Pluto to live always by himself in his gloomy kingdom. His kindness and his sadness had won her pity, and almost her love; she had grown used to the realm of shades, so that it had lost much of its terror.

Thenceforward Persephone lived on earth with Demeter for six months in the year, and during that time mother and daughter went about their old work, and the land blossomed and was fruitful. But when Persephone returned to Hades Demeter sorrowed for her daughter and refused to bless the earth, so that it lay bare and hard, and brought forth no fruits for the food of man.

Phaeton and the Fiery Steeds

Phaeton and the Fiery Steeds

In one of the lovely valleys of Greece dwelt the nymph Clymene, wife of Apollo, god of the sun. She had four children— three tall, graceful daughters and one little golden-haired son, named Phaeton. His mother when she looked at him thought of her husband and sighed because he could not see this boy who was so like himself ; for Apollo because of his many duties came but seldom to the quiet home in the valley, and Hera would not suffer his wife and children to dwell near high Olympus. So it happened that Phaeton could not remember his father, whose latest visit had been paid when his son was but a babe.

Clymene, however, talked every day to the children about their father. On summer days as they wandered in the valley she would point to the glowing sun and say, " See, your father drives his glorious chariot across the heavens, giving light and warmth to the world. None is as great as he, none as good, for without him all things on earth would fade and perish, and man himself would die. You are the children of the mighty Sun-god, bright and beautiful, from whom come all good things. Rejoice and honour your father, who is loved by gods and men."

It was natural that the children should grow up proud of their parentage and accounting themselves raised above other less fortunate children, whose fathers were but mortals. Phaeton especially gloried in his high birth ; for him his father was the greatest of all the gods, greater than Zeus himself. Deep in his heart the boy cherished a great ambition. He never spoke of it even to his mother, for he knew that to others it must appear a foolish idea. But often as he watched the rosy glow of dawn, the crimson glory of evening, or the shining pomp of noonday, he would say softly to himself, " Some day perhaps I may drive my father's chariot across the heavens," and the thought of that swift, triumphant passage would make his heart throb with fearful joy. He could not help talking to his playmates of the father of whom he was so proud, and after a time this angered them, and they began to jeer at him.

45

The Book of Myths

"If Apollo is indeed your father," they said, "why does he never come here to visit you? Our fathers dwell with our mothers at home; yours, you say, dwells on high Olympus. It is a fine tale, but we do not believe it. You cannot give us any proof of what you claim, so cease your boasting and let us hear no more about this wonderful father."

The mocking words hurt Phaeton as if the boys had struck him, and burning with indignation he rushed home and poured out the tale to his mother. Clymene was as indignant as her son, for it seemed to her a terrible thing that any should cast doubt on her children's parentage.

"I cannot give you a sign that will convince these mockers," she said, "but go, find your father, he will show you how to deal with them. You are old enough now to make the journey, and the way lies straight before you. You must travel on, always eastward, until you come to the Sun Palace. You will know it by its brightness, the glory of which can be seen from afar. Enter, and you will find your father. Greet him, and tell him your errand, and he will certainly help you."

Phaeton rejoiced when he heard his mother's words. All his anger vanished, and he was so impatient to be gone that he could scarcely wait to say good-bye to his mother and his sisters. The secret hope within him grew stronger, and the thought that it might possibly soon be fulfilled made his heart beat wildly. He went swiftly on his way, travelling ever eastward, until at last he came to the Land of the Rising Sun, and saw his father's palace shining before him. Beams of dazzling light spread from it, and he went on more slowly, shading his eyes with his hand. The palace was supported by slender, graceful, golden pillars, inlaid with precious stones; its golden pinnacles and turrets shone with diamonds and emeralds, sapphires, rubies, and amethysts. It had twelve doors of silver, on which were carved the twelve signs of the Zodiac; and when he had passed through one of these doors Phaeton saw still more wonders within. The ceiling was of polished, softly shining ivory; on the walls were painted marvellous pictures glowing with deep, rich colour. Most wonderful of all was the great golden throne on which was

Phaeton and the Fiery Steeds

seated Apollo himself. Phaeton, as he looked, felt that even his mother's loving descriptions had not prepared him for the beauty, the majesty, and the sweetness of this glorious being. He did not know that he himself was a smaller, less dazzling

THE SIGNS OF THE ZODIAC

copy of the great god, but Apollo at once recognized his child. He watched the youth who came resolutely up the hall, trying to be brave and hold his head high, then stopped, abashed as he neared his father's throne. Apollo stretched out his hands and drew the trembling boy forward.

"You are my son," he said, "come from the fair vale where

dwells my loved Clymene. Do not tremble. Apollo's son has nothing to fear in the palace of his father. Tell me of your mother and your sisters, and why you have come here to seek me."

Phaeton began to speak low and timidly, telling his father what he desired to know ; but very soon he forgot his awe, and his voice grew quick and eager as he told of his companions' gibes and their disbelief in his divine birth.

" They would not believe that the Sun-god was my father," he finished. " They asked for proofs, and I had none to give them ; and so my mother sent me here that I might beseech you, O great Apollo, to testify to my sonship, and close the mouths of those who jeer."

He looked at his father anxiously. The Sun-god rose, and laid his hand on the boy's shoulder. " It was time indeed," he said, his eyes flashing fire, " that you came to me when such things are said among the children of men, to whom each day I bring the light and warmth by which they live. Doubt not, the proof you seek shall be given you. Ask of me anything you please, and I swear to you by the dread river, the oath which the gods break not, that I will give it you. So shall you confound these mockers."

Then Phaeton's breath came fast and his heart beat wildly. The great moment had come, the thing he had longed for would be his if only he had courage to grasp it. He spoke softly, but clearly. " Grant me, O my father, this boon—that I may for one day drive your chariot across the heavens. So shall men see me in your place and know that I am your son."

The words pierced Apollo like a sword-stroke. He sat down on the golden throne, his face grave, his eyes full of tender pity, though his mouth was sternly set.

" Nay," he said, " my son, you know not what you ask. Not one of the gods on high Olympus, not great Zeus himself, can drive my chariot. I alone can drive it. Ask me some other boon. Look round on the wide earth and the spreading heavens and fear not to ask for any treasure, however great or precious. Only this one thing ask not."

Phaeton and the Fiery Steeds

But Phaeton could not give up his heart's desire, the thing for which he had yearned in secret through his childhood and his youth. All other things were as nought to him; not all the treasures of earth and heaven could tempt him to forego his request. His longing gave him boldness to say: "Your oath, my father."

Then Apollo, seeing that his son's heart was set upon this thing, was greatly troubled. He repented his hasty words and the oath that he had sworn; yet because he had sworn it he could not say to his wilful son, "This boon I will not grant you"; for the oath by the dread river is the oath that the gods break not.

"It is true, my son," he said, "that I have sworn to grant you any boon that you may ask. But this which you desire is death—death to you and destruction to the fair earth with those that dwell upon it. Think of your mother and your sisters in their quiet, happy home; think of the glories of the world, the high hills, the spreading fields, the glorious cities, the palaces and their treasures. Do not doom all these to destruction in your wilfulness. Ask of me some other boon."

Then Phaeton thought, "My father speaks as the old speak who have forgotten the fiery longings of youth. He deems me but a babe who cannot guide a team of horses. I will show him that I am able to do the work of a man, yea, of a god." So he answered: "O my father, on my head be the punishment, if punishment there must be."

"Pause yet," said Apollo, striving with all his arts to restrain the wilful boy from his own destruction. "To drive my steeds is no easy task. You see me day by day making my prosperous way across the heavens, and it seems to you that it is nought but a splendid progress from glory to glory. I tell you it is not so. The path I travel is beset with difficulties. Monsters, huge and horrible, lie in wait for me. The lion raging in anger, the bull whose strength is such that he cannot be overthrown, the sly, malicious crab, and, worst of all, the scorpion with poisonous, deadly fangs. Think of these. Think how from the chariot of the sun come scorching rays, blinding to the eyes

49

of mortals. Remember the dizzy height at which you ride. Think how difficult it is to keep a straight course, and yet how terrible will be the consequences if your chariot approach too nearly the earth or the heavens. My steeds are fiery and hard to rule, scarcely can I myself guide and restrain them. Think of all these things, and think, too, of the pangs that will tear my heart if you force me to send my own son to destruction."

Phaeton for the first time hesitated, not because he feared the dangers of which Apollo had spoken, but because he could not bear to hear how his father's voice broke over these last words. Yet he could not give up his plan. " My father will rejoice with me when I come back to him successful," he thought ; " his brief suffering will be forgotten then." So again he looked up steadfastly and said : " Yet let me go, my father. On my head be the consequences."

Apollo, for his oath's sake, could no longer refuse. Moreover, it was time his chariot was brought out, that a new day might begin. Sadly he signed to rosy-fingered Dawn, who stood near by, and she flung wide the gates of the morning. There stood the golden chariot that Hephæstus had made, diamond-studded, dazzling to look on. Its four steeds tossed their golden manes and pawed the ground, impatient to be off. The stars seeing it, retired one by one, the day star last of all ; the moon veiled her face, and a faint rosy glow shone down upon the earth. Phaeton, flushed and happy, seized the reins, while Apollo rubbed on his body a cooling unguent which should help him to bear the fierce heat.

" Drive carefully, my son," he entreated, " and keep a middle course. Hold the reins firmly, but do not use the whip." Then, looking sadly at the bright, eager face, he made a last attempt to dissuade the boy from his purpose. " Will you not now, at the last moment, let me mount in your place ? Death waits for you in the way."

Phaeton shook his head, and gave his father a farewell look of adoring love, then gathered up the reins. The horses bounded away, and Phaeton exultant, breathless, feeling that life had nothing to offer equal to the glory of this exploit, bent all his

Phaeton and the Fiery Steeds

skill to guiding the chariot aright. The horses missed the firm
master hand which had known how to control their every movement ; they quickened their pace and dashed recklessly on.

The swift motion roused in Phaeton a wild excitement, so that
with shining eyes he urged them forward instead of checking them.
Heedless of everything save the joy of that lightning rush, he
took no care to keep in the path marked out for him, and soon
he saw, with a thrill of terror, that his steeds had borne him

PHAETON

far from the track, and that the monsters of whom his father
had warned him were very near. In haste he tried to turn the
horses back, but they would not obey his guiding hand ; then, in
anger, he took up the whip and lashed them furiously. From that
moment all his control over them was lost. They dashed hither
and thither ; they approached the earth, and at once the rivers
began to dry up, the trees and plants to wither, and great tracts
to shrivel and blacken. Horrified, Phaeton tried to turn them
upward, but they took no heed to the rein. Lower they went,
and fires sprang up all over the earth. Mountain tops flamed
like giant torches, great cities fell into heaps of blackened ashes,
men were consumed in thousands, and the nymphs of wood

and river perished. Poseidon [1] himself with his wife and children took refuge in the deepest caves under the sea, fearful lest ocean itself should be dried up.

Through all this confusion and terror Zeus, in high Olympus, slept, until at last he was roused by the clamour of agonized voices calling on his name. Up he rose, and saw, dismayed, the havoc of the fair earth. He shouted to the clouds to make a screen to shield men from the heat, but there was not a cloud left to do his will. Then, in fierce anger, he took a bolt from his dread armoury and hurled it swift and sure to where Phaeton still sat in his chariot bewildered, hopeless, and miserable. Then Death, of which his father had warned him, came to the ambitious boy, and he fell in his brightness down, down like a falling star, until he reached the river Euridanus, where just enough water remained to quench his glowing ashes.

Then Apollo sadly regained command of his chariot and brought his fiery steeds back to their old obedience, while Zeus set to work to repair the damage which had been done to the homes of men. Yet when the story was told many pitied Phaeton and mourned for the daring, beautiful boy who had ventured and lost his life. Clymene and Apollo lamented together for their son ; the three sisters journeyed to the place where their brother had fallen and stood by the river side weeping day after day bitter, unceasing tears; until the gods in pity turned them into tall poplar trees, and their tears to drops of amber. Phaeton's friend, Cycnus, sought in the stream for the ashes of that loved body, searching diligently, and singing as he searched a sad song of mourning ; until the gods, pitying him too, turned him into a swan. Still he floats and sings, and often thrusts his head deep into the water, seeking ever for the ashes of his beloved friend.

Hermes, Messenger of Zeus

Atlas, the Titan who bore up the firmament on his shoulders, had seven beautiful daughters called the Pleiades who were

[1] The god of the sea. He is also known as Neptune.

Hermes, Messenger of Zeus

nymphs in the train of Diana. The second of these, named Maia, was the most beautiful of them all. Zeus saw her one day as she roamed about the fair country near Mount Cyllene ; immediately he loved her, and did not rest until he had won her love. In secret she became his wife, and because it was necessary to hide themselves from jealous Hera's watchful eye, they made their home in a cave on the slopes of the mountain. Here their little son was born, and to him they gave the name of Hermes.

When Hermes was only a few hours old the nymphs who were his nurses laid him in a cradle in the cave and left him sleeping, while his mother slept in her bed near by. As soon as they were gone Hermes raised his head and looked around him. He was tired of lying in his cradle, and he wanted to see something of the world outside. Very quietly, without rousing his mother, he crept out of his cradle and left the cave. It was drawing toward evening, and the sky was full of drifting, rosy-tinted clouds. Hermes watched them with delight as he made his way down the side of the mountain, going swiftly and easily over the rough path. Soon he came to a broad green meadow, where a great herd of cattle, belonging to Apollo, were feeding. " I am hungry," said Hermes to himself, " and a meal of roasted ox flesh would suit me very well." So he drove off fifty of the oxen, first taking care to fasten bunches of leaves round their hoofs that they might leave no tracks. Then he killed two of them, cooked some of their flesh, and made a hearty meal. The rest of the oxen he hid in a cave, and then, very well pleased with his night's adventures, he blithely turned toward home. As he was about to enter the cave on Mount Cyllene, he saw a tortoise making its slow way over the rocks. " This is a curious creature," he thought, and he picked it up and examined it. An idea struck him as he saw the hollow shell which formed its outer covering ; so he killed the tortoise and took off this shell. Across it he fastened some strings, and touching them with his light, quick fingers he drew from them entrancing sounds such as had never been heard on the earth before. He laughed gleefully, and, carefully holding his treasure, in a flash he had crossed the cave and lain down once more in his cradle.

The Book of Myths

Morning came, and Apollo looked out over the earth, seeking his oxen. In the broad meadow before Pylos he saw but a scanty sprinkling where at evening there had been a great herd. "What thief has stolen my oxen?" he cried; and then by his divine power he knew that it was the babe Hermes, news of whose birth had been brought to Mount Olympus only the day before. Swiftly he transported himself to the cave on Cyllene, and entered in a great rage.

"Where is Hermes," he cried, "the thief who has stolen my cattle?"

Maia, the lovely nymph, bowed before him, and answered, "Hermes is but a babe, my lord, scarce a day old. What can he know of your cattle?" She led Apollo to the cradle where her son lay, his bright eyes closed, and his breath coming so evenly and peacefully that it seemed impossible to doubt that he was fast asleep. He looked so tiny and so innocent that his mother turned reproachful eyes on Apollo, deeming him mad to bring so wild a charge against this one day's babe.

But Apollo knew more about Hermes than did his mother. Shaking him roughly by the shoulder he cried, "Come now, thieving rascal, rouse yourself and tell me where you have hidden my oxen." Hermes opened his eyes with an innocent baby stare, and pretended that he understood nothing of what had been said to him. To Apollo's rough words he answered only with a chuckling baby laugh and pretty gurgling noises. Apollo, not a whit deceived by this cunning, grew more and more angry. At last he snatched Hermes from the cradle, and though the frightened Maia wept, and pleaded with him to restore her child, he insisted on bearing him off to Olympus, that Zeus might judge between them.

Sternly the King of the gods looked at his son, who lay in Apollo's arms. "Tell me," he said, in the voice whose commands neither men nor gods dare disobey, "have you stolen the oxen?"

Hermes no longer ventured to pretend ignorance, and answered, quite without shame, "I have."

"Go then," thundered Zeus, "restore them to Apollo, and think not thus to trick the gods of high Olympus."

Hermes, Messenger of Zeus

Together the baby god and the great Apollo journeyed toward Pylos, and there Hermes led the cattle from their hiding-place and restored them to their rightful owner. Then he sat down on the grass by the wayside, took out the lyre he had made from the shell of the tortoise, and began to play. Apollo stayed the angry words with which he was declaring that Hermes must pay for the two missing oxen. He himself was the god of music, and had marvellous skill upon the pipes, but such sounds as these he had never heard. "Show me," he cried, "this wonderful instrument"; and Hermes, laughing within himself at the success of his device, put his lyre into Apollo's hands. The god drew his fingers across the strings, and again the sweet notes sounded. To the music-loving Apollo this new instrument was more wonderful and precious than all the treasures of Olympus.

"Give it me," he cried, "and I will forgive all that you have done, and say no more of the missing oxen."

"A music-breathing lyre for a supper!" said the secretly delighted Hermes. "That were a bad exchange."

"I will give you also my magic wand, Caduceus," said Apollo, holding out his staff to the boy; for Hermes was no longer a babe, but a tall, lithe, handsome youth, with quick-glancing, merry eyes.

"What is the good of that?" he asked, taking the staff and using it as a leaping pole. "It is but a common stick."

"It will reconcile any two—men, beasts, or elements—that are in conflict," replied Apollo.

Hermes looked around him. On the borders of the wood close by were two snakes with up-reared heads, thrusting out their forked tongues, and hissing fiercely at one another. He thrust the staff between them, and immediately they forgot their quarrel and wreathed themselves round the stick, intertwined; and from that day forward the Caduceus bore always the two intertwined serpents.

So Hermes gave the lyre to Apollo, and peace was made between them; and the next time he visited Olympus he was received by Zeus very graciously. The great King of the gods noticed with pleasure the agile figure of his son, his springing

55

step, his bright eye, his air of alertness and vigour. " This
boy shall be my messenger," he determined, " to do the errands
of the gods, and bear their commands to men." Forthwith he
called his son, and told him his will, and Hermes was well pleased ;
for to speed from place to place, busy and important, to do the
errands of the gods and know their secrets, seemed to him the
most desirable of all lots. Zeus gave him a pair of golden-
winged sandals, which enabled him to travel with marvellous
swiftness ; and the other gods gave him a broad-brimmed,
winged hat, which made his face look brighter and more charming
than ever.

After this he helped Zeus in many of his undertakings, and
was, perforce, let into many of his secrets ; and Zeus found the
quick and ready wit of his son extremely useful. Hera grew
more and more jealous, and Zeus was obliged to take many
precautions to prevent her finding out that there were mortal
maidens in whose company he delighted.

One of these maidens was Io, daughter of the river god Inachus.
She was very lovely, with gleaming, pale gold hair, cheeks faintly
rose-tinted, and softly shining blue eyes. Zeus loved to wander
with her in the meadow close by her father's river home, and
meeting her there one summer afternoon, he spread a cloud
over the place that they might not be visible to the eyes of
Hera. But the Queen of heaven, looking out, wondered to see
a cloud in one particular spot when everywhere else there was
brilliant sunshine, and she at once guessed that its object was
to hide something from her eyes. Angry and suspicious, she
searched the palace, and all the haunts of Zeus on Olympus,
and not finding her husband, she quickly set off toward the
earth. She brushed away the cloud and saw Zeus standing in
the green meadow, and by his side a beautiful white heifer ;
for he had been warned by the sudden glare of sunshine that
came as the cloud was removed, and had instantly transformed
Io into a shape in which he believed she would be safe.

Hera, though she was sure she had been tricked, did not
quite know of what to accuse her husband. She began to praise
the heifer, saying how white it was, and how graceful. " Where

Hermes, Messenger of Zeus

does it come from ? " she asked, " and to whose herd does it belong ? "

" It is of no herd," replied Zeus; " it is formed newly from the earth."

" Then," replied Hera, " I pray you, my lord, give it me ; for as soon as my eyes rested on it I greatly desired it."

ZEUS AND IO

Zeus now found himself in a fix. He was unwilling to give Io into the power of Hera, but he did not know how to deny the queen's request. So he said, " Be it as you desire, my queen," and Hera triumphantly led the heifer away. She determined that there should be no chance of Zeus recovering the animal, who she felt sure was really a maiden, so she gave her into the charge of Argus. Argus was one of her servants, a giant who had a hundred eyes, and while some of these were closed, the others kept watch. Zeus tried in every way he could think of to come to Io's relief, but he could not elude the watchfulness of Argus; so poor Io wandered miserably about the meadows all day, and at night was tied up to a tree. One day, as she stood by the riverside, she saw her father Inachus rise from the water, and she lowed piteously trying to tell him her story. Inachus saw that this was no ordinary heifer; he came and stood by her side, and she looked up at him with tearful eyes. She could not utter words, but she lifted her hoof and scratched on the sand of the river the letters of her name, " Io." Then Inachus knew that this was his lost daughter, and he wept sorely; but his power was not great enough to override that of Hera, and he was obliged to go away and leave his poor child in her painful captivity.

Argus the hundred-eyed had not failed to see everything that happened at this meeting, and the story was carried to Hera. " So the heifer is a maiden, as I thought," said the angry queen, " and her name is Io. Leave her not for one moment, good Argus, and if my lord approaches her, send me word instantly."

At last, Zeus, despairing of helping Io by his own efforts, told the whole story to Hermes, and bade him try to make a plan by which the maiden might be rescued. " Only close Argus's eyes for a short space while you bring my poor Io to me," he said, " and I will do the rest."

Hermes agreed willingly, for it was a task such as he loved. When evening came he hastened down from Olympus, laid aside his cap and his sandals, and with his staff and pipe approached the place where Argus sat on a grassy bank, watching the white heifer that wandered unhappily through the pleasant valley. Hermes took out his pipe and began to play, and Argus, who had never before heard the music of the Syrinx, as this pipe was called, was delighted. Hermes played soothing, quiet strains which he hoped would lull the giant to sleep; but although some of his eyes were closed, there were many still gleaming like stars through the dusky air. Then Hermes began to tell stories in a low, monotonous voice, and more of his eyes closed; but still points of light shone through the dusk, and Hermes knew that the giant was still watching. He went on and on, droning out the story of how Pan had invented the Syrinx whose music had charmed Argus a little while before. As he spoke he saw to his delight one after another of the starlike points disappear, and when he finished not a single one was to be seen. Argus was asleep.

Up leaped Hermes and his sword flashed out ; one stroke and the head of Argus with its hundred eyes rolled on the grass. Hermes did not stay to triumph, but bounded toward the white heifer, and began to lead her quickly away. Swift as his movements had been, they had not been swift enough to outwit Hera. From Olympus she had seen the slaying of Argus, and now, quick as a lightning flash, she sent an enormous gadfly to torment the poor heifer. Driven to madness by the agony of the cruel sting, Io rushed wildly away, disregarding all the efforts of Hermes to take her where Zeus awaited her. Through rivers, over wide plains, and across mountains she rushed in frenzy. She swam across the sea, which has since been called " Ionian " in memory of her flight, and roamed from country to country till she reached the Thracian strait, henceforward called the Bosphorus ; then on and on until at last she reached Egypt. On the banks of the Nile, Zeus, having at last gained permission from the angry Hera, restored her to her natural form. She became once more a fair nymph, and returned to her father and sisters in her river home. As for Argus, who had met such a sad fate in her service, his hundred eyes were taken by Hera and set in the tail of the peacock ; and she took this bird as her emblem in memory of her faithful servant.

Midas and the Golden Touch

It happened in the days when the gods of Olympus ruled over men that the people of Phrygia were in sore trouble. Their king was dead and had left no heir, and they knew not where to look for a ruler. In this difficulty they did as the Greeks were used to do—they consulted an oracle, that is, an inspired priest or priestess. The oracle replied that he who came riding to them in a wagon should be their king. The saying perplexed the Phrygians greatly, and a number of them were assembled

The Book of Myths

in the market-place discussing its meaning when there came riding toward them in a wagon a countryman named Gordius, with his wife Cybele, and his little son Midas. Their appearance seemed to the Phrygians a direct fulfilment of the oracle's words. At once they rushed to Gordius, acclaimed him as their king, and bore him away to the temple from which the oracle had spoken that he might be solemnly appointed to the royal office. Gordius, greatly surprised and honoured by being thus chosen, accepted with humility and thankfulness, and offered up to Zeus the wagon that had brought him his advancement. He fastened it in its place in the temple by a knot which no one was able to undo, and which in later times was called the Gordian knot.

Gordius, although he was but a poor countryman, was sensible and quickwitted, and he ruled ably over the Phrygians for many years. His son Midas was in many ways unlike his father. He loved music and dancing and revelling, and the great god of his worship was Dionysus, god of wine. But most of all he loved gold. One day when he was quite a child he had tired himself with play and was lying among the grass, quite still and half asleep, when a company of ants, each bearing a tiny grain of wheat, came toward him. They crawled over him until they reached his mouth, where each left his grain, and retreated whence he had come. This was said by the wise men of the country to be a sign that Midas would one day be the richest man in all the world. The boy was delighted at this saying, and henceforward in his dreams he saw himself always with a store of gold—chests and coffers full of the precious metal, a palace overflowing with golden treasures, gold shining on his clothing, gold everywhere, before his eyes and beneath his fingers.

In the course of time Gordius died and Midas became king, and succeeded to the treasure laid up by his father. This was not great, for the countryman, although he had kept the simple, frugal habits of his early life, had been very generous to such of his subjects as had been in want, and, besides, had not understood the arts by which riches are gathered. With Midas this was different. He had already amassed a store of gold which was a

Midas and the Golden Touch

large one for a young man, and now that he was king he set to work, steadily and resolutely, to amass more. Year by year his store grew, until he was a very rich man indeed ; but still he was not satisfied. This way of gathering gold, he thought, was a slow process. He walked about his palace, thinking how delightful it would be if everything in it were made of gold ; if the gleam that he loved to see were reflected from walls and floors and furniture, so that, to delight his eyes and charm his fingers, it would be no longer necessary to go to his storeroom and open his great coffers ; he need simply walk from room to room, sit at his meals, or lie on his bed.

One day he heard a commotion outside his palace, and presently his servant came in and said that an old man had been found lying in a drunken sleep in the royal rose gardens, and that the gardeners had brought him to the palace to ask the king's will in the matter. Midas commanded the man to be brought before him, and when this was done he recognized him at once as Silenus, the

MIDAS, DIONYSUS, AND SILENUS

tutor of the god Dionysus, and a very great favourite with his master. It appeared that in the revels of the evening before Silenus had drunk too much wine, and had been unable to join his merry companions in the dance which had ended the festivities. He had strayed into the rose garden, and after doing some damage to the flowers in his drunken antics, he had lain down and gone to sleep.

The servants of Midas were very much surprised at being told to pay all respect to this unseemly looking stranger, to provide him with robes befitting the highest rank, and to prepare the king's chariot for a journey. Midas and Silenus entered the chariot and were driven to the place where Silenus knew the god was to be found. When he heard what had happened, Dionysus rose from the couch where he had been sleeping after the night's revels, and came himself to thank Midas for what he had done. The god was young and very beautiful, with dark eyes shining in his flushed face, and red, smiling lips ; his tumbled curls were a glossy black, and on them he wore a wreath of ivy leaves.

" You have brought me back old Silenus," he said to Midas, " and I love him, though many think that a graver and more sober tutor would better beseem my godhead. Now ask of me a boon, for by the red juice of the vine which is my token, I swear to give you anything you desire."

Midas did not hesitate, for he had long made up his mind as to the thing he most desired, though he had never dreamt that the chance of possessing it would come to him. He bowed before Dionysus, and said : " Great god of vineyards, son of Zeus, grant me I pray you that whatever I touch may turn to gold."

Dionysus looked at him in astonishment, believing that he jested ; but seeing the king's earnest face he laughed out merrily. " Be it so," he said; " when you cross the threshold of your home this gift shall come to you. Fare you well."

Midas hastened back to his palace, scarcely able to believe in his own good fortune. He alighted from his chariot, and, entering his door, laid his hand on a carved bench that stood within. At once it changed from dark oak to shining gold, and Midas perceived with delight that the god had kept his word. He went from room to room, touching walls and benches and tables, until at last his dream was fulfilled, and everywhere around him, before his eyes and beneath his feet, was gold. The gleam of it dazzled him, and he felt almost dizzy with the fulfilment of his highest ambition. His robes had long since turned to cloth of gold, and he looked a splendid figure when he summoned his servants and bade them prepare a great feast in honour of the gift bestowed upon him, and to set forth the choice wines and rich dishes that befitted so great an occasion.

Midas and the Golden Touch

He sat down to the table, touched the platters and goblets, and saw them all put on the gleam that he loved; and then, for the first time, a horrible misgiving took hold of him. For when he tried to eat some of the delicious viands that had been prepared for him, he found that as soon as a morsel touched his lips it turned to hard gold; he lifted his goblet to drink the choice wine, but only succeeded in filling his mouth with melted gold. After a time he rose from the table, hungry, weary, and with the horrible misgiving grown into an over-mastering fear. Was he doomed to starve with all this treasure around him? Was it death that he had begged of the merry, laughing god? He tried to drive his fears away, telling himself that it would be absurd to give up so wonderful a gift for such a small matter as eating and drinking, and that the wise men of his kingdom would certainly find some way to overcome the difficulty. So he went, tired and dispirited, to his magnificent golden bed, and there soon fell asleep and forgot his perplexities.

Next morning, with the sun shining brightly, it was easier to be hopeful, and Midas got up early and went out into the palace garden, exercising his power there as the evening before he had exercised it within doors. His servants brought him food, and he tried to eat it; but again it was gold upon which his lips closed. He put by cup and platter with a sigh, and bade his heralds summon all the wisest men in his realm to assemble immediately in the palace and consult on an urgent matter with their royal master.

The council met, and the problem was gravely argued, but not one of the wise men could tell how this difficulty—the difficulty of keeping the king alive—could be successfully met. Some suggested one thing, some another, and trial was made of all; but still not one morsel of anything but pure gold could be placed in the king's mouth, and Midas dismissed the council with hard and angry words.

For the rest of that day he sat brooding by himself, miserable and defiant. He could not, would not, give up the power that he had won. He himself would find some way, since these use-less wise men could not. His head ached, and he was faint with hunger, but he held doggedly to his resolve, and vowed that he would not turn aside from the path he had chosen, though he saw Death waiting for him in the way.

After a night of exhausting, unrefreshing sleep, he woke to yet another new day; and now his mind was changed. As he opened his eyes and saw the bright gleam of the sun's rays on his golden furnishings he hated it with a great and bitter hatred. The sight of his golden gown filled him with loathing, and he thought of his subjects—the shepherds, the herdsmen, the peasants—moving about in their poor huts with coarse, homely things, dingy and worn with long use, around them, and he envied them with a passion that brought tears to his eyes. He thought of cool, white linen, and shuddered at the touch of his golden coverings; he remembered how he used to lave his face in cold, fresh water, and he longed with a painful longing to do so once again. He was faint with hunger, and a cup of wine would have given him a little strength; yet he could not have it because he had exchanged all the good things of life for this ugly, hard, glittering gold.

Soon he resolved what he would do. He would go to Dionysus and entreat him to take back the gift he had bestowed. He would cast forth every morsel of gold from his house, and henceforward live in simplicity among the cool, green, living beauties of the forest. Surely the god would not refuse his prayer, and would give him back his life and his happiness.

The chariot was ordered, and soon Midas was once more in the presence of Dionysus. He looked so haggard and worn and miserable as he stood before the radiant young god, that it would have been a hard heart that refused to pity him. Humbly he asked his boon : " I pray you, O Dionysus, take from me the gift you have bestowed. Take it, or I die."

Dionysus looked on him kindly, yet with a little half-mocking smile. " Go you, then, wash in Pactolus, near its source. Its waters will cleanse you from this golden plague, and will restore to their former state those things which your touch has changed."

Midas thanked the god with words of heartfelt gratitude. Then he hurried to his chariot, and bade his servant drive him

Midas and the Golden Touch

quickly to the bank of the healing river. He now longed far more earnestly to rid himself of his fatal gift than before he had longed to attain it. When he reached the river he plunged eagerly into its waters. Their delicious coolness and freshness seemed to give him new life. He held up his hands, and let the water drip from his fingers, rejoicing to see that the drops were still crystal clear, without the yellow taint of which his eyes had sickened. Then, springing from the stream, he laid his hands, all wet and dripping, upon his golden chariot; and behold! its bright hue faded, and it became once more as it had been in the happy days before yesterday; and the heart of King Midas rejoiced, for he knew that the abhorred power had passed from him.

Henceforward he hated gold as much as before he had loved it. He gave up the luxurious life in which he had delighted, and lived simply like a shepherd or a hunter whose real home is in the fields and woods. He became a worshipper of Pan, the god of flocks and herds, and often saw him in the groves of the forest and listened to his music.

Pan was the son of Hermes and of Penelope, a nymph of the woods. When he was a tiny, new-born baby he looked such a curious little creature that his mother ran away from him in fear. His body was covered with fur, he had little, furry, pointed ears, and feet like the hoofs of a goat. His father carried him up to Olympus to show him to the gods, and they were all delighted with him. They laughed at him and praised his quaint ways and his funny, bounding movements. But Pan did not care to dwell on Olympus; he loved better the woodland places of the earth where he could wander freely, and sport with the satyrs and fauns and forest nymphs, and startle travellers by jumping out upon them from behind a tree, and dance and sing through the long, sunny days.

Once he loved a nymph named Syrinx, but she, frightened at his curious appearance, fled from him in terror. He followed her, his hoofed feet pattering on the ground. Coming to the banks of a river, Syrinx called piteously upon the water nymphs to help her. They heard, and hurried to her assistance, so that

Pan, coming up and clasping as he thought his loved Syrinx, found that he was embracing a tuft of reeds. He sighed deeply, and his sigh breathed through the reeds, bringing out from them a sweet, low sound. " I will at least have something that will remind me of my love," he said, and he cut seven pieces, of different lengths, from the reeds, and fashioned them into a pipe, on which he played the most delightful music.

PAN

Midas loved the music of Pan's pipes, and would lie in the woods listening to it the whole of a summer afternoon. Pan himself was very proud of his skill; he even boasted that the music he made on his pipes was sweeter than that made by Apollo, and one day he challenged the sun-god to a contest. Tmolus, the mountain-god, was chosen as judge, and all the inhabitants of the woodland gathered round to listen. Midas was there too, very anxious that Pan should be successful. But though the forest-god played very sweetly, there was no doubt that Apollo's

Midas and the Golden Touch

music excelled his. The listeners were so entranced with the marvellous sounds he produced that they shouted in acclamation when Tmolus unhesitatingly awarded him the prize.

But there was one among the listeners who declared that the prize should have been given to Pan, and that one was King Midas, and he obstinately persisted in his opinion, though all the others exclaimed loudly at his strange lack of musical taste. At last Apollo grew angry.

" Is it possible," he said, " that anyone with ears can have so little power to use them ?   I will give you a new pair of ears, with which you may perhaps do better."

Then Midas, to his dismay, felt his ears growing long and furry, and found that he was able to move them about, just as he had seen asses do.   He was, indeed, furnished with a pair of ass's ears !

His shame at this horrid transformation was so great that he could not bear that any of his subjects should know of it. So he secretly procured for himself a cap which he could draw down tightly over his ears, and he wore this always.   But the time came when the barber, whose duty it was to cut and trim his hair, came to perform his accustomed task.   Midas did not know what to do.   His kingly dignity demanded that he should not let his hair grow long and wild, but should have it properly attended to ;   he was forced, therefore, to let the barber into the secret of his ass's ears.

The barber's astonishment was so great that he could think of nothing else ;   neither by night nor by day could he forget what he had seen.   He knew that the king would slay him if he were to tell the secret to any other person, and yet he felt that he could not keep it to himself.   Always he went in fear that the desire to tell would some day be so great that he would shout the secret aloud for all to hear.   So at last he dug a deep hole in a remote spot, and thrusting his head down into it he called aloud : " King Midas has the ears of an ass.   I myself have seen them."   This act gave him the relief that he desired, and he filled up the hole and went back to his work in the palace.

Not long afterward a bed of reeds appeared on the place where the barber had filled up the hole, and when the wind blew through them they whispered, " King Midas has the ears of an ass " ; and all the people passing by heard and repeated the marvel. So that after all the great secret became known throughout the land.

Orpheus and Eurydice

Orpheus was the son of Apollo, and Calliope, the Muse of Poetry. When he was quite a tiny boy he could play and sing with such wonderful sweetness that his father was delighted. He gave his little son a golden lyre, such as he himself used, and trained him to play upon it ; so Orpheus became the most famous musician in all the land. He could, when he chose, draw such sad notes from his lyre that those who heard him wept as if some great sorrow had fallen upon them ; and then he could change to a measure so joyous and sweet that the saddest heart was lightened and all troubles were forgotten. While he played, base and unkind thoughts were driven from the minds of his hearers ; and none could refuse any boon that Orpheus asked after they had listened to his music. Not only men, but beasts and birds, even the trees and the flowers, the sea and the mountains, loved the sweet sounds that he made and bowed before him. With his beautiful face and his magical music he was welcome everywhere, and men and gods were his friends. He took part in many adventures with the other young heroes of Greece and visited distant lands ; and after his wanderings he settled down in his native land of Thrace and used his wonderful powers in trying to help and civilize the people round him.

Soon after his return home he met the lovely nymph Eurydice, and loved her, and wooed her with enchanting strains that could not be resisted. Apollo arranged a grand marriage feast for his son, and many of the gods came as guests in splendid array. But the one to whom everybody looked most anxiously was a tall and handsome youth who carried a torch in his hand. This was Hymen, the god of marriage, and according as his torch burned bright or dimly would be the fortunes of the bride

Orpheus and Eurydice

and bridegroom. Imagine, therefore, the dismay of the guests when they saw that no clear flame rose from the torch—hardly even a glimmer of light, but thick, acrid smoke which spread through the air until it brought tears—ill omens for a marriage—into everyone's eyes. A gloom fell on the festivities, and the joy of even Orpheus and Eurydice was a little damped; but they soon forgot the evil omen in bright visions of the happiness in store for them.

For a short time they were, indeed, very happy, and Orpheus made more wonderful music than ever before. Then one day Eurydice went to join in the joyous games of the woodland nymphs, as she had been used to do before her marriage. As she wandered happily on, a certain shepherd saw her and fell in love with her beauty. He came boldly toward her, with honeyed compliments on his lips, and as she turned from him he caught her arm. Frightened, Eurydice drew her arm from his grasp and fled, not heeding where she went, and in her haste she trod on a snake that lay hidden in the long grass. The creature turned and bit her on the heel. The venom did its work swiftly, and when Orpheus came to seek her he found her lying in terrible pain and very near to death. He bore her home, but nothing he could do could save her; and so their short, happy married life came to an end. Eurydice passed to the dark land where Pluto reigned, and Orpheus was left in the world above lonely and broken-hearted.

In all the troubles that life had brought him he had ever found comfort in music, and in this worst grief of all he turned to music once more. He drew from his lyre sounds so full of woe and yet so lovely that all who heard them felt their hearts melt with pity. But neither their pity nor his music could bring any comfort to Orpheus. He flung aside his lyre, and thought only of Eurydice. Eurydice so young and fair, yet gone to live for ever in the gloomy shades of Hades. Would no one bring her back to him? And then the thought came that he himself might be her deliverer. Men and gods had said that his music could work miracles. He would try if it could work this miracle, and restore to him his lost happiness.

The Book of Myths

He took his lyre and started on his way to the palace of the gods. Arriving on Mount Olympus, he threw himself on his knees before Zeus, and begged the great god to give him back his loved Eurydice. Zeus listened, and his heart was moved at the sight of Orpheus' misery.

"I cannot restore your wife," he said. "She is in the realm where my brother Pluto holds sway. But this I can do. I can grant that you may go down to Hades and try to win her back. Yet pause before you make this rash attempt, for terrible will be its dangers, and it may well chance that you will never leave that dread kingdom."

Orpheus did not hesitate. "Fain would I be with my loved one, even though it were in Hades. Earth holds no joy for me when she is gone. I thank you, mighty Zeus, that you have granted me this boon."

He bowed before the great god, and without delaying for a moment, he took his way toward the gloomy land where he hoped to find his lost Eurydice. Through a dark cave he went, and on until he came to the great gate of Hades. Cerberus, a huge, three-headed dog, frightful to look upon, sat there on guard, but he dared not keep out one who had permission from Zeus to enter. Grudgingly he let the great gate swing open, and Orpheus passed into Hades. Down a long dark passage he hastened, where he could hear soft sighs and flutterings as the souls of the dead floated down beside him.

At length he came to the sombre and splendid hall where Pluto and Persephone sat on their sable thrones, and there once more he pleaded his cause, making his prayer a plaintive song which he sang to the music of his lyre. Such wonderful sounds had never before been heard in that dark realm. Even the spirits in its farthest depths who were condemned to never-ending tortures felt a moment's respite from their pains. Tantalus, the cruel king who had oppressed his people and insulted the gods, forgot for an instant his terrible, undying thirst, and ceased his vain attempts to drink from the cool stream which always drew away from his lips as he stooped toward its waters ; the stone which Sisyphus, thief and murderer, was doomed for

Orpheus and Eurydice

ever to push up a hill from which for ever it rolled down, rested for a moment's space; the fiery wheel to which was bound Ixion, the oath-breaker, slackened and cooled; the forty-nine daughters of Danaus, who slew their husbands, stayed in their labour of filling a bottomless cask; Salmoneus, who had dared to personate Zeus in the eyes of men, forgot the overhanging

IXION ON THE WHEEL

rock which each instant threatened to fall and crush him. Persephone wept, and even Pluto felt the power of the magic music.

"Let Eurydice be brought hither," he demanded; and so Orpheus saw his wife again, pale and shadowy, and limping painfully on her wounded foot, but still his own wife, with a great joy shining on her white face as her eyes met those of her husband.

"Take her," said Pluto, "and lead her forth from Hades, if indeed your music has power to draw her to the upper air.

But look always before you, for if you so much as glance behind the spell will be broken, and your wife will pass back again to dwell for ever with the shades."

With their hearts beating so fast for joy that they could scarcely breathe, the two happy lovers turned toward the gate of Hades. Surely never in all the ages of the world has such music been made as Orpheus made then. Eurydice must have followed even had it been against her will. On through the dark passage went that glorious music, and following it came glad-hearted Eurydice. They passed Cerberus, who lay still, unheeding, intent only on the music, and climbed the steep ascent toward the outer cave. A few more moments and they would be in the cheerful upper air. A quick fear came to Orpheus lest he should pass through and leave his wife in the lower kingdom, and, forgetting all else, he turned his head to be sure that she was close behind him. Alas! He caught just one glimpse of a slender, white-clad form, heard a soft, sad cry that sounded like "Farewell!" and his wife passed from him, caught swiftly back to the dread kingdom of Pluto.

Despair fell on Orpheus, for he knew that nevermore might he see his wife on earth. Yet he turned and rushed back on the dark way, begging, in tones of agony, that he might be given one more chance, or might be allowed to join his wife in the kingdom of the dead. But three-headed Cerberus drove him back, and Zeus would grant him no further grace. He must live out his life on earth alone,. until the time decreed by the Fates when he should pass by the way appointed for the souls of men freed by death, and join his lost Eurydice.

He wandered far away from the homes of men, and made his dwelling in the woods. Here among the groves and trees he seemed to be nearer to his wife, and often looking down some leafy glade he thought he caught a glimpse of a flitting, white-robed form and heard again the soft, sad cry, "Farewell!" "Eurydice!" he would call, and with flying footsteps follow the sweet vision, but always when he reached the place the form had vanished. Then he would take his lyre and play, pouring out all the anguish of his broken heart ; and the birds and beasts of the forest would gather silently round him, the trees would softly wave their branches, the flowers bow their fair heads; even the lofty mountain tops would bend toward him, all doing homage to the great and sad musician.

At last one day Dionysus with his train of revellers came near the place where Orpheus had his dwelling, and a troop of maidens, fair, but wild, dishevelled, unseemly in their drunken gaiety, spied the beautiful youth as he sat by the side of a stream playing his mournful strains. They rushed toward him with shouts and laughter, praising his beauty and his music, calling on him to join in their sport and sing them a merry song. But Orpheus would have none of them ; the thought of his fair, lost Eurydice made him look on these wild-eyed, loose-tressed damsels with disgust. Then their laughter turned to anger, while still he played the sad strains hated by all followers of Dionysus; they cast stones at him, but the stones fell harmless, charmed by the power of the music. Enraged, the revellers sprang upon him and slew him, and cast his body in the stream. Death came to Orpheus as a friend, and he welcomed it with a smile; as he floated down the stream he looked once more the happy youth who had wooed his bride in the fair land of Thrace.

The gods who loved Orpheus mourned for his death, and that he might always live in the memory of men they placed his lyre in the skies and made of it a bright constellation, which they called Lyra.

Hercules and the Golden Apples

One of the most famous among the Greek heroes was Hercules. Zeus himself was his father, and his mother was Alcmene, daughter of the King of Mycenæ. Hera hated him, as she hated all the children of Zeus whose mothers were mortal women, and throughout his life her hatred followed him, bringing many troubles upon him. When he was only a few days old he was lying in his cradle, in the palace of the princess his mother, when suddenly the nurses who were watching him saw two huge and horrible serpents writhing their way over the floor toward the place

73

where he lay. The women shrieked, but they could do nothing to save him, and they dared not pass the serpents to run for help. Their cries woke the babe, and he opened his sleepy eyes and looked around. When he saw the serpents he sat up eagerly, and gave a delighted chuckle; then he leaned over the side of his cradle and took one of the death-dealing creatures in each of his baby hands. Still crowing and gurgling with delight, he tightened his fingers round their necks until they were strangled; and then, throwing them from him to the floor, where they lay, limp and lifeless, he sank back in his cradle and went happily to sleep once more.

Hera was furious when she heard what had happened to the creatures she had sent; and the more she heard people talking about it, and foretelling great things of the wondrous infant, the higher her anger rose. It had seemed so easy to destroy the feeble life of such a tiny creature, and yet, behold, he had escaped her and was growing vastly in strength and stature every day. She decided that it would be of no use to lay any more plots against his life; instead she would follow him with her hatred so that he would live out his days in hardship and misery, and come at last to a cruel death. This was the plan she made and she followed it out with persistence, but she failed even to bow the bright spirit that she meant to break. The story of Hercules is the story of a brave man meeting trouble after trouble and danger after danger with high courage and tireless energy, and without moaning or complaint. The babe who laughed while he strangled the deadly serpents grew into the man who entered into countless adventures with zest and enjoyment, and took difficulties and dangers as part of the day's work.

It would take too long to tell here the stories of his wonderful deeds. One adventure only can be related fully after we have given a brief account of the hero's youth.

As soon as he was old enough, Hercules was sent to Chiron to be educated. Chiron was a centaur, that is, he had the head and shoulders of a man joined to the body and legs of a horse. Though his appearance was thus strange, he was wise and brave and gentle, skilled in the arts of war and of hunting, learned in

Hercules and the Golden Apples

medicine and music, and he possessed the gift of prophecy. All the heroes in turn were sent to him, and he trained them well, teaching them to be just and merciful as well as brave. Hercules learned to love Chiron dearly, and when his education was finished, and the day came when he must go out into the world, it was with many regrets that he left his master and his quiet home in the forest.

HERCULES AND CHIRON

At first all went well. Hercules travelled over the country, helping the weak and the oppressed and doing many wonderful deeds. He married a beautiful wife, and three lovely children were born to him. Nowhere was there a happier family than this family of Hercules, ruled over by a father who was so strong and yet so gentle and loving. But soon Hera, remembering her hatred and her vow, sent a fit of madness upon him, in which he killed his wife and all his children. When he recovered his reason be was overcome with grief, and went to the moun-

75

tains to mourn in solitude; but he was not long left alone in his despair, for the gods sent their messenger to tell him that he must purge himself of the crimes he had committed even though these had been done in madness. To this end he must serve Eurystheus, King of Argos, as a slave for a twelvemonth and a day.

This was a terrible trial for the proud Hercules, and for a time it seemed as if madness were coming upon him once more. But Eurystheus, seeing his misery, had pity on him, and told him he should be free once more if he could accomplish twelve mighty labours which his master would set him to do. Action of any kind was delightful to Hercules, and adventures, however dangerous, he loved. So he brightened at this new prospect, and prepared to do his best. The labours were difficult, and all his strength and courage and daring were needed to perform them, but in each he was successful. He had to slay or capture terrible beasts; to cleanse the Augean stables where three hundred cattle were kept, and which had not been cleansed for thirty years; to steal the girdle of the Queen of the Amazons. All these things he did; and then, as his eleventh labour, he was told to bring to Eurystheus the Golden Apples of the Hesperides.

These apples had been given to Hera on her marriage with Zeus by Ge, the goddess of the Earth. Hera had given them into the charge of the Hesperides, three beautiful maidens who were the daughters of the Titan, Atlas, and of Hesperus, the Evening Star. These maidens kept the apples in a garden, where they watched over them continually; and underneath the tree on which the apples hung lay a fierce dragon, who never slept.

Hercules was puzzled to think how he should start on this quest, for he had no idea where to look for the Garden of the Hesperides, and he knew of no one who could tell him. He was obliged to set out trusting that chance would lead him in the right way. He questioned every one he met who he thought might be able to help him, and at length some river nymphs told him to go to Nereus, god of the sea, who could probably give him some information.

Nereus was very old, and of a kindly and placid disposition.

Hercules and the Golden Apples

Like most of the ocean deities, he had the gift of prophecy, and the power of taking different shapes, one after another, to evade any person who tried to capture him. Hercules found him lying asleep on the seashore, the hot sun streaming down upon his face. Knowing what he had to expect, Hercules grasped Nereus firmly by the arm before he awoke him and put his question. Nereus did not like being disturbed, and did not wish to give any information, so he very rapidly took one shape after another, becoming a serpent, a bear, a fish, a dolphin, and many other creatures, in quick succession. But through all the changes Hercules kept his firm grasp, and at last old Nereus thought it might be better to attend to him than to fatigue himself further. So he took his own shape and listened.

" Tell me, I pray you, O Nereus," said Hercules, " where I can find the Garden of the Hesperides."

" I do not know," answered Nereus. " The sea is my kingdom, and I have nought to do with the land."

" Then tell me of someone who knows," pleaded Hercules. " I am sure that you can help me if you will."

" There is Prometheus, who for countless ages has lain bound to a rock in the Caucasus mountains," replied Nereus. " He can tell you if he will ; but you must take a long journey to find him."

" I will go at once," said Hercules ; and he started again, unwearied, on his quest.

At length he came to the rock where Prometheus lay. The Titan was worn and scarred by the storms of the long years that had passed over him, and his body was racked with pain, for the fierce eagle had never ceased to tear and devour his flesh. When Hercules saw the bird at his horrid work, his wrath flamed up fiercely. He drew his club, and sprang up the mountain side ; with one blow he smote the vulture so that it fell dead at Prometheus' feet ; then he struck at the chains that bound the Titan's body, and his mighty strength was sufficient to break the bonds that had been forged by Hephæstus himself. Prometheus, released at last from his long captivity, stood up and looked at his liberator.

"Who are you?" he said. His voice was firm and strong as ever, though his body was wasted and worn.

"I am Hercules," the other replied; and he looked with awe upon the giant he had released, for he knew what Prometheus had done for man, and how he had been rewarded. He noted how straight and firm the Titan stood, and how proud was his glance; and he rejoiced that the long and cruel punishment had not broken his noble spirit.

The name of Hercules, which by this time had become famous throughout all the land, meant nothing to Prometheus, for, chained to his rock, little news from men had reached him. Yet he knew that his liberator must be of note, for his strength was as the strength of no other that Prometheus had ever seen.

"Why have you come hither?" he asked; and Hercules told him the story of his quest.

"Go to my brother Atlas," the Titan said, "he who bears up the firmament on his shoulders. From him you will certainly learn where the golden apples are to be found. Leave me now, for I have many things to think of."

So Hercules set off once more, travelling southward toward Africa. He passed through Lybia, where lived a race of dwarfs who were called Pygmies, tiny people, only a few inches high. These Pygmies went in constant fear of the men who dwelt in the countries round about them, for they knew that these could make an end of them altogether if they chose to invade their land. When these tiny people saw great Hercules striding through their fields and cities they were terrified, though he did not attack them or work them any harm. In their alarm they went to Antæus, a giant who had undertaken to protect his little neighbours. Antæus was a great wrestler, and every traveller who passed near his home he forced to wrestle with him.

"Come," said the Pygmies, "here is a stranger, a gigantic man, who is passing through our country. Come and overthrow him that we may be safe."

Antæus, who had been victorious in every one of his many wrestling encounters, came gladly at their call.

"Ho, there!" he cried, "you who pass through the country

Hercules and the Golden Apples

of the Pygmies. Know that all who come this way must wrestle with Antæus."

Hercules turned round quickly. He had looked with amazement at the dwarfs, and had been careful not to injure either them or their dwellings. Now there started up among them this enormous giant who looked even larger than he was in

HERCULES WRESTLING WITH ANTÆUS

contrast with his Pygmy friends. But Hercules was always ready for a trial of strength, and he gladly accepted the challenge of Antæus.

The two began their struggle, and a very fierce and prolonged struggle it proved to be. At first neither could gain any advantage over the other. Time after time Hercules thought he felt the giant growing weaker, but just as he was beginning to hope that the victory was won, a renewal of strength seemed to come to his opponent, who became more dangerous than ever.

Hercules was puzzled to account for this, and as he felt his

79

own great strength failing, he set himself to find out the giant's secret. At length he noticed that the fresh spurts of strength seemed to come each time that Antæus had been for an instant forced to the ground, and this suggested to him that the giant's strength came from contact with the earth. Well, he would see ; with one tremendous effort he seized him by the waist and lifted him so that his feet no longer touched the earth. At first Antæus struggled fiercely, but soon his strength dwindled. He grew limp and helpless in Hercules' hands, gasping and piteously begging for mercy. But Hercules still held him in a firm grasp. And at last his moans grew fainter and he died.

Then Hercules turned from the land of the Pygmies and strode on. At length he came in sight of the huge Titan, who for his rebellion against the gods had been doomed to stand supporting the heavens on his broad back for ever. Long ages he had stood already, weary and alone, and although he was not tortured as his brother Prometheus had been, yet his lot was a sad one, and he longed for release from his burden. When he saw Hercules he was glad, and he listened with interest while the stranger told of the task that had been given him and the reason he had come to that solitary place.

" It is true," Atlas replied, " that I know where the golden apples are to be found, for the fair Hesperides in whose charge they are placed are my daughters. I can tell you the way to the garden, but you will never bring from it a single golden apple, for a fierce dragon guards the tree by day and by night. Yet with my help you may obtain what you seek. I am weary of holding up the heavens, and crave for a short relief. If you will take the burden on your shoulders, which are almost as broad as my own, I will hasten to the garden and bring back the fruit you desire. Then I will relieve you of your load and you can go on your way."

Very willingly Hercules agreed. He stepped forward, and the firmament, now—for it was night—studded with countless stars, was carefully transferred from Atlas's shoulders to his own. For the first time in many centuries the Titan stood upright. He stayed for a moment to stretch his cramped muscles and

Hercules and the Golden Apples

then set off on the quest he had undertaken. How he dealt with the dragon we do not know, but the nymphs, his daughters, gave him their aid, and he came back bearing the precious fruit. As he strode along it seemed to him that there were no joys so great as the free swing of unhampered limbs, the rapid movement through the cool, fresh air, the freedom to look this way and that over the fair earth. In a few moments he must give up these joys and take his burden once more, standing with cramped limbs, bent shoulders, and eyes looking always earthward. He would not do it; he had suffered enough; let Hercules take his turn.

Meanwhile Hercules was beginning to feel very weary. His spirit chafed at the inaction that had been forced upon him, and he wished that he had gone himself to seek the golden apples. "Better anything than this miserable bondage," he thought. "What matters danger if one be free?" The slow minutes, the slow hours, dragged past, and at last in the morning light he saw Atlas returning. Only a few minutes now, and he would be eased of his burden. But something in the Titan's face, and in his free, joyful stride, made the heart of Hercules sink; and when the golden apples were held up to show him that the quest had been successful, he was almost prepared for the words that followed.

"You shall keep your burden yet a little longer, and I will take the apples to Eurystheus. It is but justice that I should have some respite from my weary task."

Hercules had little cunning, but the little he had he called to help him now. He did not try to argue with the Titan and he did not complain.

"Be it so," he said sadly, "yet at least let me bear my burden with as much ease as I may. I have placed it but awkwardly upon my shoulders, not being skilled in such matters, and thinking to carry it for a short space only. Take it for one moment, I pray you, and fit it to my back in the manner your long experience has taught you."

The Titan had still less cunning than Hercules, and he was quite willing to do his best for one who had set him free from his long servitude. He threw the apples on the ground, and lifted the firmament from Hercules' shoulders to his own, at the same time beginning some wise advice as to the best manner of bearing such burdens. But as soon as Hercules felt his shoulders lightened he sprang aside, picked up the apples, and hurried away, calling farewell to Atlas as he went. So the Titan was left to ponder sadly over the way in which, by his own simplicity, he had lost the one chance of relief that had come to him ; to recall the golden moments when he had been free and happy, and to long for the end of his weary servitude.

But in the heart of Hercules there was joy, because he had escaped the horrid fate that just for a moment had threatened him, and because his task—almost the last of the twelve heavy labours that had been imposed upon him—was accomplished. The long journey back seemed short and pleasant, and he presented the golden apples to his taskmaster, feeling proud that he had brought so beautiful and so rare a present. But Eurystheus would have none of them ; perhaps he feared the anger of Hera when the theft should be discovered ; perhaps he felt that the apples belonged of right to the hero who had dared so much to obtain them. He gave them back to Hercules, and Hercules presented them to Athene, the goddess of wisdom ; and Athene after a time replaced them in the garden whence they had come.

CHAPTER II

MYTHS OF THE NORSEMEN

Mighty Odin,
Norsemen hearts we bend to thee!
Steer our barks, all-potent Woden,
O'er the surging Baltic Sea.
VAIL

NORSE mythology was born in the lands of Northern Europe, where winter lasts through the greater part of the year. The ground lies frozen and hard under a bitter sky, the sun is hidden from sight; strong winds rush in an icy torrent over the land, and lash the sea to fury round the rocky coasts. Then comes the brief summer, hot and beautiful, but passing like a flash, so that the earth has scarcely loosened itself from its bonds before the frost comes down once more. The soil is barren and niggardly, not teeming and gracious as it is in the South. It gives man nothing. All that he obtains from it he must win, as a man wins spoil from an enemy, after a hard struggle; and even after he has won his victory the spoil is but scanty. If he tries to gain his living from the sea he must fight with winds and waves, venturing out on the great waters in his frail boat, setting his strength and skill and courage against the fierce tempests that time after time attack him.

Such a life of warfare made the Norseman of those early days strong and hardy and bold, gave him a fierce delight in the exercise of his strength, made him as ready to fight against human foes as against the forces of Nature. It caused him also to be wild and rough in his joy as in his toils, so that he loved deep drinking and coarse feasting, loud merriment, rough jests. But it gave him besides a sense of strength and lordship, so that he held his head high and bore himself with a large and careless confidence that had in it a certain dignity. And the

83

memory of the brief bright summer which for so short a space transformed his land bestowed upon him a sense of gracious, fleeting beauty which, though it came so seldom, was the most precious of man's possessions.

The gods which the imagination of such men created were naturally very different from the gods of the Greeks. Strength, not beauty, was the object of their worship; and so we get a race of deities, the Æsir, who are mighty giants, armed with magic, unfailing weapons, to whom fighting is the great business of life, and whose greatest feats are feats of strength. They are not beautiful to look at, and some of them bear disfiguring marks of their many combats, but they have majesty in their bearing and eyes that can flash fire. Their wrath is terrible, but they have a rough kindliness and a homely, sometimes even a coarse, humour. They are not quick-witted or subtle; with the exception of Loki, they are inclined to be slow in apprehension; their followers regard them with little reverence, though they stand in wholesome awe of their strength. Only one of them— Balder, the bright Sun-god—is beautiful and beloved; he is, to the Norseman, the personification of the fleeting summer. The goddesses—Frigga and Sif and Freya—are beautiful, but they have little power in comparison with Hera and Demeter and Athene among the Greeks. They reign as queen-consorts rather than as sovereigns in their own right.

The Wild Huntsman

Odin, the Allfather, sat one day on his throne Hlidskialf, set high in his palace of Valaskialf, in Asgard. He looked around, and saw his glorious city with its shining palaces built of gold and silver; he looked away to the North and saw the desolate lands of his enemies, the giants; to the South, and saw the quenchless fires of Muspellsheim, the land of flame. But he looked longest and most earnestly at the earth beneath, where men, his own special charge and delight, lived and toiled and fought, and his heart swelled within him as he saw that the creatures he had made bore themselves well and were valiant in warfare.

The Wild Huntsman

" To Valhalla shall they come," he cried, " to live and feast as heroes should. They shall not languish until age or sickness cuts them off, and then die cows' deaths under a roof; in the open air, with their swords in their hands and dealing brave thrusts against their enemies shall they die, and the white-armed Valkyrs, the warrior-maidens of Asgard who do my will, shall bring them to me, that I may give them the praise and honour that is their due. I will rouse me now and stir up warfare on the earth, and great deeds shall be done before the high gods." So he rose and called aloud for Sleipnir, his eight-footed steed, and at his voice all his train came eagerly round, impatient to know what was going forward.

Then Odin said : " To-night you shall follow the Wild Huntsman, and hunt the wild boar through the sky, so that all men may see us, and say, ' Lo, hear the hounds and see the hunt as it rushes past. It has come to tell us that war is at hand, and fierce fighting, and that many will die the hero's death.' "

So he mounted his horse and rushed onward, his huntsmen following with lusty shouts of " Hallo-ho ! " and the hounds in full cry after them. Men heard the tumult a long way off, and came and stood at their doors and looked up into the sky ; women and children trembled, whispering to each other, " The Wild Huntsman ! "

Soon they saw, rushing headlong through the heavens, that dark and terrible train. First came the leader on his coal-black horse, and behind him, stretching right across the sky, came his huntsmen ; and still more and more came in sight, leaping from the bridge Bifrost that led from Asgard to the earth, which the gods called Midgard, and urging on their horses with deep and terrible cries. " I am glad," said one man to his neighbour, " that I remembered to leave the last sheaf of wheat in my field as fodder for the Huntsmen's horses. His messengers will find there a goodly store awaiting them." But the other man said nothing, for he knew that in his field the messengers would search in vain.

Still the wild cries went on, and men, as they listened, felt their blood stirred, and longed to join in that glorious chase.

longed to rush wildly, unarmed and unarmoured as they were, against a worthy foe. There was a goatherd, named Halfdane, very poor and despised, who lived in a miserable hut among the mountains, yet who had a brave and a noble heart. He, as he saw the mighty form of the Wild Huntsman, could not help joining in the hunting cry, and shouted " *Hallo-ho !* " as if he were in truth one of the train. Something dark fell at his feet,

HALFDANE WATCHING THE HUNT

and when he picked it up he found it was the leg of a horse. His companions, standing round, laughed loudly. " Behold," cried they, " the steed that is given to the valiant Halfdane. Mount, my friend, and join the flying huntsmen. We too will join in the cry, and ride with you." So in mockery they shouted " *Hallo-ho !* "

Then Odin was angry because men had mocked him, and, laughing, had proposed to join his terrible hunt. So he made a fierce wind blow round about those men, which caught them up and swept them in dreadful eddies up to the skies, and they were never seen on earth again. Halfdane looked on in terror,

The Wild Huntsman

but he could do nothing to help his unfortunate companions. He felt within himself that this was the work of the gods; and so he went home sadly to his poor hut, taking with him the horse's leg that had so strangely fallen to him from heaven. But on the morrow when he woke up he found that it had been changed to a lump of pure gold.

All night long the Wild Huntsman rushed through the sky with his mad following, and louder and louder grew their cries, till the whole earth seemed in tumult. At last their leader saw a faint gleam in the East, and then his speed grew more headlong and his shouts wilder, for he knew that Day, in his glittering chariot, drawn by the white horse Shining Mane, would soon appear over the rim of the earth; and before that time every steed of the wild hunt must be stabled in Asgard. One after another they galloped over Bifrost, and the tumult gradually sank, until the last rider disappeared, and a great calm fell upon the earth.

Not many days after, Odin again looked out from his throne, and saw that war had suddenly broken out among men, and there was fierce fighting in many places; and he gloried in the strength and courage of the creatures he had made. When night fell he sent out his twelve Valkyrs, clad in shining armour and riding fleet steeds, to search the battlefields and bring back to him those who had shown themselves most valiant in the strife. No long time passed before he heard the beat of their horses' hoofs returning over the shining bridge, Bifrost; and then he hurried to Valhalla, ready to welcome the heroes whom the Valkyrs had brought. He stood at the great door, above which was perched the red, golden-crested cock, Fialir, with his sons, Hermod and Bragi, on either hand; while the warriors who had been long in Valhalla trooped from the tilt-yard, and entered the hall by its five hundred and forty doors, through each of which they could pass eight hundred abreast. Here they awaited the new-comers; and these soon entered, not bleeding and exhausted as they had fallen on the field of battle, but whole and fresh, like men who had risen and arrayed themselves after a night of peaceful sleep. They saw a huge hall, where, mighty as the concourse was, every one could find a place. Its roof was covered with shining golden shields, and its walls with flashing spears, which sent forth gleams of light, like rays from the sun. In each man's place was a suit of fine armour, Odin's gift to his heroes. The tables were spread with huge dishes of flesh from the divine boar, which was daily killed to provide the feast, and daily came to life again before the time for the next meal. Great horns of mead were carried round by the Valkyrs, who had taken off their armour, and put on beautiful white robes ; and for goblet, each man had the skull of his greatest enemy.

Odin smiled proudly to see his happy warriors, who drank and sang and told to each other stories of great deeds done in warfare. " Drink, my heroes," he shouted, " drink deep and sing, for this is Asgard, the home of the high gods, who love and honour the brave. Feast until the morning, and then in the tilt-yard you shall fight once more, and give and receive blows such as heroes love ; and in the evening, cured and refreshed, you shall feast again in Valhalla, the hall of the chosen slain."

Geirrod and Agnar

Once more Odin sat upon Hlidskialf, watching what men were doing on the earth below ; but this time his mood was softer and more genial, and he thought, not of fighting men and fierce battles, but of the joys of home, the love of children, the kindly intercourse between friend and friend. He listened to the voices of his two ravens, Hugin (Thought) and Munin (Memory), who sat one on each of his shoulders, waiting until he should send them forth to their daily task of gathering news for him throughout the world.

" Remember," said Munin, " what you saw when you last visited the earth. Remember King Hrauding's two fair-haired little sons, with whom you made friends, while they believed you to be a poor, wayfaring man, who could tell them many stories of strange lands and wonderful adventures."

Geirrod and Agnar

Then Hugin took up the tale : " You have watched them since from your throne in Asgard, and seen them grow up to handsome little lads. Geirrod is now ten years old, and Agnar eight, and they are the delight of their father and of the whole country."

Then Odin, prompted by these two ravens, sat long in thought. At last he rose from his seat and went to find Frigga, his wife. Frigga sat in her palace of Fensalir, the hall of mists, her jewelled distaff, which shone like a cluster of stars, before her. Around her floated in soft glowing masses the webs she had been weaving, which by and by would form the sunset clouds in the sky below. Near her were grouped her maidens—golden-haired Fulla ; swift-footed Gna ; Lofn, beautiful and gracious ; Eira, the skilful physician, and many others.

Frigga stood up as Odin came in, a tall, stately woman in a long, flowing white robe, bound by a golden girdle.

" Frigga, my wife," said Odin, greeting her, " do you remember the little lads, Geirrod and Agnar, with whom you played when last we visited the earth. I should like to speak to them once again, and see their bright faces looking trustfully in mine. Will you come with me to visit once more those two whom we loved ? "

Frigga was as glad as Odin could be at the thought of seeing the lads again. " I will joyfully come with you, my lord," she said. " Robe me, my maidens."

So her maidens took off the white robe and shining jewels, and attired her in the clothes of a peasant woman ; and she made her eyes look dim and her cheek withered, and bowed her stately height so that she seemed stricken in years. Odin, meanwhile, had put on the cloudy-blue mantle, the grey kirtle and broad-brimmed hat which he always wore for his wanderings on the earth ; and the two set out, crossing the bridge Bifrost and alighting unnoticed on Midgard.

It was a chill autumn morning, but as Frigga passed along the wind lost its keenness and played like a soft breeze about their faces, and the sun shone with the clear radiance of spring. Frigga looked at the clouds above, and smiled to see how blue they were, remembering how she and her maidens had spun them in Fensalir the evening before.

The two made their way to a small island far out at sea. " Look ! " said Odin. " The sun shines pleasantly upon the waters. Geirrod and Agnar and many another will be tempted to make one more voyage before the winter storms begin. But I will raise a tempest which shall drive them upon this island.

ODIN TEACHES GEIRROD THE USE OF THE BOW

Let us make ready for their coming." So by his magic power he made a hut, poor but comfortable, and stored with all that shipwrecked voyagers might need ; and then he loosed the storm wind. The sky was darkened, and the sea rose in angry waves.

Odin and Frigga watched a little boat which rose and fell on the waters and was driven ever nearer to their island. Soon it came near enough for them to see the two lads striving manfully against the storm. But their efforts were vain ; their boat was driven upon the island, and a great wave overwhelmed it, washing them high up on the beach. As they rose, shaking the water

Geirrod and Agnar

from their eyes and from their hair, Odin came to meet them. With pleasant words he led them to the hut, where Frigga received them, gave them dry clothes and food, and warmed them by her fire. Their boat was lost, and they had no means of getting away, so they stayed for many days with their kindly host and hostess, passing the time happily enough, and watching for a ship that would carry them home.

Each day Odin took Geirrod to an open space on the island and taught him to use the bow and the spear, to wrestle and to run ; and Geirrod learnt rapidly, so that his teacher was proud of his strength and courage.

Agnar, who was younger and gentler in disposition, stayed at home with Frigga, or took long walks with her, while she taught him the names of birds and trees and all happy woodland lore, and told him long stories of brave and noble deeds and how men might best please the Allfather.

So the winter passed away, and when spring came once more Odin knew that it was time for the boys to return. By his magic power he provided a boat, in which he sent them out to seek their home. Straight and swift it sailed over the waves until it touched the shore of their own land.

Then Geirrod, who had nourished evil, jealous thoughts in his heart, and did not wish his brother to share with him in the welcome which awaited them in their father's house, felt a sudden temptation assail him. He jumped quickly on shore, then violently pushed the boat with his brother in it far out to sea, bidding him go back whence he came. Then he walked away toward his father's palace, where he was received with wonder and delight. His brother, he said, had been drowned in the wave that had overwhelmed the boat, and the king grieved sorely for his little Agnar ; but he had received back one of the sons whom he had thought to be dead, and in that he found comfort.

The years passed away. The king died, and Geirrod reigned in his stead. No one heard anything of Agnar, but Frigga, watching him sadly from Asgard, saw that the drifting boat carried him swiftly far away over the sea, until he reached the land of the giants. They received the shipwrecked boy in friendly fashion, and he lived among them for many years, and at last married one of their daughters. But his heart always yearned for his own land and his own people, and he knew that, sooner or later, he must return to them.

Odin, meanwhile, occupied with the many matters that concerned his rule, thought little of the two princes whom he had loved in their boyhood. But one day as he looked out from Hlidskialf over the world, he remembered Geirrod, and turned his eyes to the country of King Hrading to see what manner of man the little boy had become. He saw Geirrod, honoured and powerful, ruling his country with a firm hand, and feared by all his foes.

Then Odin thought of Agnar, and his eyes travelled over the world until he found him living among the giants and married to one of their race, an obscure, unhonoured man. He turned to Frigga, who sat by his side. "Look now at the two lads," he said. "Geirrod, whom I trained to arms, is now a king, ruling his people wisely ; and Agnar, whom you loved and petted and valued above his brother, is poor and humble ; more, he is married to one of the giant race, foes to the high gods."

But Frigga, who knew more about the two boys than did Odin, for she had watched them closely during the years that had passed, replied quietly : "Better to be poor, O my lord, than to be highly placed and have a hard heart and an ungenerous spirit, to work evil to a brother, and be an ill host to those who come to ask hospitality."

Odin was wrath to hear Frigga speak in this way, and cried, "Who is it that says Geirrod has not an open hand and heart for his guests ? " For the high gods of Asgard looked on hospitality as one of the greatest of the virtues.

Frigga, however, held to what she had said, and Odin, when he found he could not convince her that she was wrong, said that he himself would go to Geirrod as a poor pilgrim and see how he would be received.

He set out at once. But Frigga, knowing Geirrod's cunning, and fearing that he would recognize Odin in spite of his disguise,

Geirrod and Agnar

sent a swift messenger to bid the king beware of a stranger who would shortly arrive at his palace and who was destined to work him ill. Even to such an one the Norsemen counted it a sin to refuse hospitality; but Geirrod's evil and suspicious nature caused him to act as Frigga had guessed that he would. As soon as Odin arrived he was seized, brought before the king, and questioned roughly as to his name and his business. Odin replied that his name was Grimnir, but he refused to say where he came from, and why he wished to visit the king's palace. Then Geirrod commanded that he should be bound and placed between two fires, yet so that the flames did not actually touch him. Here for eight days Odin remained. He was given nothing to eat, but for that he did not care, as he seldom tasted food; but he would have suffered terribly from thirst had not one of the lower servants of the palace brought him, secretly by night, the horn of ale given him for his own drinking. This servant was really Agnar, whose longing for his own country had become so strong that he had returned in secret, and had hired himself as a menial to serve in his brother's house.

On the eighth day of Odin's captivity Geirrod, whose cruel heart delighted in the sufferings of others, came, as he often did, to look at his victim. As he entered the hall he heard unexpected sounds, and to his utter amazement he found that the man, in the midst of his tortures, was singing. The song came, low at first like a mourning chant, then gradually rose until it became a shout of victory.

> The fallen by the sword
> Ygg shall now have;
> Thy life is now run out:
> Wroth with thee are the Æsir:
> Odin thou now shalt see:
> Draw near to me if thou canst.

So startled was the king that at first he stood perfectly still, then drew his sword, meaning to strike the daring captive.

The last triumphal notes died away, and the flames of the two fires flickered and died with them, leaving only a few dead ashes; the chains fell from the singer's limbs, and he stepped forward into the hall, a poor wanderer no longer, but of godlike form and majesty, beautiful, though terrible to see.

Geirrod started back in terror, and his feet became entangled in his drawn sword ; he stumbled and fell, and the sharp blade pierced to his heart so that he died.

All the servants and dwellers in the palace had crowded into the hall, and Odin called aloud for Agnar, who came, full of fear, hearing that dread voice. Then Odin took him by the hand and led him to his brother's throne. His poor garments fell from him and he stood before them all clad in kingly robes, a crown upon his head. And between grief for his brother who lay dead, and awe in the presence of the mighty Odin, and a certain secret joy which ran through him at the god's favour and kind words, Agnar was wellnigh broken down ; yet his princely blood and his honest heart upheld him, and he stood there, brave and steadfast, looking earnestly in the face of the high god.

Then Odin said : " Agnar, whose youth I watched over, whom my wife, the divine Frigga, loved ; who had pity on the poor prisoner in his agony, and risked a great punishment to bring him the drink he craved. Many years have you lived in exile and weariness and longing, but now have returned to your home. Take then the kingdom that was your brother's and rule with justice and mercy. So will I bless you and give you length of days and prosperity."

So Agnar became king in his brother's place and ruled his happy kingdom for many years.

The Wolf Fenris

Loki, god of fire, had two brothers, Ægir, god of the sea, and Kari, god of the air. These three belonged to a race older than either the Æsir or the Vanas, the gods of the sea and the wind, and were quite distinct from them. Loki, however, was allowed to come and go in Asgard as he pleased. He was from the beginning a worker of mischief, always contriving some trick or deceit that he could practise upon the high gods ; but at first

The Wolf Fenris

his mischief amused the Æsir, and therefore they permitted his presence among them. Loki was, besides, very cunning, and sometimes when they were in a difficulty he could show them a way out which their slower brains had not perceived. But gradually Loki's fun grew more and more malicious, and at times he only just escaped a terrible punishment at the hands of the angry gods.

He offended them, too, by his marriage. He secretly took for his wife a hideous giantess named Angurboda, and three monstrous children were born to him—the wolf, Fenris ; Hel, a horrible-looking creature whose body was half blue, half flesh colour ; and Iörmungandr, a venomous serpent.

Loki was terribly afraid of what would happen when the Æsir found out that he had brought into the world such horrible monsters, so he hid them for as long as he could in a dark cave in the depths of Jotunheim ; [1] but they grew so quickly it was impossible to keep them there for very long.

Before he could think of a more secure hiding-place, Odin from Hlidskialf had seen the cave and its inmates, and at once a terrible rage possessed him. With the speed of lightning he made his way to the cave, and first dragging out Hel he flung her over into Niflheim, the region of the dead, telling her that she might take, if she would, the rule of that dismal kingdom. Then he seized Iörmungandr and threw him into the sea, where very soon he became so big that he was able to wind himself right round the earth and hold his tail in his mouth.

Fenris was more difficult to deal with, and at last Odin decided to take the wolf back with him to Asgard and try if his fierce nature could be tamed by kindness. But very soon he saw that there was no hope of any such change in the creature's disposition. Fenris ate and drank and exercised himself in his own uncouth manner, regardless of any about him ; and every day he grew bigger, uglier, stronger, and fiercer. Odin was troubled and anxious, and the other gods murmured against him because he had brought such an unpleasant monster to beautiful Asgard.

At length the Æsir became really frightened. If Fenris were

[1] See page 98.

95

The Book of Myths

left alone he would soon become strong enough to be a real danger in their midst; so they held a consultation to decide what should be done with him. They could not kill him, for no blood might be shed within the borders of Asgard. So they resolved to bind him so firmly that he would not be able to work any mischief. They obtained a very strong chain, and one day they went up to Fenris in friendly fashion and proposed that they should bind him with this chain for sport, and see if he could break it. Fenris guessed their object, but he was not afraid of being bound, as he knew his own strength. He let them put the chain on him, binding it as closely and cunningly as they could, and then he gave one mighty stretch, and the chain fell off, broken in many places.

All the gods clapped their hands and shouted in applause, though they were really very angry that their plan had failed. "We will try again," they said, "and this time perhaps you will not find it so easy to get free." They searched until they found a much stronger chain. This time Fenris was a little unwilling to allow himself to be bound, but the gods flattered him, saying that such a chain would be nothing to his great strength, and at last he let them put it on. He freed himself, but not as easily as before; he was obliged to struggle and put forth all his strength, and he determined that the experiment should not be tried a third time.

The gods, greatly disappointed, gathered together to discuss what they could do next. "It is clear," they said, "that no ordinary chain, however strong, will bind this outrageous wolf. Our only hope is in the dwarfs who made Thor's hammer and Odin's spear and Frey's boar.[1] Let us send to them and ask them to make us a chain which Fenris will not be able to break." So Skirnir, the servant of Frey, was sent to Swart-alfa-heim, the home of the dwarfs, and before very long he came back with a chain so light and soft that it looked as if a child might take it in his tender fingers and pull it apart as he might pull the petals of a rose. But Skirnir said the dwarfs had assured him that this chain, which they called Gleipnir, could not be broken.

[1] See page 111.

The Wolf Fenris

It was made of the sound of a cat's footsteps, the beards of women, the roots of a mountain, the voice of fishes, the longings of the bear, and the spittle of birds ; and strong spells had gone to its weaving.

The gods, though they were rather distrustful of this slight chain, knew what wonders were constantly being worked by the dwarfs, and determined to try it. They persuaded Fenris to go with them to an island in the middle of a lake, and then, after they had all joined in various sports, one of them brought out Gleipnir and proposed that Fenris should once more give an exhibition of his strength. It looked so slight a thing that Fenris's suspicions were at once aroused ; they would not, he was sure, propose to bind him with such a chain unless it possessed some magic power which made it dangerous. Yet he looked at it again, and could not believe that he need fear it. He had grown enormously, and was much stronger than when he had been bound before.

" See," cried the gods, " Fenris is afraid of a thread of silk. How weak he must have grown since he broke the strong iron with which we fettered him but lately. Poor Fenris ! See how fear has taken him. Leave him alone, frighten him no more."

" Frighten me ! " shrieked the wolf. " Who says that I am frightened ? It is you who are the cowards, and I will prove it. You shall bind me with what you will, if one of you will hold his hand in my mouth meanwhile."

The gods drew back in dismay, for no one was willing to lose his hand by the jaws of the fierce wolf.

Then Fenris in his turn cried, " Cowards ! " and taunted them, until Tyr, the bravest of all the gods, could bear it no longer. " Stop your mocking ! " he cried. " I will put my hand in your mouth. A god is not afraid of a wolf."

Then Tyr put his right hand between those cruel, ugly jaws, while the other gods made haste to bind the creature fast with the silken chain. When they had finished Fenris put out all his strength in one mighty effort to free himself, but the bonds held fast.

At once a panic of rage and terror came upon him, and his

97

jaws closed with a vicious snap, severing Tyr's hand at the wrist. Then he struggled and tore and rolled over and over on the ground, striving frantically to free himself, but the dwarfs had done their work well, and Gleipnir still remained closely bound round his terrible neck and savage paws.

The gods, throwing off their pretence of friendship, shouted in glee, and drew him from one side to another to show him how powerless he was ; and Tyr, in spite of the pain in his bleeding wrist, shouted as loudly as the others. They drew the chain through a rock and fastened it to a boulder which was sunk deep in the earth ; and there they left Fenris, bound fast until Ragnarok, or the last great day when the gods should be overthrown, when he would be released to join in the final battle.

Thor's Visit to Jotunheim

Away on the very edge of the world lay the frost-bound, desolate land of Jotunheim, the home of the Jotuns, or giants. The giants had been from the beginning the enemies of the gods, and were always looking out for a chance to work them ill. They feared to attack Asgard while the gods were in their full strength, but hoped that a time might come when their power would decay ; while the gods on their side guarded carefully against an attack by the giants, whose success, they knew, would mean that their day of power was over, and that the twilight of the gods, foretold from the beginning, was at hand. Meanwhile it behoved them to keep the foe in order and stop at once any attempt to work ill either to the abode of the gods or to Midgard, which was under their protection. Therefore, when complaints began to be made that flowers and fruit were not appearing in their due season because cold blasts were continually coming out of Jotunheim which nipped the tender young buds as soon as they ventured to show themselves, the gods were at once roused. They knew who was sending the cold winds. It was Hraesvelgr, the great giant who sat in the extreme north of the heavens, where dwelt the icy winds, ruled over by their god Vasud.

Thor's Visit to Jotunheim

Hraesvelgr looked like a monstrous bird, for he wore a covering made of eagle's feathers, and eagle's plumes were fastened on his arms, making them look like wings. With a movement of these feathered arms he wafted the icy winds from their resting-place, and then they rushed forward, eager to show their power by cutting off all tender green things, and smiting with the keen thrust of their spears all that came in their way.

Hraesvelgr, the gods decided, must be punished and made to stop sending out the winds unseasonably, and Thor was chosen to make a journey to Jotunheim and deal with the spiteful foe.

Thor was quite willing to go, and quite confident that his errand would be successful. He took Loki with him, for though Loki often angered the gods with his tricks, they liked to make use of his cunning and resourcefulness.

So Thor and Loki mounted Thor's brazen chariot, which was drawn by two goats, Toothcracker and Toothgnasher, and they set off.

It was a long and difficult journey, for Thor could not, like all the other gods, pass lightly over Bifrost to the earth below. His tread was too heavy, and his lightnings too fierce for that, so he was forced when he visited Midgard to ford the river Ifing, and ride through many miles of desolate country.

The companions did not reach the borders of Jotunheim until night had fallen, black and bitterly cold. A peasant's hut stood close to the edge of the giant's land, so Thor knocked at the door and asked for shelter. The poor peasant very kindly bade them enter, and began to get ready the best food that he had for their supper. Thor eyed the preparations ruefully : this would never satisfy the huge appetites of himself and Loki. So he went outside the cottage and killed his two goats, which had been stabled in a shed, and he cooked them by the peasant's fire. " Come," he said to the good man and his family. " Here is roasted goat's meat. Sit down and eat your fill ; only do not break any of the bones, but throw them into the skin which I have spread upon the floor."

Eagerly the peasant with his wife and children helped themselves to the savoury meat, and the whole company feasted

99

merrily. But Loki, curious to see what would happen if the god's will was disobeyed, spoke to the peasant's son, who sat beside him. " Goat's meat is good," he said, " but goat's marrow is better. It is of marvellous flavour and wondrous power. Thor doubtless wishes to carry away the bones, but he will never miss one. Here now is a small marrow-bone ; one tap with that piece of iron that lies in the corner, and it will break. See, Thor is not looking, he is already nodding over his meat. Haste now, and you will wake to-morrow with power in your arm and wit in your head such as you never had before."

The young man listened and was persuaded, though when he tasted the marrow, he failed to perceive the marvellous flavour of which Loki had spoken ; yet he trusted that on the morrow he would receive the promised benefits.

But on the morrow, when Thor was ready to depart, he struck the goat skin on which the bones lay with his hammer Miölnir,[1] and up sprang the goats as fat and as lively as if their flesh had never furnished the evening's feast. Only Toothcracker limped a little on his left fore-leg as he trotted toward his master.

Then Thor knew that his command had been disobeyed, and one of his great rages came upon him. Sparks flew from his hair and beard, and he cried out in a terrible voice : " One of you has dared to break the bones of the goat that belongs to Thor, and therefore shall all your bones be broken."

He lifted his hammer to strike, but the boy fell on his knees, owning his fault and begging for mercy. The father, too, in terror, besought the god's forgiveness, and offered him as a peace offering his son Thialfi, and his daughter Roskva, to be his servants for ever.

Thor's gust of anger quickly passed at this ready confession, and, smiling and kindly once more, he accepted the services of Thialfi, bidding him be ready to depart at once with them on the journey through Jotunheim. The goats he left with the peasant, charging him to care for them well.

Then Thor, Loki, and Thialfi set off. All that day they travelled painfully on foot through a thick mist that allowed them to see

[1] See page 112.

Thor's Visit to Jotunheim

little of the country save that it was more bare and desolate than any they had known before. When night fell they could find no hut or lodging of any kind, until Thor chanced upon what he took to be a house, though its shape was strange, and it had no door, the whole of one side being open to the air.

Glad of any shelter, the three entered this curious dwelling. Inside there was no light or fire, or sound of voices, and certainly no hope of supper. But they were too tired to make any attempt at exploring their quarters that night, so groping their way in through the thick darkness, they laid themselves down, hoping to sleep.

Scarcely were they settled when they heard a curious noise, which made them start up again in affright. The sound rose and fell, low at first, then swelling to a mighty volume, as if all the winds of heaven were shut up in a small space, and were fighting desperately with each other to find a way out. At the same time the earth beneath them quivered and the walls of the house seemed to rock. They were all puzzled to think what was causing this commotion, but by Thor's advice they rose and went into a smaller apartment, where they thought they would come to less harm if the roof did fall in, as it threatened to do ; then, though the noise continued and the earth still shook, they were soon fast asleep.

In the morning they rose early and went out quickly to try to learn what was the cause of the strange sounds which had disturbed them, and which were still to be heard.

" Yonder," said Loki, " is a great hill, and the noise seems to come from the top of it. Let us climb up and see what is happening. But as he spoke the sounds stopped, and the hill began to move, stretching out first along the ground, then narrowing at the base and rising to a great height toward the heavens. " By Odin ! " cried Loki, " it is a man—a giant, rather—a giant who slept near us and frightened us with his snores ! "

" Giants have I seen often," said Thor, " but never one like this."

All three, smitten with amazement, gazed for a moment, and then laughed loud and long. But they were more amazed still when they saw the giant stoop and pick up the house, as they had thought it, where they had spent the night. It was his mitten, and the apartment where they had taken refuge was the division which received his huge thumb!

" *Ha !* " roared Thor in his mightiest voice ; but the giant was putting on his mitten, and took no notice.

THOR AND THE GIANT SKRYMIR

" *Ha !* " Thor screamed again. " Who are you, and which is the way to the house of Utgard-Loki, your king ? "

The giant looked about him in a puzzled fashion, and after a time he saw the three small creatures who crept about his feet. " *Hullo !* " he exclaimed, " and who are you little fellows who want to go to Utgard ? "

He would have picked them up and held them in his hand, but Thor, drawing himself proudly to his full height, thundered : " I am Thor, the mighty Æsir, one of the high gods of Asgard, rulers of all the world. I come on an embassy to the giants, to tax them with their evil ways."

There was something about Thor—some majesty of bearing, some air of more than mortal power and dignity—which, in spite of his small figure, impressed the monstrous giant. He thought for a moment. " Come then," he said, " we will go together. My name is Skrymir, and I travel toward Utgard."

All day they journeyed, and at night rested under a great oak tree. " I am weary," said the giant. " I will lie down at once to sleep ; but if you would like supper, you will find what will serve you in this wallet."

Thor and Loki, who were very hungry, took the wallet eagerly

Thor's Visit to Jotunheim

but try as they would, they could not undo the knot with which it was fastened, and Thor's quick anger rose. He seized his mallet, and wielding it with both hands, struck a furious blow on the giant's head.

Skrymir stirred uneasily, and asked in a sleepy voice, " Is that you, Thor ? Are you ready to lie down and sleep ? " And Thor replied that he was quite ready.

But, tired and supperless, he was not in a very good humour, and the giant's loud snoring annoyed him even more than it had done on the previous night. At last he got up, determined that he would make an end of the trouble, and this time he put such strength into his stroke that he actually made a dint in Skrymir's skull. But the giant only murmured something about birds in the tree above throwing down leaves and twigs, then turned over and slept once more.

Thor lay still till morning dawned, and then he resolved to make one more desperate effort. This time he drove his mallet deep into the giant's skull, and Skrymir sat up, rubbing the injured part. " That acorn hit me quite a hard blow," he said. " This is no place in which to rest. I will stay no longer ; and indeed it is time that I went on with my journey." He stretched his huge length and stood up. " And here, Thor, we must part," he said. " Yonder toward the east lies the way to Utgard, while I am bound toward the north."

So Thor and his two companions travelled on toward the city. Long before they came to it they could see the palace of Utgard-Loki, its giant ruler, for this palace was built of ice blocks, wth icicles for pillars, and in the morning light it gleamed like a great diamond against the cold blue sky. When they reached it they found the gates open, and they went boldly in. All round the courtyard and the entrance they saw mighty giants, and when they were brought to the king they perceived that he was the biggest and most terrible looking of all.

Utgard-Loki knew that he must be wary in the presence of one of the high gods ; he spoke civilly, but made a great show of his surprise at seeing the small stature of his visitors. " Yet,"

The Book of Myths

he said, " I have heard much of you, Thor the Thunderer, and it is true that a man's deeds are not always proportioned to his size. Show me then some sign of the greatness for which men and gods praise you ; for this is the hall of heroes, and none are welcome here save the doers of mighty deeds."

But Loki, who was by this time very hungry, interposed. " As for me," he said, " the feat that would be most to my liking just now would be to eat something ; and in that I will promise to outdo any that may be set against me."

" Well," replied the giant, " that would certainly be a feat worthy of praise and glory. Come then, Logi, my cook," and he called to one of his followers, " come and see who will eat the most, you or this stranger."

A great trough of meat was set before them, and Loki began to eat at one end, Logi at the other. It was soon clear that they were well matched, for they met in the middle ; but Logi pointed out that he had eaten meat and bones and trough, while his opponent had only eaten the meat, and so he was adjudged the victor.

" So," said Utgard-Loki, with a scornful smile, " it is clear that, whatever great feats you may be able to accomplish, in the matter of eating, you are outdone."

The smile enraged Thor, who called out : " Whether he win at eating or not, I will win at drinking. I wager that I will drain any vessel you give me, however large it may be."

" Let him try then," said the king, and ordered a horn to be brought in. " This horn," he said to Thor, " a good drinker can empty in one draught ; he who has only a moderate thirst must take two ; and we call him a small drinker indeed who needs must sup thrice."

Thor took the horn, and drank and drank till he could drink no more. Then he set it down and looked into it—and the liquid had sunk only a very little below the rim. Again he tried, and again, while the giants called out mocking words of encouragement ; but still he could not empty the horn.

" Ah well ! " said Utgard-Loki, " Thor the mighty is no drinker, that is plain. Yet we have heard many tales of his strength and

Thor's Visit to Jotunheim

his skill. Tell us, then, dweller in Asgard, what it is you can do that you are called strong among the gods."

"Strong I am," answered Thor, angry, and eager to silence his gibing enemies. "Give me some real trial of strength and I will show you what I can do."

"Try then," said the king, "to lift this cat"; and he pointed to a large grey cat who at that moment appeared in the hall. Thor was almost affronted at being asked to do so small a thing, and he put his hand under the cat, expecting to lift her without effort. But though he tried and strained and put forth all his strength, he could only raise one of her feet, and he was obliged once more to own himself beaten.

"Ah!" mocked the king. "It is as I thought. Thor is too little to pick up the cat of the giants."

"Little though I may be," shouted Thor, now thoroughly enraged, "I will wrestle with any one of you who will come against me."

The king looked round on his followers. "Not one of these but would think such an encounter too poor a trial of courage," he said; "but if you will, there is my old nurse, Elli, who has thrown many a man in her day. If you can overcome her, we will say perhaps that you have strength to meet a man."

So, to Thor's deep disgust, the nurse was brought in—a withered, toothless old woman who seemed no fit opponent for the mighty Thor. But when he seized her he found that she stood firm against his strongest efforts; and after a desperate struggle he himself was brought down on one knee.

Shamefaced and furious, Thor obeyed the king's gesture and stood aside, while Utgard-Loki turned to Thor's servant. Thialfi declared himself a runner, and offered to race with any one of the giant's followers who would run against him; and a young man named Hugi answered the challenge. But Thialfi was hopelessly outdistanced from the very first, and a second and a third trial gave the same result. So Thor had, perforce, to own that he and his companions had been beaten at all points in the contest, and to join with what good temper he might in the feasting and revelling with which the evening ended.

The Book of Myths

Next morning at dawn the three prepared to depart, and Utgard-Loki himself escorted them to the gate of the city. "And now," he said, "that you are out of my city—and I will take good care you never enter it again—go back to your home and tell the gods how mighty are the giants of Utgard."

"They are mighty indeed," said Thor, "and I am only grieved that I have so ill upheld the honour of the gods among them."

THE GIANT VANISHES

"As for that," replied the giant, "you did not do so badly. When I met you first as the giant Skrymir the blows from your mallet would easily have ended my life had I not slipped aside, so that they fell upon the mountain. Three glens they formed there, which will remain to witness to your strength. So with the contests in my hall. Loki really contended with Fire, which devours everything, and Thialfi ran against Thought, whom none can outpace. As for you, one end of the horn I gave you reached the sea, and your draughts actually caused its waters to sink. The cat you tried to lift was the Midgard serpent,[1] and when you managed to raise one of its paws we were all in terror, lest it should no longer be able to encompass the world. Elli, with whom you wrestled, was Old Age, who overthrows every man in his turn. And now beware of coming back again, for you see how by my arts I can bring to nought all your prowess, great as it is, and make your strength seem as weakness."

On hearing the giant's words Thor's rage rose high, and he lifted his hammer to destroy both Utgard-Loki and his city; but lo! when he would have launched it, both giant and city

[1] See page 95.

Sif the Golden-haired

had disappeared, and Thor and his companions stood alone on a broad, grassy plain.

And so Hraesvelgr never received the warning which Thor had set out to give him.

Sif the Golden-haired

Thor the Thunderer took for his wife Sif, and lived very happily with her in the splendid palace he had built for himself, which he called Bilskirnir, the Hall of Lightning. The great god was kindly natured, though he was so tall and strong and terrible in battle. He was the friend of the poor man, and all who fared humbly or were in bondage ; while they lived he was their protector, and when they died he received them into one of the five hundred halls of his great palace, and there they feasted and made merry, as did those of higher rank in Odin's hall, Valhalla. He loved his son Lorride, and his daughter Thrud ; and most of all he loved his beautiful wife Sif. Her long golden hair was his glory and delight ; his mighty face would glow and his wide-glancing eyes shine with pride when she stood beside him, with her wonderful hair loosened and hanging in a shimmering, glorious veil which covered her, tall though she was, from her head to her feet. All the glory of the world's cornfields, he thought, was in it ; all the bright beauty of the harvest fields on which men love to look and which the gods cherish.

Then a morning came when there was grief and dismay in Bilskirnir. Sif came to meet her husband weeping and downcast, her head bare as a cornfield when the reaper has passed over it and only the stubble is left. In the night a thief had come to the Hall of Lightning and robbed its mistress of her shining tresses. How it had been done none knew ; her maidens had heard nothing of the cowardly intruder, but, waking, all had cried out upon his work. And Sif covered her shorn, unhappy head, and hid her face, and wept in shame and anger.

But Thor knew who had done the thing. There was one, and one only who would dare to affront the high gods in the very sanctuary of their homes. In wrath terrible to see the

Thunderer rose ; one of his great rages came upon him ; sparks flew in showers from his red beard and hair, and fell from Asgard on to the sky beneath, where they made fierce lightning in the eyes of men.

"*Ha!*" shouted Thor, and his voice rolled through Asgard, and travelled in deep thunderings over the world below. "Loki, mischief-maker, malicious one, you it is who have dared to rob and insult the wife of Thor. I will crush you as you would crush a fly ; I will lay waste your dwelling and drive your children far away. I will hurl you into Niflheim, where you shall freeze for ever in torments." He seized his weapons, and turned to go ; but before he went he spoke lovingly to his unhappy wife : "Do not fear, my Sif. Soon you shall be Sif the golden-haired once more. The rascal shall give you back the beauty of your locks. I, Thor, will see to it."

Then began a contest in which the agile, quick-witted Loki, terribly frightened now that his mischievous trick had roused the dire anger of the Thunderer, matched himself against the god whose strength was much greater than his own, but whose brain was less nimble.

Loki had the power of changing his shape at will, and now when Thor came to look for him he changed from one forest creature to another, hoping that his pursuer would be puzzled and give up the chase.

Thor was too much in earnest to be baffled by such tricks as these, and Loki soon saw that he must be caught. So he took once more his proper shape, hoping to overcome the god by argument and persuasion. But Thor, when he came up to him, waited for no words ; he seized him furiously by the throat so that he was nearly strangled.

Poor Loki, breathless, not able to speak, feeling his life going from him, made desperate and humble signs to his captor, entreating his mercy, until at last Thor dropped him to the earth while the life was still in him.

But the anger of the god was not appeased, and it was in vain that Loki in panting, painful breaths entreated and promised and pleaded.

Sif the Golden-haired

" Rascal," shouted the enraged god, " you who are at the bottom of all the ill that is done in Asgard, who love to make mischief and do crookedly, I will make an end of you that the gods may be at peace. I will hurl you from Asgard that you may be seen there no more."

But Loki, still relying on the god's good nature and on his own often-tested power of wriggling out of what seemed a desperate scrape, still entreated and promised, till Thor said : " Go then, and bring back Sif's gold locks, not as hair that is severed and lifeless, but as living gold that will grow again on her fair head. Then you shall have pardon, but with nothing else will I be content."

Loki, in dire fear of his life, readily agreed, and Thor, his anger beginning to cool a little, left him, saying : " Bring me the hair again before morning, or all that I have promised I will do." Then he went back to his home, and the lightnings died away over the Middle Earth and the thunder rumbled into silence.

Loki, left alone, felt very unhappy. The task that Thor had set him was a hard one, and how it was to be accomplished he did not know. But he knew that the Thunderer would keep his word, and that somehow or other Sif's loss must be made good. So he set his brains to work to find someone who would help him.

Down below the earth, in Svart-alfa-heim, lived the dwarfs, small, misshapen, cunning creatures who searched out the gold and silver and precious stones that were hidden away in the earth's secret places, and stored them up for their own use. These evil, cunning creatures Loki knew well, and in his schemes of mischief he had sometimes found them useful. So now he went swiftly to their dark home, and seeking out Dvalin, famed above his fellows for his skill in working in the precious metals, he besought him to fashion hair of gold that would grow upon Sif's head. " Make me also," he entreated, " some cunning present for Odin and for Frey, for when they hear Thor's tale, their anger will be hot against me, and they will be swift to punish, if I cannot appease them."

Dvalin, won by Loki's entreaties and seeing a chance of gaining glory in Asgard by an exhibition of his skill, readily set to work.

Soon the fire blazed and the gold was ready for the anvil, and then with skilful strokes Dvalin fashioned the spear Gungnir, which in warfare should never fail of its aim. This was for Odin the Allfather. For Frey, the ruler of the winds, Dvalin made a wonderful ship, Skidbladnir, which could sail over sea or land or through the air, which was always sure of favourable winds,

and, most wonderful of all, could, when its owner wished, carry the twelve Æsir with their steeds, and yet, when its work was for the time done, could be folded up so small that it could be carried in the hand or stowed in a warrior's belt.

Then, from a gold thread finer than ever mortal spun, Dvalin made the hair for Sif, and he gave to it a magic property which would protect it from being again stolen or injured by force or cunning or charm.

Loki was delighted, for now he felt sure of his pardon. " Of all smiths," he cried, " in Asgard, or Midgard, or in the under-world, Dvalin is the greatest.

THE SHIP SKIDBLADNIR

None can work as he can, none other can fashion gifts worthy of the high gods, even for Odin who sits on Hlidskialf, highest in Asgard."

Dvalin swelled with pride as he heard these words, but Brock, another dwarf who stood by, was not so pleased. " 'Tis good work indeed," he allowed, " but Sindri, my brother, can do better. He is a greater smith than Dvalin."

Swiftly Loki turned upon him. " Let him show then what he can do. Let him make three gifts for the gods which shall be better than Gungnir, Skidbladnir, and the golden hair of Sif. As for me, I hold by Dvalin, and I wager my head against yours that your brother cannot surpass his work. The gods themselves shall give the award."

" Done ! " exclaimed Brock, and ran to fetch Sindri, who for his part agreed to the contest.

Then Sindri's fire was lit, and Brock worked lustily at the bellows that it might burn up fiercely.

" Do not stop for an instant," said Sindri, " if you wish me to succeed, for work such as this I have in hand can be spoiled even in the space in which one draws a breath."

The forge burned and the great flames rose, lighting up the blackness of Svart-alfa-heim. Sindri threw gold on the fire, and went out to one of the secret places where he could obtain the magic help by which his wondrous works were to be fashioned. Brock blew steadily, and Loki, watching, began to fear the loss of his wager. So, with his usual love of crooked dealing, he turned himself into a gadfly and stung Brock sharply on the hand. But Brock, remembering his brother's words, bore the pain without flinching and went on blowing the bellows ; and he forgot the pain altogether in triumph when Sindri returned and drew out of the fire a huge wild boar, covered with golden bristles. " Gullin-bursti is his name," cried Sindri. " He can fly through the air faster than the swallow, and as he goes golden rays dart from him so that all the world is light. Frey, who travels daily through the sky, shall ride him, for he is a steed fit for a god."

Loki could not but agree to himself that Gullin-bursti was indeed a marvellous piece of work, and that Brock stood a good chance of winning his wager. So when Sindri, after throwing more gold on the fire, and exhorting his brother to blow steadily, went out once more, Loki, still in the form of a gadfly, flew over to Brock and again stung him cruelly, this time on the cheek.

But Brock was proof against this attack also, though a sharp burning pain went through his body. He did not stop working the bellows even for a moment, and when Sindri came back the second piece of work was ready. From the fire was drawn the magic ring Draupnir, which had the power of multiplying itself, and on every third night dropped from its rim eight other rings similar to itself.

The Book of Myths

Sindri next threw a piece of iron on the fire before he went out, and Loki determined that somehow or other Brock must be stopped and this last piece of work spoiled. With venomous spite he stung the dwarf just above his eye, so deeply that the blood streamed down, and Brock raised his hand to clear it from his eyes. It took only a second, and then he blew more vigorously than ever, but that second had its effect.

When Sindri came back and drew from the fire an enormous hammer, he found that it was slightly short in the handle—only an inch or so, but enough to spoil the perfection of his work. Both the dwarfs were deeply disappointed, but Loki rejoiced—yet still with fear and doubt in his mind, for in spite of its imperfection the hammer Miölner was a marvellous weapon. It returned always to the hand of him who threw it, and it never failed of its aim.

Brock and Sindri agreed that it was a gift that would rejoice the heart of Thor, and they still hoped that the award of the gods would be given in their favour.

Night was now coming on, and Brock might safely mount to Asgard; like all the other dwarfs, he was forbidden to leave Svart-alfa-heim by day, on pain of being turned into stone. So he set off bearing Draupnir, Gullin-bursti, and Miölnir, while Loki brought Gungnir, Skidbladnir, and the golden locks of Sif.

The gods were all assembled in council. Odin seated high in the midst, with Thor and Frey on his right hand and his left. Thor had told of Loki's theft, and of the compact that had been made, and all had agreed that if Loki failed his punishment should be a heavy one. But long before the first rays of the morning sun shone on Asgard, Loki and Brock stood before Odin's throne. Loki looked as impudent and self-satisfied as usual, for he felt sure that the presents he had brought would appease the gods, and he would be restored to his place. Brock, confident in the merits of his brother's work, and longing for the triumph over Loki, stood before the mighty ones, humble but not abashed. Each in his turn presented his gifts, and the high gods deigned to accept them with thanks and praise.

Thor's fiery eyes were fixed on Loki's face, until the offender

Sif the Golden-haired

produced the golden hair which Dvalin had made. Then Thor rose and called for Sif. She came in, veiled and shrinking, and Thor gently uncovered the bowed head and placed upon it the glittering golden hair. Just for a moment the gods held their breath and Loki trembled. Then Sif raised her face, smiling and lovely once more, and tossed back the shining locks and held her head proudly ; and warmth and light seemed to spread throughout the hall. Thor passed his great hand over the recovered locks and laughed his mighty laugh. " 'Tis lovelier than before," he said ; " a golden harvest field with the sun shining bright upon it."

A shout of assent came from the rest of the gods, and they rose to acclaim Sif, now once more the golden-haired ; and she, with rosy, happy face, bowed low before the throne of Odin.

Then Loki triumphed, for he thought his cause was won ; but Brock, eager for his brother's honour, and even more eager to save his own head, craved leave to speak, and cunningly set forward the merits of the gifts he had brought.

The gods deliberated long, but even Thor's delight in his wife's recovered beauty could not make him forget the wonderful hammer which Sindri had fashioned, and he gave his vote for Brock. The other gods assented, and so Loki was doomed to lose his head.

Out from the hall rushed Loki, but after him came Thor, and the chase of the previous morning was repeated. It ended in the same way, and Thor bore Loki back on his shoulder. But on the way the frightened rascal represented to his captor that though he had wagered his head, nothing had been said about his neck. Thor, who could never help feeling some amusement and even admiration at Loki's nimble wit, agreed ; and passing his captive over to the dwarf, he warned him that Loki's neck must not be touched.

Here was a disappointment for Brock ; and the gods sat enjoying his bewilderment and Loki's fears, and waiting to see whose would be the triumph at the last.

At length Brock decided that he would sew up Loki's mouth, and all looked on while he tried to make holes in Loki's lips with his sword. But the weapon was too big and clumsy, and

113

finally Brock was obliged to use his brother's awl. With this the holes were made in workmanlike fashion, and Loki's mouth was tightly sewn up.

The gods laughed loud and long to see the impudent rascal, whose tongue had always run so fast and so smoothly, now stricken with silence. "How now, Loki?" they cried. "Not a word! What ails you? Quaff you a cup of wine, 'twill cheer your heart! You will not! Has Loki then forsworn the wine-cup? Come, feast with us, we go to the banquet. Sing us one of your merry songs. Laugh, bend those stiff lips to a smile."

Loki bore their gibes perforce in silence, and hung his head, and pretended that he was very sorrowful and repentant; but in his heart he rejoiced, for this punishment was trifling and easily removed.

And so when the high gods passed out to the feast prepared for them, Loki, the mischief-maker, the impenitent, cut the string that fastened his lips and straightway was as before.

And Sif, Thor's wife, in her chamber at Bilskirnir, combed out her bright tresses and rejoiced; and to Thor it seemed that he stood once more among the happy fields golden and ready for harvest.

The Apples of Youth

Bragi, god of poetry, the son of Odin and Gunlod, married Idun, the fair goddess of immortal youth, and brought her to Asgard, where she became the delight of the whole company of the gods. For Idun possessed a treasure which was coveted by the giants, the dwarfs, and the great Æsir themselves. This was a magic casket, containing the apples of youth. Whoever ate one of these apples every day would never show signs of age, but would remain young and blooming for ever; and however many apples were taken from the casket the same number remained, so that the supply never failed. The gods of Asgard were subject to age, like the rest of creation, though their lives were prolonged through countless ages; and therefore they received with great rejoicing the apples which Idun served out

The Apples of Youth

at their daily banquets, and were eager to help her in guarding her magic fruit from the giants and the dwarfs who made many attempts to steal it.

But the cunning of their foes was on one occasion too great for all their watchfulness. It began with an excursion made by Odin, his brother Hœnir, the bright and blameless one, and Loki, to the earth, where, according to their custom, they wandered about in various disguises, that they might mingle freely in the affairs of men. At last, when they were tired out, they found themselves in a vast open region where not one house and not one human being could be seen. The only living things near them were some oxen feeding in a green pasture, and as the gods were very hungry, they slew one of these animals, made a fire, and proceeded to cook its flesh. As they did so an eagle came and sat on a tree near by and looked down at the flames as they roared about the meat, and at the gods lying exhausted on the ground, waiting for their meal to be ready. After a time the Æsir rose and took the meat off the rough spit which they had made to cook it ; but to their great disappointment they found that it was red and raw just as it had been when it was put on. They built up a larger fire, which crackled and roared like an angry dragon ; but still the meat remained uncooked.

"This is not the fault of the fire," quoth Odin ; "there is magic at work," and he looked round to see if he could find out whence the magic came.

There on the tree above him sat the eagle, black and lowering, his staring eyes fixed on the fire. But nevertheless he saw the angry and suspicious looks of the three hungry gods, and he knew that they would not easily bear to be robbed of the meal they needed so much. Therefore he judged it best to speak. "It is true," he said, answering their looks, "that I have bewitched the fire so that it will not cook your meat, but if you will promise to let me have as much of it as I can eat, I will take off the spell, and the fire will do its work."

The gods, thinking that they could well spare as much as the bird would be able to devour, readily agreed ; and the eagle flew down from the tree and hovered over the fire, flapping its enormous wings so that the flames roared more fiercely than ever.

Very soon the meat was ready, and the gods removed it from the fire and prepared to eat ; but before they had tasted a mouthful the eagle swooped down, seized three-quarters of the animal in his strong beak, and prepared to make off with it.

Greedy Loki, seeing his dinner thus about to disappear, seized a large branch that was lying on the ground close by and struck the eagle as hard as he could, just as the bird had spread its wings and was rising in the air. But when he tried to lift the branch for a second blow, he found that it had stuck fast to the eagle's back, and feeling that he was being lifted from his feet as the bird flew upward, he unclasped his hands, meaning to let the branch go. To his intense dismay, however, he found that he could not, for it had stuck to his fingers.

Away went the bird, first rising swiftly so that Loki was breathless with the rush through the air, then flying low and dragging his unfortunate captive over stones and brambles till he was torn and bleeding and exhausted. His arms were strained and aching, yet he could not let go the branch, and the eagle took no notice of his prayers for mercy.

At last in despair he promised to give anything his captor might ask if only he might be borne safely to the earth and allowed to loose his horrible grip.

"There is only one thing that will serve you as ransom," answered the eagle, "and that is the casket of magic fruit belonging to Idun, the wife of Bragi."

Loki protested that it was quite impossible for anyone to steal Idun's fruit, for all the gods in Asgard would unite to protect it.

"You must get it for me or you must suffer worse tortures than those you have borne already," answered the bird. "I am Thiassi, the giant of the storm, and I can toss you about like a leaf blown by the wind, and hurl you against rocks, and cast you into the middle of the ocean, and these things I will do if you do not bring to me the magic casket."

Then Loki, trusting to the cunning that had so often served

The Apples of Youth

him in his difficulties, swore solemnly that by some means he would lure Idun out of Asgard with her wonderful apples and put her in the power of the giant.

" Do so," said the eagle, " and you shall be free ; but if you fail, I will have no mercy."

Loki went back to the place where he had left Odin and Hœnir, who exclaimed loudly when they saw his bruised and bleeding limbs. Loki said nothing about the compact he had made with the eagle, but groaned piteously and declared that he must hasten back to his home for rest and healing. His crafty brain was busy trying to form some plan for betraying Idun into the giant's power, but some days passed before he could find any opportunity of speaking to her alone. Then, fortunately for him, Bragi left Asgard, as he often did, to travel as a minstrel through the Middle Earth, and Loki at once went to seek Idun. He found her alone, and began to tell her of some wonderful apples he had seen growing in an orchard just outside the city, of such marvellous flavour and fragrance, and so lovely in appearance that none like them had ever been known, except those contained in her casket. Idun could not be convinced, and replied that there were no apples like hers to be found though one sought them through all creation ; but Loki still declared he could show her some identical with her own. Thus they argued for a long time, and at last Idun, eager to prove that the apples Loki had seen were far inferior to those in her casket, agreed to his proposal that she should accompany him next day to the place where the apples were growing, bringing her casket with her that the fruit might be compared.

So in the morning they set off together ; but no sooner were they outside the safe shelter of Asgard, than Loki disappeared. Idun, finding herself alone, turned to go back to the city ; but suddenly it seemed as if a black cloud hid the light of the sun, and looking up she saw a huge black bird with outstretched wings swooping down upon her. She shrieked and looked round wildly for some place to hide herself, but there was no refuge from those terrible claws. They fastened themselves in her flowing garments, so that she felt the cruel pressure on her

117

tender body. Then, rising as easily as if he held nothing at all in his talons, the great eagle flew swiftly away northward.

Soon Asgard was left far behind and he was flying over the desolate wastes that led to Jotunheim, the land of the hated giants.

When at last the eagle alighted Idun was breathless and almost fainting with fright; but she strove bravely to conquer her terror that she might guard the precious apples, which in that giddy rush through the air she had held with desperate grasp. She sat up and pushed back the fair hair which had fallen over her eyes, and there before her she saw a giant, terrible and grim, who held out his great hand threateningly.

" I am Thiassi," he said, " the giant of the storm, and this is my stronghold. Here you are far from Asgard and no help from the gods can come to you. Give me that crystal casket in which are the apples of youth, and you shall be my queen and the lady of this castle, and live here with feasting and merriment, with many to serve and obey you."

But Idun shrank from his outstretched hand. " I will not give you the apples," she said, " neither you nor any of your race shall touch the fruit which has fed the gods of Asgard."

Then Thiassi's rage was terrible to see, for he knew that he could not take the apples by force. He shouted with his dread voice, and his people came running in—giants and giantesses, ugly and misshapen, with fierce faces and twisted limbs and streaming hair that seemed always as if it were tossed by the wind. They carried Idun away to a chamber in a rock-built tower round which the wind shrieked and the lightning played and the thunder crashed.

Here for many days she was shut up, seeing no one but her fierce gaolers and Thiassi, who came every morning to demand the magic apples. But Idun resisted bravely, and gave always the same answer that she had given at first; but she pined and grew weak and pale in her gloomy prison. All day she sat and thought of her bright home in Asgard, and wondered if she should ever see it again. " Bragi! beloved!" she cried, "when will you come?" And sometimes she fancied that through the

The Apples of Youth

noises of the storm she heard, faint and wavering, the sweet notes of Bragi's harp.

But Bragi knew nothing of his wife's captivity, thinking her safe in Asgard; while Odin and the other gods, missing her from their banquet, believed her to be travelling with her husband. As the time passed, however, they grew uneasy. It was now many days since they had tasted the magic apples, and they feared that age would creep on them unawares. So they began to make inquiries, and found that Idun had not left Asgard with Bragi, but had been seen after his departure walking toward the city's gates in company with Loki. The mention of Loki at once roused the gods' suspicions; they sent for him and questioned him closely. Loki tried craftily to evade their questions, but they all knew him too well to be content with anything less than a solemn oath that he knew nothing of Idun's disappearance. So at last he was obliged to confess what he had done, and at that the anger of the gods was so fierce that Loki began to fear that this time he had really gone too far, and that his life would be forfeited. He pretended great sorrow, and he promised to try and restore Idun; but nothing would appease the angry gods until he offered to set off then and there and by some means bring her back to Asgard. Freya consented to lend him her falcon plumage, and he flew away, while the gods, sternly bidding him keep his word and that quickly, made their way to the ramparts of the city to watch for his return.

Urged on by fear of what would befall him if he failed in his enterprise, the nimble Loki sped like the wind toward the giant's stronghold. There, entering by a window in Idun's tower, he changed her into a swallow, and without waiting to give any explanation, he took her between his claws and began to fly homeward as swiftly as he had come.

The giant's servants, seeing a falcon take flight from the tower, rushed up, in fear for their prisoner, and found her gone. They stood helpless and dismayed, and just at that moment Thiassi, who had been away fishing, returned. In fear and trembling they told their tale. The storm-giant raged and shrieked in anger when he found that his captive had escaped; but a moment

119

later he had changed himself into an eagle once more and had started in pursuit.

Soon Loki was aware of what seemed like a mighty tempest raging behind him, and knew that Thiassi was coming with whirlwind speed; but Asgard was not very far off, and he still hoped to escape. He spread out his falcon plumes to their widest extent and hurried desperately on, while Idun, trembling in his grasp, cried: " Quicker! quicker! he will catch us! I can see his great black wings. O, quicker! quicker! "

THE APPLES OF YOUTH

The gods from the ramparts of Asgard could now see Loki like a speck in the far distance, and they raised a cry of rejoicing; but a moment later a darker speck appeared behind him, and they knew that the giant was in pursuit. Nearer and nearer came the two birds, and now they could plainly see that Loki held something carefully within his claws. " Idun! " they cried, and they leaned over the ramparts and shouted encouragement to the panting, labouring Loki, while some ran and fetched huge bundles of fuel, which they piled high on the ramparts. On came the giant, his great wings almost fanning Loki's falcon plumes. The gods shouted wildly, and Loki made a last despairing effort. He sped forward like an arrow shot from a bow, and was drawn by eager hands over the ramparts where he fell breathless and exhausted. Quickly the gods brought blazing torches and set light to the great pile of fuel; so that when Thiassi, unable to stop in his headlong flight, followed Loki over the ramparts, he was choked and blinded by the great clouds of smoke that rose from the pile, and his feathers were singed and shrivelled by the leaping tongues of flame. He fell helpless on the ground, and the swords of the gods quickly put an end to his life.

Turning from this act of vengeance they saw Idun standing before them in her natural form, as fresh and lovely as when they had last seen her in their banqueting hall ; and in her hand was the casket of apples that she had brought safely through so many dangers. She held it out to them, bidding them taste once more the fruit they loved, and the gods eagerly obeyed. At once they felt a new sense of youthfulness and joy run through them, and they surrounded Idun with joyous greetings and thanks. So light-hearted were they that they felt kindly disposed even to the fallen Thiassi. What wonder, they said, that the giant ventured much in the hope of tasting this magic fruit ; and as a sign of their goodwill they set his eyes in the heavens as a constellation, to shine for ever in the sight of men.

Ægir's Brewing-kettle

Ægir, god of the sea, was a tall, thin old man, with long silvery hair and beard, and hands that looked like the claws of some terrible bird of prey. He was cruel and greedy, and loved to lie in wait for the ships of men, overturn them, and drag them down to his caves at the bottom of the sea. His wife Ran was as cruel as he was ; she had an enormous net in which she used to catch the ships, and laugh as she saw how the men in them struggled vainly to get away. This dread pair had nine beautiful daughters, the Waves, who floated about on the sea clad in long, flowing robes of green or blue or grey. Usually they were gay and sportive, but at times they would fall into terrible tempers, and rush violently about, dashing themselves on the rocks and uttering wild, piercing shrieks.

Ægir often paid visits to the gods in Asgard, but they had never visited him in return, when one day he suddenly made up his mind to invite them to spend the harvest feast with him at the palace he had built for himself on an island in the Cattegat.[1]

[1] Arm of the North Sea between Sweden and Jutland.

The Book of Myths

The Æsir were rather surprised when they received this invitation, for the sea-god was not noted for his hospitality, and it was generally believed that the fare in his palace was both plain and scanty. So one of the gods—most likely Thor, as he was fondest of eating and drinking—mentioned to Ægir that in Asgard the board was richly spread every day and that wine was poured out freely. "You will need to prepare a goodly feast and brew

THOR AND TYR IN THEIR GOAT-DRAWN CHARIOT

much mead," he said, "if you think to entertain the gods of Asgard." But Ægir answered that his meats were ready and rich dishes would be plentiful, but that he was a little doubtful whether he would have enough mead. "For," he said, "my brewing-kettle is small, and the liquor that it will hold may not suffice for so large a party."

"Oh, if it is only a question of the size of the brewing-kettle," said Thor, "I will soon put that right. Hymir the giant has a kettle that is a mile deep, and so wide that you cannot see both sides of it at once. He will lend it to you I am sure, and Tyr and I will go and fetch it."

Ægir's Brewing-kettle

So Thor set off in his goat-drawn chariot with his brother Tyr, the god of war. He took the same road as he had taken when he visited Utgard-Loki; he left his goats at the peasant's house as he had done then, and the two gods walked thence to Hymir's house.

The giant was out when they arrived, but his mother and his wife were at home—the mother a horrible old giantess with nine hundred heads, the wife young and beautiful. They received the two gods very hospitably and set meat and drink before them; but they were very doubtful as to what Hymir would say to Thor's request.

The younger giantess advised them to hide under one of the huge kettles hanging at the end of the hall, while she told her husband of their coming. "For," said she, "sometimes when he is in a bad temper he will kill unbidden visitors with a look." The gods took her advice, and were hardly settled in their hiding-place when Hymir came in.

"Two gods from Asgard have come to visit you," said his wife. "They want to borrow your big brewing-kettle to lend to Ægir, who is making a great feast."

At this Hymir's wrath began to rise, and he looked so angrily toward the place where Thor and Tyr were hidden that the rafters cracked, and all the eight kettles fell with a crash. Seven of them broke in pieces; only one—that which the gods had come to borrow—remained whole. Through all the clatter and din Hymir's angry voice was heard, and he came threateningly toward Thor and Tyr, who were trying to get clear of the fragments that had fallen all around them.

But the giant's wife knew how to manage her husband when he fell into these sudden fits of rage, and after some trouble she convinced him that the two gods had come with no evil intentions, but solely desiring to show him honour, seeing that there was no brewing-kettle in Asgard equal to his, or fit to prepare mead for the great feast that was getting ready.

Then Hymir's mood changed, and he became good-tempered and jovial, and welcomed the two gods with heartiness. He went out into his field, killed three of his best oxen, and brought them in to be cooked for supper ; but he felt rather dismayed when Thor ate up two of the oxen, leaving only one for him, to share with his wife and Tyr. "To-morrow," thought the giant, "I must go to my fishing early, or I shall never catch enough to make a breakfast for such a hungry fellow as this Thor." So next morning he got up in the faint light of the dawn and went down to the shore. Before he had got the boat ready to launch, down came Thor, and offered to go fishing with him. Hymir was not very well pleased at this, but he did not quite know how to refuse, so he answered : "Very well, only I have no bait for you. You must find that for yourself."

"Easily done !" replied Thor, and he very calmly went to the field where the giant's oxen were feeding, picked out the biggest, killed it, and came back with its great head under his arm. He threw the head into the boat where the giant was already seated, jumped in himself, took the oars, and with great strokes carried the boat out to sea.

Very soon the giant cried out, "Hold ! We have gone far enough. Here is my fishing-ground."

But Thor took no notice, and the boat went rapidly on.

"Stop !" cried Hymir, beginning to get frightened. "I will go no farther. Put back I tell you. We are getting near the place where the Midgard snake lies below the water, and at any moment its terrible head may be raised to see who is daring to come this way."

Now Thor wished above all things to meet and fight the awful Iörmungandr, so the giant's words only made him row faster. When he thought that he was probably just above it, he took the head of the ox, fastened it to his strong fishing-hook, and lowered his line very carefully.

The giant meanwhile had caught two whales. "These," he thought, "will surely be enough for breakfast, so now we can go home, and glad enough I shall be, for I have no fancy for an encounter with the Midgard snake."

He was just about to tell Thor to turn the boat, when the god gave a great shout of triumph, and began to pull his line in with all his might. The water round about the boat rose in great waves, foaming and swirling as if an enormous whirlpool had suddenly been formed there.

"Hurrah!" shouted Thor, "I have hooked the snake I am sure. No other creature could be so heavy or struggle so fiercely!" In spite of the giant's horrified entreaties he pulled and tugged until, after a terrific struggle, the horrible head of Iörmungandr, raging and sending out his poisonous breath in all directions, came to the surface.

This was too much for Hymir, and taking out his great knife he cut the fishing-line through, so that the snake sank back again to the bottom of the sea.

Swift and terrible rage descended upon Thor. He had taken his hammer and was just going to deal the snake a crushing blow when it had disappeared from his sight. Now, his hammer still poised to strike, he turned toward Hymir and dealt him such a blow that the huge giant toppled overboard. But Hymir, not a whit perturbed, only made haste to get out of the way of the dreaded snake, and waded quickly to the shore, in time to meet Thor as he landed. The Thunder-god, his gust of anger over, greeted him jovially; and Hymir, taking up the two whales, strode away to the house. Thor, not to be outdone, took up the boat, oars, and fishing-tackle, and followed him; and very soon they were seated at breakfast together, where the whales quickly disappeared.

After breakfast Hymir called upon Thor to do some feat which would prove his boasted strength. "Come," the giant cried, " show me that you can do something better than drag a wretched serpent from the depths of the sea. Try, for example, if you can break my tankard."

Thor took the tankard and flung it with all his might against the stone pillars supporting the house; but when he went to pick it up he found it unbroken, and without even a dint upon its surface. Again and again he tried, but still the tankard remained uninjured, and the giant shouted with delight.

The giant's wife, who was moving about on household tasks, passed near Thor, and managed to whisper in his ear, " Throw it against Hymir's forehead." Quickly Thor turned and flung the tankard with all his strength, and it fell to the ground shattered.

" Well then," said Hymir, a little put out at the god's unexpected success, " there is the kettle you came to fetch. Take it, and go your way." So Tyr went to take the kettle, but found to his surprise that he could not lift it. He tugged and strained, but it would not move. Then Thor came to see what he could do. Long he strove, but could only raise it an inch or so from the floor. He girded himself with his magic belt, Migin-giörd, which doubled his strength, and drawing this to its last hole, he took up the kettle and laid it on his shoulders. But the great pull that he had given shook the giant's house, so that the pillars were cracked and great pieces fell down from the roof ; and he had planted his feet so strongly on the floor that at the last effort they had gone through and made a great hole.

Hymir looked on indignant ; and when in triumph Thor clapped the great pot on his head like a hat, and strode off with Tyr to begin the journey homeward, the giant could contain his anger no longer. He rushed from the house and called loudly upon his brothers, the storm-giants, to help him make an end of these two audacious gods, the eternal enemies of the Jotuns, now that they were in their power.

The storm-giants came flocking at the call, and they all started in pursuit. Thor, looking back, saw them coming, with angry shouts and gestures. He took his great hammer, Miölnir, and hurled it at the foremost, who fell dead ; and when the hammer came back to his hand he threw it again, and the second giant perished. So Thor slew all the giants, and then, with the pot on his head, he journeyed merrily on with Tyr toward Asgard.

Balder the Sun-god

While the elder gods spent the time they could spare from graver matters in fighting and feasting, their sons and the younger inhabitants of Asgard found time for lighter and more joyous pastimes. The sport they liked best was the throwing of the golden disc or quoit, and very often they would assemble on

Balder the Sun-god

their playing-field of Idavold, part of the fair green plain on which their city was built, and try who could throw the disc the farthest and with the surest aim. Here would come Hermod, nimble and swift-footed; Vida, the strong god, who spoke but seldom; Heimdall, whose hearing was so keen that he could hear the grass grow in the fields and the wool on the backs of the sheep; Bragi, young and fair, whose sweet songs could make the trees bud and blossom; Balder, the Sun-god, more beautiful still; Hodur, Balder's twin brother, blind from his birth, and dark and sad in aspect; and Uller, stepson of Thor, and the special friend of Balder.

The elder gods—Thor the Thunderer, one-handed Tyr, and even Odin himself—came sometimes to look on at the sports of the younger ones, and Loki came too, not so much that he cared for the sport as that his mischief-loving nature saw a chance of some trickery wherever a number of others were gathered together.

In all beautiful Asgard there was no more delightful sight to be seen than this playground of the gods when the sport was going on, and always it was clear to every onlooker that the most joyous movement and the blithest laughter came from that quarter of the field where Balder played his part. His bright head and fair face passed like a flash of light among the darker forms of the others, and his voice was the clearest and the happiest of any. There was no strife where Balder was, no harsh words or complaining. All felt better and happier when he was present, and everybody loved him—not only the gods of Asgard but men who lived in the world below, and even the giants of Jotunheim.

When the sports were over and Balder went home to his beautiful palace, whose silver roof was held up by golden pillars, he brought happiness there too. His young wife Nanna loved him dearly, and was full of joy when he came back to her. Odin and Frigga loved him the best of all their sons, and watched him proudly day by day, happy to see his unclouded face and to note how easily he won the hearts of all who came near him. "And yet," they said one to the other, "how unspoiled he is, how wise in council, how dutiful, how brave!"

The Book of Myths

But there came a heavy day when a change was seen in Balder. He rose from sleep troubled and absent-minded, and all day long there was a cloud on his bright face. He went about his duties soberly, without laughter or song, and spoke little. Next day it was the same, and for many days that followed his trouble seemed to increase, and he walked the city ways as if he bore a heavy load.

Asgard was no longer a joyous city, for Balder's unhappiness was reflected in the faces of all who loved him. The gods did not care now to assemble on Idavold for their sports since Balder kept away, or if he came was so silent and sad that it pierced their hearts to see him so unlike the radiant Balder of old.

Odin and Frigga looked on with dread and misgiving, for they feared some terrible trouble was coming to their beloved Balder. At last they called him to them, and begged him to tell them the cause of his sorrow, and in answer to their pleading Balder unwillingly confessed that his trouble was caused by his dreams. All his life before he had dreamed of beautiful and happy things, but lately dark visions had come to him in the night, and he had awaked not clearly remembering what he had seen, but oppressed with a vague yet terrible sense of coming evil that he could neither shake off nor explain.

Odin looked very grave when he heard this, for he himself was seldom free from dark forebodings of that dread time, foretold from the beginning, when the giants would triumph over the gods of Asgard, and the end of all things would come. He did his best to comfort his son, telling him that no harm could come to one whom everybody loved; but when Balder had gone, Odin and Frigga looked at one another, a terrible fear in their hearts. "What can we do?" asked Odin, for though long ago he had given one of his eyes for a draught from the well of wisdom, and was called Odin the all-wise, he could not think of anything that would help in this great trouble.

Frigga, who was always practical and resourceful, answered, " I will send messengers through all creation, and they shall ask everything that exists—living creatures, trees and plants

ARTEMIS AND HER NYMPHS
Chapter 1

THE RIDE OF THE VALKYRS
Chapter 2

THE OLD GODS VANQUISHED
Chapter 4

THE CHEST OF SET
Chapter 5

TOTH AND THE CHIEF MAGICIAN
Chapter 5

HANUMAN SETS FIRE TO LANKA
Chapter 7

JIZO, THE CHILDREN'S GOD
Chapter 8

Balder the Sun-god

and flowers, stones and water and metals—everything—to take an oath that it will not injure Balder."

So Frigga hurried and sent out her messengers, but still Odin's heart was ill at ease. He could not rest in uncertainty, and always the dread was upon him that the Fates had some evil thing in store for the son he loved.

"I will go," he said to himself, "I will visit the terrible regions of the dead, and question the prophetess there concerning the future of my son. Better to know the worst than to remain in this horrible doubt."

Sadly he mounted his eight-footed horse, Sleipnir, and rode out of Asgard over the bridge Bifrost, taking the northern road toward Niflheim. Along rough ways, in darkness and in bitter cold, he rode for nine days and nine nights, until he reached the river Gioll. Over this was a bridge of crystal, arched with gold, which hung suspended by a single hair, and guarding the bridge sat a grim skeleton. With difficulty Odin persuaded this dread creature to let him pass, and then he journeyed on, the way becoming darker and more difficult at each step. He passed the tall, gaunt trees of ironwood, and reached Hel-gate. Out from a dark hole at the side of the gate rushed Garm, Hel's fierce watch-dog. But fierce as he was, those whose hearts were kind had no cause to fear him, for all who had ever given bread to the needy found themselves provided with a Hel cake, and Garm at once became mild and tractable when this was offered.

Through Hel-gate Odin entered the hall—not one of the terrible chambers where the spirits of the wicked were undergoing punishment, but the place prepared for the innocent, who came to Niflheim because they had been killed by an accident, or had died of disease or old age, and therefore could not pass to Valhalla, which was reserved for those who fell in battle.

The hall was large and commodious, but sunless, and a chill fell on Odin's heart when he saw Hel's attendants busy preparing a feast, and spreading the couches with costly coverings, as if some new-comer of high rank were expected. He strode hurriedly through the hall, and in spite of horrid sights and sounds all around him pressed on until he came to the secret abiding place of the Vala, the prophetess who dwelt in Niflheim. Then three time in solemn tones he chanted a magic spell, and three times he traced on the ground the signs that had power to wake the dead. As he finished the prophetess stood before him, and demanded angrily who it was that had dared to rouse her from her long rest. Odin, not wishing to be recognized, gave a name that was not his own, and said he had come to ask for whom the preparations were being made in the hall beyond.

"For Balder," said the Vala, in tones so deep and terrible that they added to the horror of her words. "Hodur his twin brother will kill him, and he will pass ere long to the place that is made ready for him. Now let me rest again, for I will tell you no more."

But Odin, miserable as he was, had yet one more question to ask. "And who is he who shall avenge the death of Balder?"

"A son of yours who is yet to be born," answered the Vala, and then, refusing to speak another word, she passed back into her cave.

Very sad was Odin as he rode back to Asgard, and he scarcely noticed the roughness of the way in thinking of his well-loved son, who was so soon to depart and be seen by him no more. For Odin knew that the decrees of the Fates could not be avoided, and with a heavy heart he prepared to tell the waiting Frigga that she must lose her son.

But when he entered his palace he found there, instead of anxiety and suspense, a general rejoicing. Frigga came to meet him with the glad tidings that everything throughout creation had promised not to hurt Balder. "Everything?" asked Odin, afraid to believe such good tidings; and Frigga answered, "Everything—giants, men, and all created things—except, indeed, the mistletoe which grows on the oak outside the gate of Valhalla, and that is a thing so weak and insignificant—not having even a root of its own, but living on another tree—that no harm can be feared from that."

Odin could not forget the words he had heard from the Vala, and the preparations he had seen in Hel's hall. "But," he thought to himself, "if all things have sworn not to hurt Balder, what

Balder the Sun-god

evil can possibly come to him ?   Frigga's wise action, so promptly
taken, has robbed the Fates of the power to do him harm.   I
will trust that my dear son is safe, and to-night we will make a
feast and rejoice at the passing of this peril."

So they made a great feast, and not only Odin but all the
dwellers in Asgard felt that a dark cloud had passed from the
sky above them.   The faces at the banquet were joyous and
smiling once more.   Even Balder was able to shake off the vague
terror that had oppressed him, and once more appeared as the
radiant and happy god from whom light and joy proceeded.

Next day the younger gods met again on the playground which
of late they had deserted, and made merry, throwing the disc
and running races.   But at length they grew tired of these
sports, and to one of their number there came suddenly a new
idea.   " Let us," he cried, " aim at Balder.   Nothing will hurt
him, so we may throw anything we please.   Come, let us bring
swords, axes, darts, spears, and see how all will fall to the
ground, having worked him no harm."

The gods shouted with delight at this suggestion, and each
ran eagerly to fetch weapons, stones, anything that would do to
throw at Balder.

The Sun-god stood in the middle of the field, joining merrily
in the sport ; he laughed as loudly as any and incited his friends
to further efforts.   A shower of missiles rushed through the air,
touched Balder with a light touch that was almost a caress,
and dropped harmlessly to the ground.   Bolder and bolder grew
the gods at play, more and more strength they put in their aim,
louder and louder grew the din as shouts of laughter mingled
with the clanging of weapons.

Frigga, who as usual sat busily spinning in Fensalir, heard
the noise, and asked an old woman who was passing by what
it was all about.   The old woman explained, and Frigga smiled,
well pleased at this proof of the success of what she had done.
" 'Tis a merry sport," she said, " for all things have sworn that
they will not hurt Balder."

" All things ? " asked the old woman.

" Every created thing," replied Frigga, " save, indeed, the

131

mistletoe that grows on the oak at the gate of Valhalla. But what could that do ? ''

" What indeed ! " answered the old woman. " Balder is safe from harm. Good day to you, O noble lady, for I would see more of the sport," and she went with slow and feeble steps upon her way.

But as soon as she was out of Frigga's sight, she straightened her bent back, and a wonderful change came over her, and lo, here was no old woman, but Loki, the doer of evil. For Loki, who at first had only played tricks upon the gods through love of mischief and adventure, had become as time went on malicious and cruel in his fun, and at last had grown to love the doing of evil for its own sake, so that those who had before laughed at his cunning now shunned and hated him. He had for a long time been jealous of Balder, and had been looking out for a chance to work him ill. Now the chance had come, and he was determined to use it in the most direful way.

He hurried to the gate of Valhalla and picked a spray of mistletoe, and by the magic arts that he knew he made it hard and keen like an iron dart. Then he went back to the field where the gods were at play. Hodur stood moodily leaning against a tree. He had, in spite of his blindness, learnt to throw the disc with a good aim and to join in the usual sports, but at this new game he could do nothing, and he was feeling injured and ill-tempered when Loki came up to him.

" Why are you not playing with the others ? " asked the tempter.

" Because I am blind," Hodur answered sullenly; " I have nothing to throw, and could not see to aim a missile if I had one."

" Oh," said Loki, " it is necessary that you join in the game and throw at least once, or it will seem as if you alone of all the gods wished to slight Balder. Come, let me lead you to a good place, and I will give you a missile and direct your aim."

So Hodur allowed Loki to lead him forward, and the evil one put the spray of mistletoe in his hand, and guided his arm so that he aimed straight at Balder. The aim was true, and without a cry Balder fell to the ground lifeless.

Balder the Sun-god

The laughter of the gods ceased suddenly, and there was a terrible moment while each one held his breath in horror; then all rushed toward Balder. They lifted him up and tried every art they knew to bring the life back to the still form; but all was of no use. Balder was dead.

The scene grew chill and gloomy, the sun was hidden from sight, and an icy breath touched the faces of those who bent in sorrow over the lifeless body. Loki, the prime mover in the evil deed, had stolen away, and Hodur stood still on the spot from which he had thrown the fatal branch, horrified and bewildered at the deed he had unwittingly done. Cries and fierce threats of vengeance arose, but none dared to touch him and so violate the peace-stead of the gods.

Then there came a cry so shrill and piercing and full of bitterest suffering that the others stopped their lamentations and stood silent in awe and pity, for this was Balder's mother.

Kneeling down, Frigga clasped the bright head of her son, refusing to believe that he was really dead. Then, as her desperate hope slowly died, she laid him gently down and stood erect. "Go," she cried, "some one of you, down to Niflheim, and implore Hel to give up my son. Tell her to ask what ransom she will, it shall be paid. Tell her that with him happiness is slain, and that neither in Asgard nor on earth can any heart be glad if he is taken away."

No one stirred, and she cried again, "Will no one go, will no one do my bidding? Him who will do this for love of Odin and Frigga they will requite with love and thanks and will hold him in their hearts above all others."

Then Hermod, moved with pity to hear the great queen plead and none reply, stepped forward. "Lady, I will make the dread journey, for love of Odin, and of you, and of my brother Balder."

A gleam of joy shone on Frigga's grief-stricken face, and from the gods came a murmur of awe and admiration. Odin commanded Sleipnir to be brought forth, and although never before had the steed of the Allfather suffered any but his master to ride him, yet now he stood sad and quiet while Hermod mounted,

133

and turned obedient to his will, and took once more the dreary road to Niflheim.

"Take up now," said Odin, "the body of Balder, and bear it to his palace, and after go into the forest and hew down the giant pines to make a worthy funeral pyre for my son."

So the gods laboured and brought down huge trunks which they laid on the deck of Balder's dragon-ship *Ringhorn*. Then

BALDER'S FUNERAL SHIP

each brought the most precious thing that he had as a last offering to his dead comrade, and they hung garlands of flowers on the ship and decorated it with rich tapestries.

When all was ready the body of Balder, finely arrayed, was carried in sad and stately procession to the shore and laid upon the pyre, and one by one the gods stepped forward and looked their last upon the dead face. Nanna his wife came in her turn, and as she looked her loving heart broke and she fell lifeless. Reverently the gods lifted her body and laid it beside her husband. They slew his horse and hounds and placed them too on the pyre. Last of all came Odin. He bent over his

Balder the Sun-god

son, and gave as offering the magic ring Draupnir. Then, as it seemed to the watching company, he whispered some words in his dead son's ear, and covering his face withdrew.

All now was ready for the launching, but with all their efforts the gods could not move the ship. After long trial they sent for aid to the giants, many of whom had gathered round in mourning, for they too loved Balder. A mighty giantess came quickly to their aid, riding upon a fierce wolf, with a bridle of writhing snakes. When she dismounted no one could hold her terrible steed, and she herself had to throw it down and bind it fast. Then she strode forward to the ship *Ringhorn*, set her shoulder against it, and with one tremendous push sent it rushing out upon the waters.

By this time the fire was burning fiercely and great flames arose, lighting the sea and sky, and roaring louder than the rushing waves. Farther and farther out the great ship drifted, and more fiercely burnt the pyre. The shades of evening fell, and still it burnt on, with tongues of fire upleaping toward the skies. Then it flickered, and the flames died one by one, and left a mass of glowing fiery red; sank still more, lower and lower, till the last spark was quenched in the waters.

The gods went sadly home, silent and heavy-hearted; only Frigga had any hope that Hermod would return with good tidings.

Nine days and nine nights Hermod rode on the dreary way toward Niflheim. He passed Giallur bridge and leapt Hel-gate, and faring onward reached at last the banqueting hall. Here on the couch that Odin had seen prepared sat Balder, and beside him his wife Nanna. The brightness had faded from Balder's face, and Nanna's bloom was gone. The pale ghosts of their former selves, they sat listless and dejected and listened to Hermod's hopeful words unmoved and cheerless. Only when Balder looked on his young wife his heart was moved, and he besought Hermod to take Nanna away from these gloomy shades. But Nanna clung to her husband and refused to be parted from him, even to return to Asgard.

All through the night the three talked together, and in the morning Hermod went to Hel and pleaded with her for Balder's

release, until it seemed as if she would relent. " If," she said,
" all creation loves Balder, let all weep for him. Then and
then alone I will let him go ; but if one created thing, however
small, refuses a tear, then he must stay in Niflheim until the
great day which shall see the end of all the gods of Asgard."

This was more than Hermod had dared to hope, and with his
heart full of gladness he took leave of Balder and hurried back.
Sleipnir carried him bravely, and at the end of the ninth day the
watching gods saw the black horse galloping at full speed over
Bifrost. Very quickly the news went round, and an anxious
group gathered at the entrance to the city. " Surely it is good
news," they said, as they saw how Sleipnir raced along ; and
they thought that there was something in Hermod's figure, too,
which spoke of cheerfulness and confidence. When he came
nearer and they saw his face, the faint hope that had risen
within them was strengthened. He sprang down, and hurriedly
gave his message, and then amid cries and sobs of joy, and eager
praises of Hermod and Sleipnir, and a bustle of hasty preparations,
messengers were sent once more throughout creation to bid every
created thing weep for Balder. Only Odin remained doubtful,
for he mistrusted the evil offspring of Loki, and feared that
Hel's fair-seeming offer held a snare.

Everywhere the messengers went they found all things eager
to obey, and soon a sound arose as when a thaw comes after a
great frost, and waters are loosened. Loki, baffled and angry,
saw his nearly successful plan in danger, so taking upon himself
the form of a giantess, Thok, he passed into a dark cave, close
by the roadside where the messengers must pass. On they
came, calling on all things to weep for Balder, but Thok mocked
at them, and vowed that no tear should fall from her eyes.

> Thok she weepeth
> With dry tears
> For Balder's death—
> Neither in life nor yet in death
> Gave he me gladness.
> Let Hel keep her prey.

The messengers tried by every means they could think of to
induce her to give way, but in vain, and they went back sadly

to Asgard. Again the eager crowd gathered, this time in joyful anticipation of hearing the words which should release Balder. But at the sight of the messengers' faces their own fell, and when the black tidings were told, despair, deep and terrible, reigned among them. Balder, the bright and beautiful, would come no more ; the light that had shone so radiantly on Asgard was quenched. In their palace Odin and Frigga mourned with bitter tears. A gloom hung over the city and thick clouds hid the sun, for Balder, god of light and gladness, happy and beloved, was dead.

Loki's Punishment

Asgard was never the same happy place after the death of Balder. His bright face and joyous voice were missed by every one, and the gods did not care for their accustomed sports now that Balder was not there to take part in them. A shadow hung over the whole city and Odin's heart was very heavy, for he knew that the fatal day was fast coming when his race must pass away and be seen no more.

It happened that soon after Balder's death Ægir paid a visit to Asgard, and when he saw how depressed his friends were, and how gloomy the banquets that used to be so joyful, he was grieved and thought what he could do to bring back some of the former brightness. So he made a great feast in his coral caves at the bottom of the sea, and invited all the Æsir, and he greeted them so heartily and entertained them so well that for the first time since Balder's death they almost forgot their sorrow and made merry in their old fashion. But all their grief came back, and anger with it, when in the middle of the feast Loki appeared and impudently tried to take his place at the board.

Ægir sternly bade him depart, and then Loki let loose the evil temper which his cunning had always before managed to keep hidden. In a fury of rage he poured out wild and insulting words, trying to sting the gods into anger ; then seeing that none cared for his wrath he turned on a servant of Ægir, whom he had heard praised for waiting on the company skilfully. With a sudden blow he killed him, and then the gods were roused indeed. They drove Loki from the cave, and threatened him with terrible punishment if he came into their presence again.

But scarcely were they reseated when Loki appeared once more. This time he controlled his passion, and used his wicked tongue more cleverly. He jeered at Odin's one eye and Tyr's maimed right hand, at Hodur for having been so easily beguiled, and at Thor who had made such a poor show in the hall of the giant Hymir.

But it was dangerous work to gibe at Thor, and when Loki heard his mighty voice roar out "Silence!" and saw the great hammer Miölnir raised in his strong hand, he fled hurriedly from the cave.

He knew that the gods would not forgive this outburst, and that their vengeance would now certainly fall upon him, so he set his wits to work to frame some crafty plan by which he might escape them. He went away far into the mountains, and there built for himself a hut which had four doors opening toward the North, South, East, and West. These he kept always open, so that he might escape his enemies from whatever direction they came, and he decided that when he saw them coming he would change himself into a salmon, and jump into the cataract which dashed down the rocks close by.

"If they guess my device," he thought, "and fish for me with a hook, I can easily avoid that; but I am not sure what will happen if they drag the stream with a net such as Ran uses. But Ran will not lend them her net, and I do not believe that they can make one. I do not believe I could do it myself." He set to work with some string and a mesh to try what could be done, but he had not half finished when he saw in the distance Odin, Thor, and Kvasir, the god renowned for his wisdom and goodness. He threw the net he was making into the fire, rushed out through the opposite door, changed himself into a salmon, and hid himself among the stones at the bottom of the cataract.

The three pursuers reached the hut and went in, but as they could find no trace of Loki they thought that he must have had warning of their coming, and had for that time escaped them.

Loki's Punishment

But Kvasir looking about saw the half-burned net on the hearth and guessed something of what had been in Loki's mind when he made it. "Let us make such a net as this," he said, "and with it search the waters of the stream that dashes over the rocks close by." They set to work at once, and thanks to Kvasir's wisdom, they made a net that answered their purpose very well. Then the chase began. Loki doubled and twisted

THE PUNISHMENT OF LOKI

and hid and wriggled and for a time evaded them; but the gods, guided by Kvasir's advice, fished skilfully, and at last the big salmon was caught. He tried to free himself by a sudden leap, but Thor grasped him by the tail, and in spite of his slippery skin he held him and squeezed him so tightly that his tail was crushed together; and this is why salmon have narrow tails to this day.

Seeing that his tricks could not save him, Loki, in a very bad temper, took his own shape again. The gods bound him very firmly, hand and foot, and when the thongs were tied and secured they changed them into iron, so as to be quite sure that Loki could not break them. They then carried him into a deep and dark cavern and fastened him securely to the rock, where he was doomed to remain until the day of the last great battle.

But Loki had other enemies besides the offended gods. Skadi, a giantess of the cold mountain stream, hated him. Many a time the two had met in conflict without either gaining a complete victory. She gleefully watched the gods bind her enemy, and then she added the last unbearable touch to his misery. She fastened a serpent directly above his head, so that its poison fell drop by drop upon his face, which his fetters would not allow him to turn away. The pain was terrible, and Loki cried out in anguish. Then Sigyn, his faithful wife, came hurrying to his side, and held up a cup to catch the drops as they fell. Here for all the years that must pass before Ragnarok she remained, only moving from her husband's side when her cup was full and threatened to overflow. Then she hastily went to empty it, and while she was gone the drops fell on Loki's face, so that he writhed in anguish and shook the whole earth, doing terrible damage; and men called this shaking an earthquake.

CHAPTER III

MYTHS OF THE NORTH AMERICAN INDIANS

> Ye whose hearts are fresh and simple,
> Who believe that in all ages
> Every human heart is human,
> Listen to this simple story.
>
> LONGFELLOW, *Hiawatha*

THE North-American Indian, up to the late nineteenth century, lived a much freer and somewhat simpler life than the European settlers who came to the continent—not so unlike that which our own early forebears lived many years ago. In his religion and beliefs, therefore, we find a mythology in its early stages ; in the stories told around the Indian's camp fire we see legends in the making. So the mythology of the Red Man is especially interesting and valuable because it helps us to understand something of the older and more highly developed mythologies, such as those of Egypt and Babylon, whose origins are hidden in the remote past.

The dwelling-place of the North-American Indian is the forest and the plain. He knows nothing of cities or of civilization. In his village he sees small patches of ground planted with maize or wild rice, but he has no idea of the cultivation of the soil on a large scale. He has no flocks and herds, no stores laid up from last year's harvest, no means of bringing in food from other lands. He depends almost entirely upon the results of his hunting in the forests and his fishing in the lakes and streams. If he is not successful he goes hungry ; if the winter is especially long and severe, so that he cannot hunt, he stays in his cold wigwam, and when he has eaten his small store of frozen meat he starves. His whole life is a struggle against the forces of Nature. He matches himself single-handed against cold and storm and darkness, against the bewildering pathlessness of the forests, the treachery of the waters, the strength and cunning of the wild creatures who are fighting for their lives as he is fighting for his. He cannot help seeing that their efforts are far more successful than his own. Their bodies are infinitely better suited to resist cold and wet, and to live safely and comfortably in the forest. They are furnished with natural weapons against which he is powerless if he meets them in close conflict. They can run faster, their scent is keener, their sight stronger. Their instinct teaches them a thousand cunning tricks for self-preservation of which he himself would never think. Only by much toil and watching and patience can he manage to kill one here and there out of the great hosts that live in the forests.

The Indian has a great respect for the animals. He looks upon them as far superior to himself in all the qualities that really matter. So it happens that when an Indian admires particularly a special quality possessed by a certain animal—the cunning of the fox, the swiftness of the deer, the wisdom of the owl—he puts himself under the protection of that animal, making of it a sort of god. Often whole tribes attach themselves in this way to a certain animal, and devote themselves to cultivating the quality they admire, offering prayers to him for his help. In time they grow to believe that there is a certain kinship between them and the object of their worship, and finally he comes to be regarded as their ancestor. This belief in a descent from animals is called totemism, and is very common among primitive peoples; indeed, it seems likely that all races have passed through this stage at some early period in their history.

Remembering these things, we shall expect to find that stories of animals form a large part of North-American mythology, and that some of their gods have the form of animals. Totemism explains much that might seem strange to us in the Indian's conception of some of his deities. He himself is dignified and grave in his demeanour, and many of his gods—Manitou, the Great Spirit, the Sun, the Moon, the Morning Star, for example— are represented as being of high and austere majesty. But many of them are childlike and undeveloped compared to the elder gods of other nations. They do strange, unaccountable things, for which we can find no motive or purpose ; their actions are often grotesque, sometimes laughable. The Indian has watched the inhabitants of the forests very carefully, and noted their characteristics, habits, and antics with an attentive eye. All these he faithfully reproduces, but he cannot look into their mind and follow its workings. So he presents them as strange, inconsequent, powerful, delightful beings, a mixture of man and beast and god.

Glooskap and the Baby

One of the favourite gods of the Algonquin Indians is Glooskap. His name means ' The Liar,' and the Indians when they call him by it mean to pay him a very high compliment. They have a great admiration for any person who is cunning and skilled in deceiving others, so much so that they regard as a god one who possesses these qualities in a high degree. Glooskap was, they believe, a wise and beneficent deity, who in the beginning created man, and afterward spent his time going about the world trying to remove the evils with which his wicked brother, Malsum, afflicted mankind. He warred against the horrid monsters, the witches and the giants who were his brother's servants ; he made desolate regions fertile and held frost and storms in check. He fought against the Kewawqu, monstrous giants and magicians much feared by the Algonquins, and exterminated the whole race ; he subdued the Medecolin, a body of cunning sorcerers, and, single-handed, after a terrible conflict, he killed Pamola, a wicked spirit of the night.

This last victory pleased him mightily, and the next day as he walked through the forest, seeking if there might be yet more evil creatures for him to destroy, pride in his own prowess swelled his heart, and made him long to recount his victories to someone who would give him the praise that he felt to be his due. In this mood he entered the wigwam of an Indian to whom he was well known ; the man was absent, but his wife was within, and with her a baby who sat on the floor sucking a piece of maple sugar. Glooskap told the woman all about the great

The Book of Myths

victory he had gained. "And now," he said, "I am supreme upon the earth, all creatures acknowledge my power and there is not one that dares to disobey me."

The woman listened attentively and respectfully to Glooskap's narrative. At the end, very much to his surprise, she laughed aloud. "Are you quite sure of that, Master?" she said. "I could tell you of one creature you have not conquered, and whom you will never conquer, try as you may."

Glooskap was surprised and rather angry at the woman's words. "Who is it," he asked, "that can withstand the power which has subdued giants and demons?"

"It is my baby, Wasis," answered the woman; "you have not conquered him, and if you listen to me you will not try to do so, for it would only be wasting your time."

"Ha!" replied Glooskap scornfully, "a baby! Nothing could be easier than to deal with him."

"Be careful, Master," said the woman; "you have never had wife or child of your own, and you do not know anything about a baby like my Wasis. Be content and leave him alone, and own that there is one creature at least whom you cannot bend to your will."

"Not at all," replied Glooskap with dignity. "Here, Wasis, come to me," and he held out his hand and smiled pleasantly.

The baby lifted his little face and smiled back, then seemed to wait expectantly to see what the stranger would do next.

Glooskap bethought himself of a device that he believed could not fail. He was skilled in imitating the songs of birds, and now he filled the wigwam with clear, beautiful notes. But Wasis took no notice. Evidently he had no ear for music, so he gave all his attention to the maple sugar, and seemed to have forgotten that Glooskap was there at all.

The god began to grow angry. Wasis' lack of interest appeared to him almost as an insult.

"Come to me!" he shouted, "come at once, I command you!"

Wasis was frightened by the noise. He took his maple sugar from his mouth and howled dismally. But he did not move. The more Glooskap shouted the louder Wasis roared, until the

144

How Glooskap Overcame Winter

god realized that in a screaming contest the baby was well able
to hold his own. So he stopped shouting and tried what magic
arts would do. He recited in a low and solemn voice the most
terrible spells he knew, spells which would bring giants and
monsters from their secret hiding-places. Wasis looked at him
for a moment as if wondering what was the meaning of this
new form of noise, then, deciding that it had no interest for
him, he returned to his maple sugar.

More and more powerful grew the incantations of Glooskap.
No demon that ever haunted the earth could have withstood
them, but must have obeyed in fear and trembling. To Wasis
it all began to grow really tiresome. What was this strange
man doing, and did he really expect an intelligent baby to be
pleased at such a performance? He sat on the floor patient
and politely attentive, but quite evidently hoping that he would
soon be left in peace, and obviously without any intention of
moving from his place. At last Glooskap gave it up and rushed
in fury from the hut.

"Goo, goo," said Wasis contentedly, and settled down to the
uninterrupted enjoyment of his maple sugar.

Ever since that day, when a baby cries 'Goo, goo,' the Indians
say that he is thinking how Wasis successfully resisted the great
god Glooskap.

How Glooskap Overcame Winter

To the north of the Indians' country lies the Great Cold Land
where the giant Winter has his wigwam. But he is not satisfied
with this dwelling, and once every year he travels quietly and
stealthily southward and builds himself a strong palace in the
land of the Elves of Light, hoping that he will be able to live
in it for ever. He brings with him the North Wind, who is
stern and terrible, and ranges far and wide, roaring and blustering; he storms loudly at every person that he meets, nipping
and shaking them, and if they will not go away he drenches
them with sleet or buries them in snow. So the little Elves of
Light are frightened, and run away and hide themselves, and

145

The Book of Myths

the land is gloomy and very cold; the people who inhabit it find life very hard and are often hungry.

For a little while Winter is quite comfortable, and makes up his mind that this time he has really established himself and will never be driven out. But the Elves of Light have brave hearts, although they are so small, and soon they come peeping out, two and three at a time, bringing just a gleam of light to help the people of the land through the gloomy days, and though North Wind always finds them and sends them scurrying back to their hiding-places, he cannot kill them, or even hurt them very much.

This South land does not suit him, and now he grows weaker every day. The Elves soon discover this, and then they venture out in companies and harry and torment him until he lies down and tries to hide whenever he sees them coming. So they are able to get near the palace that Winter has built, and they dance round it until Winter, who hates light and warmth, begins to feel very uncomfortable. Time after time the little Elves do this, until at last he makes up his mind to move a little farther to the North. They follow him, and drive him out of his new resting-place, and so they go on until they have driven him back to his wigwam in the Great Cold Land.

By this time the Elves themselves are having a bad time of it, for North Wind's strength has all come back to him, and he is so wild and fierce, and has gathered so many followers to help him, that the Elves, though they keep on trying, cannot step over the borders of the Great Cold Land without being attacked and driven back; so although they are very sorry for the poor people who have to live all the year under the rule of Winter, they could not do anything to help them until Glooskap came.

Glooskap in his travels came one day to the Great Cold Land, and after he had wandered a long way and was very cold and tired he saw a large wigwam, and went in and asked for shelter. Inside he found a mighty giant—Winter himself, though Glooskap did not know this. He received Glooskap very kindly, gave him food and a pipe filled with tobacco, and after Glooskap had eaten they sat down to smoke together.

How Glooskap Overcame Winter

The giant was surprised to see a mortal who seemed to be travelling about as he liked without being frightened by North Wind and the rest of them, and he determined to make the daring stranger feel his power. He chatted away in such a pleasant manner that Glooskap thought he was really one of the most delightful old gentlemen he had ever met. He told Glooskap story after story of things that had happened long and long ago, ages before the Indians came to dwell in the land. Gradually his voice became more and more like a monotonous chant, and it acted as a lullaby to Glooskap, who was very tired. He began to nod, his eyes closed, and the giant's voice became just a droning sound in his ears. Then the atmosphere of the wigwam grew colder and colder, and Glooskap fell into a heavy sleep.

For six whole months Winter was able by his spells to hold the god in this torpid state, but after that time his magic became powerless and Glooskap awoke. The heavy frost was gone, though it was still very cold. At once the god roused himself and left the wigwam, travelling as quickly as he could toward the South. At each step he felt the ground under his feet less hard-bound by the frost, and the air less biting on his face, until at last he came to where the grass was growing and pale, fragile flowers blooming among it. Then Glooskap was glad, but still he had not found that which he sought, so he journeyed on, still southward. At last he came to a great forest, where giant trees enclosed fair, grass-grown glades, and through their leafy branches one could see the blue of the sky and the shining gold of the sun's rays. Glooskap looked down the green glades, and on the soft grass he saw crowds of tiny people dancing. They were very lovely, with bright faces and gleaming hair, and garments that looked like the petals of gay-hued flowers. They lit up the shady forest, and as they danced their wings fanned the sweet air so that little breezes came to touch Glooskap's cheeks. Then he knew that these were the Elves of Light, and that here he should find that which he had come to seek.

In the midst of the dancers, more radiant and lovely than any of them, was their queen, whose name was Summer. Glooskap stole quietly along behind the trees, put out his hand, and

147

very gently lifted her from the ground. The Elves ran toward
him, but he quickly took from his belt a coiled lassoo of moose-
skin, and tied one end carefully round the waist of the queen.
The other end he dropped on the ground, and the crowd of little
people seized upon it, thinking to draw their queen from his
arms. But Glooskap began to run, and as he ran the lassoo,

GLOOSKAP SEES THE LITTLE PEOPLE DANCING

which was very long, uncoiled behind him, so that, pull as they
might, the Elves could gain no advantage. Soon Glooskap had
passed on out of their sight, and then he took the cord from
the little queen's waist and held her carefully under his soft fur
coat. She was not frightened, for she was a brave little sprite,
and Glooskap's kind face told her that he would not hurt her;
so she rested quietly in her warm hiding-place.

Quickly Glooskap travelled back by the way he had come,
northward and still northward, until he reached the wigwam of
Winter. Again the giant received him kindly, filled a pipe for

The Four Wishes

him, and began, in his chanting, monotonous voice, to tell the old tales which before had charmed his visitor. But this time Glooskap was on his guard, and had, moreover, his own plan to carry out. Instead of quietly listening, he too began to talk, fixing his eyes on the giant's face, and soon he saw that Winter was growing very uncomfortable. Little Summer, nestling under Glooskap's coat, was sending out the warmth and light that were her gifts to mankind, and the air of the wigwam lost its chill, and grew soft and balmy. Drops of perspiration appeared on the giant's face; he wiped them away, but they came faster and faster, and soon were running down in streams. Moisture fell from his garments, and drip, drip, came from the walls of the wigwam. Still the gentle but powerful heat radiated from little Summer, and still faster and faster the giant and his wigwam melted away, until where they had stood was seen only a pool of clear water.

Then Summer came out from Glooskap's coat, and danced merrily over the hard, frozen snow that covered the ground as far as could be seen; and as she danced the snow disappeared, the air grew soft, green blades of grass appeared, and bright flowers showed their joyful faces.

Thus Summer conquered Winter; and every year now she visits the Great Cold Land, so that for a little space its inhabitants know warmth and light and joy.

The Four Wishes

For many years Glooskap lived upon the earth, and toiled and fought to make men better and happier. But the more he did for them the worse they became, and when he destroyed evil in the form of monsters and wizards, a blacker evil seemed to spring up in the hearts of men themselves. At length Glooskap grew disheartened and resolved to leave the world to get on as best it could without him, and to go and live at peace in the country of the gods. But before he went he made it known that for the next seven years any man might come to him and ask what boon he would. All who desired things good and

149

reasonable should have their wishes granted, but punishment should fall on any who made requests that were unwise or evil.

The home of Glooskap was in a fair and pleasant land, but the way to it was long and difficult. Many people made the painful journey and came to him with prayers for every kind of thing that the heart of man can imagine, and to all of them he fulfilled his word. One day four Indians arrived together, and Glooskap welcomed them kindly and brought them into his tent. Then he said to the first, " Tell me now why you have sought me, and what it is that you will ask."

The Indian answered, " My heart is black and evil, O Glooskap, and often a demon of anger rises within me and becomes my master, and drives me whither I would not go. Make my heart clean, I pray you, and drive out this demon, that I may live in peace with my people."

Glooskap listened, but answered nothing. " And you," he said to the second Indian, " what is it that you desire ? "

" I am poor," the man replied: " give me, I pray you, many buffalo skins and a fine wigwam, bows and knives, headdresses and mocassins and wives to serve me."

"And you?" said Glooskap to the third, and the man bowed low.

" I am little thought of in my tribe," he said ; " my fellows make a mock of me, and laugh at my low estate. Raise me up, O my lord, that I may sit high among them, and they may look on me and give me honour."

The fourth man stepped forward holding his head high and turning his face this way and that as if he wished to say to all beholders, " Look on me and see how handsome I am." He was very tall, but because he was conceited and wished to appear even taller, he had stuffed fur into his mocassins. " My wish," he said, as he stood on tiptoe, threw out his chest, and spread his arms, " is that I may become bigger yet, bigger than any man of my tribe, and that I may live for many ages."

Glooskap listened, still silent; then he went to his medicine bag and took out four little boxes. " Take this," he said, giving a box to each man, " and do not open it until you reach your home. Go in peace."

Glooskap's Farewell

The four men went out and started on their journey homeward. The first three travelled as quickly as possible, eager to reach their wigwams and see what gift the god had bestowed upon them. Each as soon as he arrived home opened his box ; at once a delicious odour arose filling the air with sweetness, and within the box each found an unguent of grease, very rich and precious. Each rubbed his body with the sweet-smelling ointment, and soon each found that his prayer was answered, and that he had been given what he had asked of the god.

The prayer of the fourth man was answered too. He could not wait until he reached his home, but stopped in an open space in the forest and rubbed himself with the ointment he found in his box. As he rubbed he felt himself grow taller and taller, but at the same time he grew stiffer and darker, until at last he became a pine-tree, the tallest tree in the forest, and he lived for many ages.

Glooskap's Farewell

At last the sad day came when the god whom the Indians so dearly loved must leave them and go to his own land far away. On the shores of the great Lake Minas Glooskap spread a feast, and to it he bade the beasts and birds from every part of the land. They came by hundreds and by thousands, all eager to see Glooskap once more and to hear his farewell words. Great as the crowd was, there was food and drink for all ; such a feast had never been made before, nor such guests assembled.

When the feasting was over Glooskap began to sing—sweet, mystic singing, telling of the place to which he was going, where those who loved and served him might follow in the happy days that were to come. Then, still singing, he entered his great canoe, which came drifting toward him over the waters of the lake; and the crowd watched in silence as it bore him farther and farther away, until they could see his face no more, nor hear the sweet, wild notes of his song. Then they turned toward their homes, each speaking sadly to his neighbour words of mourning for the good Glooskap. But to their surprise, whereas before

The Book of Myths

beast had spoken to beast and bird to bird, and all had understood, now each spoke a different language, and the wolf could not tell what the bear was saying, nor the otter answer the words of the fox. With Glooskap their fellowship was gone, and only with Glooskap could it return.

The Indians believe that in a fair land very far away Glooskap

"GLOOSKAP BEGAN TO SING"

still lives. Beside a great lake he has built for himself a wigwam, large and wonderful, and he sits within it, making arrows. Each arrow stands for a day, and when he shall have made so many that the wigwam is full, the last great day will have come. Then all the good spirits will rise at Glooskap's call, and come flocking to him, a great army eager to do his will. They will sail over the lake in a wonderful canoe, which will grow larger and larger, so that it will carry them all, however many they be, and yet when they land on the opposite shore one of them will be able to take it up and bear it away folded in his hand.

The Story of Scarface

Then this great force will attack Malsum, the spirit of evil, and will destroy him with his followers to the very last man ; and they themselves will be destroyed also, every one. But they, and all those on earth who have been true followers of the good Glooskap, will go to his bright country and live with him in happiness for countless ages.

The Story of Scarface

There lived once among a tribe of Indians a poor boy whose father and mother were dead, and who had no friends to take care of him. The kindly Indian women helped him as well as they could, giving him what they could spare of food and clothing, and shelter in the hard days of winter ; and the men let him go with them on hunting expeditions, and taught him the Indian woodcraft, just as they taught their own sons. The boy grew up strong and brave, and the men of the tribe said that he would one day make a mighty hunter. While he was quite young he met on one of the hunting parties a great grizzly bear, and fought a desperate fight with him, and at last killed him. But during the struggle the bear set its claws in the boy's face and tore it cruelly ; and when the wound healed there was left a red, unsightly mark, so that he thereafter was called Scarface.

The boy thought little of the disfigurement until he fell in love with the beautiful daughter of the chief of his tribe, and then when he saw all the handsome young braves dressing themselves in the splendid dress of the Indian warrior and going to pay court to this maiden at her father's wigwam, his heart ached very sorely because he was poor and friendless, and above all because he bore upon his face the terrible disfiguring scar.

But the maiden did not care for the finery and boastful talk of the young Indians who crowded round her, and each in turn, when he ventured to ask her hand in marriage, found himself refused. Scarface scarcely dared to approach her, but the girl often saw him as he went about the forest, and she felt that he was braver and truer than the other lovers who boldly sought her favour.

The Book of Myths

One day, as she sat outside her father's lodge, Scarface passed by, and as he passed he looked at her, and his eyes showed the love and admiration that possessed him. A young Indian whose suit the girl had refused noticed the look, and said with a sneer, " Scarface has become a suitor for our chief's daughter. She will have nothing to do with men unblemished, perhaps she desires a man marked and marred. Try then, Scarface, and see if she will take you."

Scarface felt anger rise hot within him against the man who thus mocked him. He stood proudly, as though he were a chief's son instead of a poor, common, disfigured warrior, and, looking very steadily at the young brave, he said, " My brother speaks true words, though he speaks them with an ill tongue. I go indeed to ask the daughter of our great chief to be my wife."

The young brave laughed loudly in mockery. Some other young men of the tribe came up, and he told them what Scarface had said, and they also laughed, calling him the great chief, speaking of his vast wealth and of his marvellous beauty, and pretending to bow down before him. Scarface took no notice, but walked away quietly and with an unmoved face, though in his heart he yearned to spring at them, as the great grizzly had sprung at him in the forest. But when he came down to the river, following the chief's daughter, who had gone there to gather rushes for the baskets she was weaving, his anger died away. He drew near to her, knowing that if he did not speak at once his courage would leave him, for though she was so gentle and so kind, he trembled in her presence as the fiercest warrior or the most terrible bear could not make him tremble.

" Maiden," he said, " I am poor and little thought of, because I have no store of furs or pemmican, as the great warriors of the tribe have. I must gain day by day with my bow and my spear and with hard toil the means by which I live. And my face is marred and unsightly to look upon. But my heart is full of love for you, and I greatly desire you for my wife. Will you marry Scarface and live with him in his poor lodge ? "

The maiden looked at him, and in her face he saw the love for which he asked.

The Story of Scarface

"That you are poor," she said, "matters little. My father would give me great store of all needful things for a wedding portion. But I may not be your bride, nor the bride of any man of the tribe. The great Lord of the Sun has laid his commands on me, forbidding me to marry."

The heart of poor Scarface sank at these terrible words, yet he would not give up hope. "Will he not release you?" he asked; "he is kind and gives us many good gifts. He would not wish to make us both miserable."

"Go to him, then," said the girl, "and make your prayer to him that he will set me free from my promise. And ask him that I may know that he has done so to take the scar from off your face as a sign."

"I will go," said Scarface, "I will seek out the bright god in his own land, and beseech him to pity us." So he turned and left the maiden by the riverside.

Scarface started at once on his journey, and travelled for many, many miles. Sometimes he went cheerfully, saying to himself, "The Sun-god is kind, he will give me my bride." Sometimes his heart was sad, and he went heavily, for he thought, "Maybe the Sun-god desires to marry her himself, and who could expect him to give up a maiden so beautiful?" Through forests and over mountains he went, searching ever for the golden gates which marked the entrance to the country of the great god. The wild animals that he met knew that this time he had not come out as a hunter to take them, so they drew near to him and willingly answered his questions. But not one of them could tell him where lay the Sun-god's land. "We have not travelled beyond the forest," they said; "perhaps the birds, who fly swiftly and very far, can tell you what you want to know."

Scarface called to the birds who were flying overhead, and they came down and listened. But they answered, "We fly far and see many things, but we have never seen two gleaming gates of gold, nor looked on the face of the bright god of the sun."

Scarface was disappointed, but he went bravely on. One

day, when he was very weary, he met a wolverine and asked him the question he had asked so many times before. To his great joy the wolverine answered, "I have seen the gleaming gates, and have entered the bright country of the Lord of the Sun. But the way to it is long and hard, and you will be tired indeed when you reach the end of your journey. I will put you

SCARFACE CROSSING THE GREAT WATER

on your way, and if your heart does not fail you, some day you will see what I have seen."

With fresh courage Scarface went on. Day after day he journeyed, walking until he was weary, and taking but short rest. Each morning when he started he had hope that evening would bring him to the golden gates, and then one day he came to a great water, very broad and deep, so that he could not cross it.

Now it seemed that his labour and weariness had been all for nothing, and he sat down on the shore of the great water and felt hope dying out of his heart. But very soon he saw drawing

The Story of Scarface

near to him from the other side two beautiful swans. "We will take you across," they said, "step on our backs, and we will swim with you to the farther shore." Up started Scarface, joyful once again, and poised himself carefully on the backs of the two swans; and they glided across and landed him safely on the opposite shore.

"You seek the kingdom of the Sun-god?" they said, "go then along the road that lies before you, and you will soon come to it." Scarface thanked them with all his heart. He felt happier than he had done since he had started on his journey, and he walked along with quick, light steps. He had not gone far when he saw lying on the ground a very beautiful bow and arrows. He stopped for a moment to look at them. "These belong to some mighty hunter," he thought, "they are finer than those of a common warrior." But he left them lying where he found them, for though his hunter's heart coveted them, Scarface was honest, and would not take what was not his own. He went on, even lighter of heart than before, and soon he saw a beautiful youth coming gaily along the road toward him. It seemed to Scarface that a soft, bright light shone around as the youth stopped and said, "I have lost a bow and arrows somewhere along the road. Have you seen them?"

"They lie but a little distance behind me," said Scarface, "I have but just passed them."

"Thank you many times," said the youth; "it is well for me that it was an honest man who passed, or I should never have seen my bow and arrows again." He smiled at Scarface, and the Indian felt a great joy in his heart, and all the air seemed flecked with golden points of light. "Where are you going?" inquired the stranger.

And Scarface answered, "I seek the land of the great Lord of the Sun, and I believe it is very near."

"It is near indeed," replied the youth; "I am Apisirahts, the Morning Star, and the Sun is my father. Come and I will take you to him."

So the two went down the broad, bright road and passed through the golden gates. Inside they saw a great lodge, shining

157

and glorious, gaily bedecked with such beautiful pictures and carvings as Scarface had never in his life seen before. At the door stood a woman with a fair face and bright clear eyes that looked kindly at the wayworn stranger. "Come in," she said. "I am Kokomikis, the Moon-goddess, and this youth is my son. Come, for you are tired and footsore and need food and rest."

Scarface, almost bewildered by the beauty of everything around him, went in, and Kokomikis cared for him tenderly, so that he soon felt refreshed and strong. After a time the great Lord of the Sun came home to the lodge, and he, too, was very kind to Scarface. "Stay with us," he said, "you have travelled a weary way to find me, now be my guest for a season. You are a great hunter, and here you will find good game. My son who loves the chase will go with you, and you will live with us and be happy."

Very gladly Scarface replied, "I will stay, great lord." So for many days he lived with the Sun-god and Kokomikis and Apisirahts, and every morning he and Morning Star went hunting and returned at night to the shining lodge. "Do not go near the Great Water," the Lord of the Sun warned them, "for savage birds dwell there, who will seek to slay the Morning Star."

But Apisirahts secretly longed to meet these savage birds and kill them, so one day he stole away from Scarface and hastened toward the Great Water. For a little while Scarface did not miss him, but believed him to be near by; but after a time he looked round and could not find his companion. He searched anxiously, and then a terrible fear came into his heart, and he set off as fast as he could toward the haunt of the dread birds. Horrid cries came to his ears as he hastened on, and soon he saw a crowd of the monstrous creatures surrounding Morning Star, and pressing on him so closely that he could use his weapons to little purpose to defend himself. Scarface feared to loose an arrow, but he dashed in among the hideous creatures, taking them by surprise, so that they flew off in alarm. Then he seized Morning Star, and hurried him back through the forest to safety.

When they returned to the lodge that night Apisirahts told his father of his own disobedience and the courage of Scarface.

The Story of Scarface

The great Lord of the Sun turned to the poor stranger. "You have saved my son from a dreadful death," he said; "ask of me some boon, that I may repay you. Why was it that you sought me here? Surely you had some desire in your heart or you would not have travelled so far and fared so hardly."

Now all the while he had been at the Shining Lodge the thing he had come to ask had been ever in Scarface's mind. Many times he had thought, "The hour is come when I may speak"; but because it was so great a boon he craved his heart failed him, and he thought again, "I will have patience just a little longer, it is too soon to beg so great a favour of the god who has already been so kind to me." But when he heard the words of the Sun-god, so graciously spoken, he took courage and replied, "In my own land, O mighty Lord, I love a maiden who is the daughter of the chief of my tribe. I am only a poor warrior, and as you see, I am disfigured and hideous to look upon. Yet she of her goodness loves me, and would marry me, but for the reverence in which she holds your commands laid upon her. For she has promised you, O great Lord, that she will marry no man. So I came to seek you in hope that you would free her from her promise that she might come to my lodge, and we might live in happiness together."

Then the Sun-god smiled, and looked kindly upon the Indian, who spoke bravely, though in his heart he trembled. "Go back," he said, "and take this maiden for your wife. Tell her that it is my will she marry you, and for a token"—he passed his hand before the Indian's face, and immediately the disfiguring scar vanished—"tell her to look upon you and see how the god of the Sun has wrought upon your face."

They loaded the Indian—Scarface no longer—with gifts, and changed his poor clothes for the rich dress of an Indian chief. Then they led him out from the country of the Sun, through the golden gates, and showed him a short and easy path by which he could return to his own land.

He travelled quickly, and soon was at home once more. All his tribe came out to look at the richly clad young brave, who walked with such a quick, light step, and looked so eager and happy; but none knew him for Scarface, at whom they had mocked and jeered. Even the chief's daughter did not recognize him when she first looked upon him, but a second look told her who he was, and she called his name; then, realizing that the scar was gone, and remembering what its disappearance meant, she sprang toward him with a cry of joy. The story of his wonderful journey was told, and the chief gladly gave his daughter to this warrior on whom the great Sun-god had looked with favour. That same day they were married, and the chief gave his daughter a splendid wigwam for her marriage portion. There the two lived happily for many years; and Scarface lost his old name and was known to all the tribe as Smoothface.

The Maize Spirit

When a boy belonging to the Indian tribes reaches the age of fifteen years he is considered old enough to take upon himself the duties of manhood. He must first observe a fast of three, four, or even seven days, according to his powers of endurance, and during this time he must be quite by himself that he may meditate and commune with the Great Spirit of his tribe. It is customary for his mother or his father to build a little wigwam for him in the depth of the forest, and one of them usually visits him after about three days, to see if his strength will endure a longer fast, and perhaps brings him a little water to refresh him. A legend of the Chippeway Indians tells how maize was first given to men by the Great Spirit through an Indian boy who was thus keeping his fast. Longfellow has told the story very beautifully in his poem of *Hiawatha*.

The boy, the legend says, was one of a large family, and his father was a hunter, upright and unselfish, and very kind to all his children. They lived happily together, though they sometimes went hungry when the father was unsuccessful in his hunting. The eldest boy, whose time for fasting had now come, was good and unselfish, and the great wish in his heart was that he might do something to help his fellows. So when he was left by himself in the lonely wigwam he asked the Great

The Maize Spirit

Spirit who had given men so many gifts to allow him, poor as he was, to be the means of bringing some good to his tribe. Most boys at their time of fasting prayed for courage, or skill in hunting, or success in war, but this lad's heart was full of love, and he forgot himself in thinking of his fellows.

The prayer pleased the Great Spirit, and he decreed that it

THE BRIGHT FIGURE APPEARING TO THE BOY

should be granted. On the third night of his fast the boy lay, very weak and exhausted, on a bed of leaves inside his wigwam. During the day he had rambled through the forest, seeing in the beauty spread around him the signs of the love with which Manitou, the Great Creator, loved his people, and his own heart had yearned still more strongly than before to add something, however small, to the happiness of men. Then when his strength had failed him he had come back to the shelter of his wigwam, and now he lay there drowsy and half unconscious through his weakness.

The Book of Myths

Suddenly he saw a bright figure standing in the doorway. It was a young man, tall and slender and beautiful, dressed in green robes and bearing on his head waving golden plumes. " The Great Spirit has heard your prayer, and will grant it if you follow the commands that I am sent to lay upon you," he said, in a voice that seemed to bring rest and healing to the weary boy. " Rise now and wrestle with me."

When the boy had lain down only a little while before, it had been because his limbs were too weak to hold him up; but at the words of the bright messenger he sprang eagerly to his feet. The two struggled together in silence. The boy bore himself well, for as his body touched that of his opponent his weariness passed away and new life seemed to run through him. After a time the messenger said, " It is enough. To-morrow I will return, and we will try our strength once more."

He disappeared, and the boy sank down exhausted. All through the day and night that followed he lay in the helpless, half-conscious state that comes of fasting and fatigue. But his brain was clear, and he rejoiced as he recalled the words of the messenger, " The Great Spirit will grant your prayer if you do as he commands you."

Next day the youth appeared again, and again the boy wrestled with him, feeling even more strongly than before the flow of strength and life at contact with his divine visitor. He fought valiantly, so that again the Great Spirit's messenger praised him for his strength and courage. " To-morrow I will come again," he said, and so on the morrow the struggle was renewed. This was the sixth day of the boy's fast, and he had lain for many hours prostrate and almost lifeless, yet he fought so well that very soon the youth cried, " Hold, it is enough ! To-morrow will be the last day of your trial. Your father will bring you food, so that your strength will return to you. Then, when evening comes, you will see me once more and we will wrestle together. This time I know you will overcome me, so that I shall fall before you and die. Then you must strip from my body the green garment and the golden plumes, and make for me a grave at the place where I fell, and lay me therein,

The Maize Spirit

piling the earth gently over me. When you are once more living happily in your home, come back sometimes to this place and see that the earth is fresh above me, and not overgrown with weeds, or upturned by the beasts of the forest. Tend my grave carefully, and then in the spring-time you shall see me again in my shining garments as you saw me when Manitou first sent me to you."

Then he disappeared, and the boy was left to think over his words and the promise of the Great Spirit. Next morning his father brought him food, but he said, " Lay it aside, my father, until sunset, and then I will eat." In the evening came the youth once more, and again they wrestled until he was overthrown and fell lifeless before the victor. Then the boy, sorrowing deeply, stripped from him the green garments and the golden plumes, and made him a grave, and laid him in it, and covered him lightly with the cool earth.

The time of fasting was now ended, and the boy returned home with his father, and set himself diligently to learn the forest lore and the arts of the Indian hunter. But he did not forget his promise to the beautiful youth whom he had overthrown ; he went regularly to his grave and weeded and watered it, until one spring day he saw green leaves pushing through the soil. They grew quickly, and the boy tended them with care, until when summer came there stood a tall and graceful plant, with broad green leaves, above which waved shining golden tassels. Then the boy said to his father, " Come with me, for I have something to show you in the forest." He took his father to where the plant stood in green and golden splendour, and the father looking upon the ripening seeds that it bore said reverently, " It is Mon-da-min, the gift of the Great Spirit ; let us thank him, my son, that he has thought upon men, to feed them with the good grain."

But the boy said softly, " It is my friend come again as he promised that he would, and he has brought with him the answer of Manitou the Great Spirit to the prayer which I prayed."

Then, when autumn came, and the seeds ripened, the Indians gathered the grain and thanked the Great Spirit that he had sent maize to feed his people.

The Medicine Man

When the Indian is ill he calls in his medicine man, just as we should call in a doctor. But the medicine man does not examine his patient's symptoms and prescribe for him such medicines as his study of the human body leads him to believe will correct what is wrong. Instead he listens carefully while the patient tells him, first, all about his ailment, and then anything that he has lately done or that has happened to him which he thinks might have angered one of the spirits of his tribe and brought vengeance upon him. Neither the medicine man nor the patient has any idea that the pain or the illness has arisen from something that is wrong within the man's body. Both are firmly convinced that it must be the work of an offended spirit. For the Indian believes that in almost every created thing there dwells a spirit who has power to work him harm, not only in his body, but also in his belongings. If his corn does not grow or his cattle do not thrive, it is because a spell has been laid upon them ; and if he has a terrible pain in his stomach, it is not because he has eaten unwisely, but because some spirit whom he has offended has entered his body and is tormenting him. So the medicine man must prove himself a match for the enemy ; he must be able by charms and spells and incantations and potions to drive him away ; in other words, the medicine man is really a wizard skilled in all magic devices for the protection of the human body.

The various Indian tribes have different legends to account for the introduction of this ' medicine,' or magic, among them. One of the most interesting is a tradition of the Senecas, who say that once, long ago, an Indian went alone into the woods on a hunting expedition. For several days he hunted, coming back at night, very weary, to the camp that he had made for himself, and sleeping soundly until dawn. One night he was awakened by hearing the beating of drums and the voices of many people singing. He sat up, and for a moment thought that he was back in his native Indian village, for he had often heard sounds like these at the festivals which his people regularly

The Medicine Man

held. But quickly he remembered where he was, and started from his bed in amazement, for how, in the depths of the forest where for many days he had seen no signs of a human being, could these sounds have arisen? He went quickly in the direction from which they seemed to come, but could see no one, though he still heard the singing and the beating of drums. But on the ground he saw a heap of corn, a squash plant with three squashes on it, and, laid apart from the rest, three large ears of corn, ripe and yellow. He was very much puzzled, for he could not imagine who had brought these things and placed them so near his camp. He watched for some time, then, as he was very weary, he fell asleep once more; and in the morning all was silent and he went out as usual to hunt.

In the middle of the next night he woke again, and saw a man bending over him. The man said in a stern tone, "Beware! What you saw was sacred. You deserve to die." The hunter started up in terror, but he was more frightened still when he heard all round him the branches rustling as if a great concourse of people were moving them. He could say nothing in answer to the words addressed to him, only look round in utter bewilderment; and perhaps the folk who were regarding him from the bushes saw by his face that he had not intentionally pried into their secrets. They came out from their hiding-places and gathered round him. "Your curiosity shall be pardoned," said one, "and we will tell you the meaning of the things that have puzzled you."

"That which you saw," said the man who had awakened him, "was our medicine. The great medicine for wounds is squash and corn. Come with me, and I will show you how we use it."

The hunter followed the mysterious beings to the place where he had seen the heap of corn the night before. There was now a great fire burning, and near it a bush which looked something like the laurel, but whose leaves and stem were hard and rigid as iron. The people slowly circled round this tree, chanting a strange, wild song, and loudly rattling gourd shells.

"What does all this mean?" asked the hunter. "You said

165

The Book of Myths

that you would explain your medicine to me, but I am now more puzzled than I was before."

One of the men stepped from his place in the company, and, taking a stick, thrust it into the fire. He drew it out, hot and glowing, and then quite calmly he pressed the end against his cheek until it burnt right through the flesh. Then he applied to the wound some of the medicine that had been prepared, and immediately it healed, leaving no scar. The hunter was astounded; he begged to be shown how such wonderful things were done, and his strange companions sang to him their magic 'medicine song,' until he knew it by heart. Then, seeing that it was nearly morning, he thought that he ought to return to his camp, and turned to say good-bye to his companions. But as if some spell had been taken from off his sight, he saw now that those whom he had thought to be men were really animals of the forest—foxes, wolves, bears, beavers. While he looked at them they fled, as wild creatures are used to fly from a hunter, and he was alone.

The Indian stayed no longer in the place where he had seen so many marvels, but made haste to get back to his own familiar camping ground. Later, when he thought over his adventure, he found that he had not forgotten the prescription he had learnt at that strange midnight gathering. "Take one stalk of corn, dry the cob, and grind it to fine powder; take one squash, cut it up and pound it; take water from a running stream near its source, and mix all three together." When he returned from his hunting expedition he made up the medicine and used it when any member of his tribe had need of healing, and in each case it was successful. It became the great medicine of the Senecas, and every year at the time that the deer changes his coat, they assemble, prepare the mixture, make a great fire, and dance round a bush to the rattling of the gourd shells, singing the strange, wild song that the hunter learnt from the people of the wood.

The Cherokees have a legend of quite a different character concerning the way medicine was first introduced into their

166

The Medicine Man

tribe. They go back to the far off time when men and beasts lived as friends together, understanding one another's speech, and mixing as equals in all the business of everyday life. But this Golden Age did not last. Men increased in numbers so quickly that they wanted the greater part of the world for themselves, and the animals were driven into the wildest depths of the forest, and the most barren and desolate spots on the earth where men did not care to live. Then man forgot his old friendship for the beasts and began to hunt them for the sake of their flesh and their skins; he invented marvellous weapons, which made him, weak and small as he was, the superior of the mightiest beasts that ranged the forests.

The animals saw what was going on with alarm. "If something is not done quickly," they said, "there will be none of us left. Man will go on and find out more and more deadly devices to make an end of us." The bears, who had suffered specially from the hunters, summoned a council, at which the Old White Bear, who was the head of the tribe, and renowned for his wisdom, presided. All those present decided that since man had declared war upon the beasts, the beasts must make war upon man with all the strength and craft of which they were capable. The question arose, how could the bears, with only the claws that Nature had given them, make themselves equal with man, who already had weapons far more deadly than bears' claws, and who, it must be expected, would invent others of even greater destructive powers as time went on. Man could, even now, send death flying from his bow, while he himself was out of reach of the bear's claws.

"We too must have bows and arrows," one of the bears exclaimed, and the others eagerly agreed. Quickly a piece of wood, from which could be fashioned a bow such as they had seen in the hands of man, was procured, and one of the bears bravely consented to be sacrificed that from his dead body the gut required for the bow-strings might be taken. Eagerly the bears set to work, and made a bow which seemed to them quite as good as those used by their enemies. The arrows were an easy matter in a forest where birds of all sizes made their homes.

167

The Book of Myths

The next thing was to practise shooting the arrows from the bow, and then, to their great disappointment, the bears found their claws sadly in the way. One after another tried, but with small success; not one could send the arrow straight and strong and true as the arrows of men had come to them. One of the bears cut his claws, and then he succeeded much better. The

THE BEARS PRACTISING SHOOTING ARROWS

others were rushing to do the same when Old White Bear stopped them. " It is all very well," he said, " to wish to shoot with the bow, but think what will happen if we cut off our claws. We shall not only be defenceless against our enemies—for I do not believe we shall ever use weapons to such good effect as we can use our claws—but we shall not be able to climb trees. Then we shall catch no game for food, and we shall starve." The bears saw the wisdom of their leader, and sadly gave up the hope of using bows and arrows; so their grand plan came to nothing.

Next, the deer called a council, and Little Deer, their leader,

The Medicine Man

invited them to propose some way in which they could avenge
themselves on man for his treatment of them. They decided
that any man who killed a deer should be afflicted with rheumatism unless, at the time of slaying, he asked pardon of his prey.
They sent messengers to the nearest Indian settlement, with
instructions as to the way in which this was to be done, and
the Indians sent the message on from tribe to tribe until all
had heard it. Ever since then, when a hunter kills a deer, he
must be sure to use the form of words in which he has been
instructed; for after he has borne away his prey Little Deer
will come along, and bending over the bloodstains will ask:
" Did the slayer ask pardon, O my brother ? " If the blood
replies " Yes," the hunter is left in peace with his spoil; but if
it says " No," Little Deer follows on the trail of the offender,
and however far he has to go, he tracks him to his wigwam,
and smites him with rheumatism, so that he is crippled and can
no longer go hunting.

The Indians fear Little Deer's vengeance so much that if any
one of them does not know, or cannot remember the proper
form to use, he lights a huge fire across his trail, hoping by that
means to prevent Little Deer following him.

Next came a council of the fishes and reptiles. " We cannot
fight these men," said the fish, " but we will afflict them in their
night slumbers. They shall dream that they are eating fish, de-
cayed and horrible, and shall wake with the taste of it in their
mouths."

" And we," said the reptiles, " will send them dreams of serpents, huge and hideous, twining round their bodies, so that
they shall wake gasping with fear."

Last of all, the birds and insects and smaller animals held a
joint meeting. The grub worm presided, and urged the company
to do its utmost against man, the common foe, and although
some were not inclined to begin active warfare, they all agreed,
finally, to do their part. " We will afflict man with various
diseases," they said ; and each named the special disease that he
would bestow upon the enemy.

The trees and plants in the forest listened to all that the

169

animals said, and resolved to do their utmost to bring their plans to nought. For man had done no harm to the vegetable creation. He had, indeed, of late acted toward the trees and plants in a more friendly fashion than he had ever done before, sometimes even digging the ground, and watering and planting. So they decided that for every disease that might fall upon man through the ill-will of the beasts they would provide a remedy. Every single plant, from the huge trees down to the delicate moss, was given a part in this curative scheme, and they became the 'medicine' by means of which man is cured of all the ills that may afflict his body.

Blue Jay

The Indians of the Chinook tribe, who live on the north-west coast of America, had a deity to whom they gave the name of Blue Jay. He was the god of mischief, but he was not at all like the Norse god, Loki, who was cunning and subtle, as well as mischievous. Blue Jay was conceited, impudent, and blundering ; he was constantly trying to play tricks on every one around him, but he usually succeeded in making himself, and not his victim, appear ridiculous. He chattered and bragged until no one took him seriously or believed anything he said. He was, in fact, the comic figure of Chinook legend, around whom all the stories of blunders and absurd actions collected. Many tales of his adventures have come down to us, and we may feel fairly certain that there were many more, and that when the Indians gathered round their camp fires after a day's hunting, and stories of heroes and gods were told, there seldom failed some tale of Blue Jay and his tricks to lighten the more serious talk of the meeting.

Many of Blue Jay's adventures had to do with the Supernaturals, a race of beings whom the Chinooks imagined as living in a country which lay next to the earth, and could be easily reached by earth-dwellers. They were not the spirits of men departed, but an independent creation of spiritual beings, superior to man, but not divine. Blue Jay often visited the land of the

Blue Jay

Supernaturals, and played his tricks upon them as freely as he did upon man.

One of the stories told about him relates how the sister of an Indian chief married a Supernatural, and went to live with him in his country of shadows. Some time after the marriage the chief wished to visit his sister, and caused a large canoe to be prepared, in which his people rowed him across the sea which separated the two countries. Blue Jay went with them, boisterous and irrepressible as he always was. When the canoe came in sight of the land of the Supernaturals, their chief, who was walking by the shore, saw it.

"There are mortals approaching our land," he said to his attendants, "and I fear they come to work us ill. I will by my magic cover the sea with ice, that their boat may approach no nearer to our shores."

By means of charms he caused the air to grow colder and colder till ice began to form on the water. The people in the boat shivered. "*Ugh !*" cried Blue Jay, "it is getting horribly cold ! I shall jump into the water and get warm." He gave a great leap and fell splash into the sea.

"*Ha ! ha !*" shouted the Supernaturals, "Blue Jay has fallen into the water and will be drowned."

The Chinooks heard the shouts and were angry, and their chief rose, gathered up the ice from the surface of the sea as one would gather in a fishing-net, and cast it far away. The Supernaturals were dismayed. "These beings," they said to one another, "are more powerful than even our chief." They hurried away from the shore, and shut themselves up in their houses, waiting to see what these marvellous visitors would do.

When the Chinooks landed—Blue Jay among them, quite unsubdued by his dip in the icy water—they found the place quite deserted. They looked about, and saw what they supposed to be the house of the chief, and they went toward it, hoping to find someone who could direct them to the person they had come to seek. At the door they saw two sea-lions guarding the entrance.

"Beware !" cried the chief; "these are fierce animals, and you must approach them carefully."

171

The Book of Myths

"As for me," cried Blue Jay boastfully, "I am not afraid. See me leap over them!"

He leapt, but not far enough. Up jumped the sea-lions, fierce and terrible, and bit Blue Jay, so that he began to howl and shriek with pain. With another leap he came back to his companions, and ran away as fast as he could, still uttering loud and doleful cries.

The Chinook chief was a proud man, and he had intended to enter the land of the Supernaturals with such dignity as would have impressed them with the importance of himself and his country; so that to see one who had come in his train act in this absurd manner annoyed him very much. He felt sure that the Supernaturals, though none of them were to be seen, were laughing at Blue Jay's antics, and in a fit of anger he grasped a sea-lion in each hand and threw both so far away that no one could see where they fell.

The Supernaturals laughed no longer. All around could be heard cries of fear, and angry voices denouncing the new-comers, and threatening vengeance. Blue Jay came bounding back. "See what I have done," he cried. "I told you I was not afraid of the sea-lions. I have cast them far away. Look, all you people, the fierce beasts that guarded the chief's house are gone. All may follow safely where Blue Jay leads, for I have killed beasts a hundred times wilder and fiercer than these. No one, man or beast, can stand against the strength of my arm." He strutted about, tossing his head, and giving himself such foolish airs of importance, that the Supernaturals, in spite of their anger, roared with laughter, and the Chinooks, all except the chief, laughed too.

Now that the sea-lions were gone, the way into the house lay open, so the Chinooks entered. They found inside no one except the sister of their chief, whom they had come to see. All the Supernaturals had vanished. They had left no food behind for the refreshment of their visitors. "I am dreadfully hungry," complained Blue Jay, "I am dying of hunger. Such great deeds as I have done take away one's strength. Bring me food."

172

Blue Jay

He made such a fuss that his elder brother Robin, who was as quiet and correct in his behaviour as Blue Jay was unruly, turned on him sternly.

"Cease your complaints," he said. "An Indian suffers pain and hunger in silence and does not squeal like a hungry jackal."

As he spoke a most remarkable thing happened. Blue Jay

"FROM UNDER THE BED CAME OUT A SUPERNATURAL WITH AN ENORMOUS BEAK"

stopped his cries in sheer astonishment. From under the bed came out slowly a Supernatural with an enormous beak in place of a mouth. He took no notice of anybody, but went toward a heap of wood, split it up with his beak, and made a large fire.

"Robin," said the shameless Blue Jay, in a very loud whisper, "this is the spirit of our great grandfather's slave."

The fire began to smoke terribly, so that the Chinooks could only see one another dimly, and were almost choked.

"Where is the Smoke-eater?" cried a voice; and then several times it called, "Smoke-eater, Smoke-eater!"

The Book of Myths

Through the dimness the form of a huge man appeared. With great gulps he swallowed the smoke so that the house was clear. Then, by unseen hands, a very small dish, with one piece of meat on it, was brought in. Blue Jay began to grumble, " What is the good of that ? I am famished," when the mysterious voice again cried out, " Whale-meat-cutter, Whale-meat-cutter ! " and another curious long-beaked creature appeared, who began slicing up the small piece of meat. Slice after slice he cut, until the dish was filled and would hold no more. Then he blew upon it, and the dish became a great canoe filled with meat. The Chinooks fell upon it and finished it up, Blue Jay eating twice as much as anybody else, so that the Supernatural people, who were hovering near, unseen, were astounded at their appetites. They began to come out and make themselves visible to their visitors, and after a time sent them a message proposing a diving contest, in which the defeated competitor was to lose his life. The Indians agreed, and Blue Jay at once began to proclaim loudly what an excellent diver he was, and what prodigious feats he had done; so he was chosen as the champion of the Chinooks. The other side chose a woman.

Blue Jay slyly swam out to the Indian chief's canoe, in which he had placed some bushes, and threw these out so that they floated in a heap on the water. Then the contest began. Blue Jay dived bravely, making a great show of skill, and when he was out of breath he came up slyly to the surface hiding his face under the bushes, so that none of the spectators discovered his trick. Four times he did this, crying each time when he descended, "Where are you ? " " Here I am," answered the woman, but each time the reply came more gaspingly, until at last in her effort to outstay Blue Jay she became unconscious, and lay stretched out at the bottom of the sea. Then Blue Jay struck her a blow on her neck, and came blustering to the surface. " I have won ! " he cried. " The woman lies dead at the bottom of the sea." They waited a little while, but the woman did not appear ; so the Supernaturals, very much disappointed, were obliged to acknowledge Blue Jay as victor.

Another contest was proposed, this time in climbing. Blue

Blue Jay

Jay, made more conceited than ever by his success, eagerly put himself forward as champion once again. " If you are beaten," the Supernaturals warned him, " you will be dashed to pieces."

" I shall not be beaten," replied Blue Jay boastfully. " No one can climb as well as I can," and he looked with contempt at the chipmunk who was matched against him. He took a piece of ice, so tall that it reached the clouds, and set it upright. Then the two began to climb. When they had gone so high that the watchers below could not see them clearly, Blue Jay slyly began to use his wings. The chipmunk was climbing with her eyes shut, and did not see what her opponent was doing. Soon after, Blue Jay took out his club and gave her a blow on the neck, so that she fell in the midst of those below. Then Blue Jay flew down in triumph, and once more claimed the victory.

The Supernaturals were by this time really angry, and ready to do anything to prove that they were superior to the Indians. They proposed a shooting match, in which the competitors were to shoot at each other. Blue Jay saw no chance of winning this by trickery, so he allowed another champion to be chosen. The cunning Chinooks set up a beaver, in front of whom they fastened a millstone, and of course they won this match also. The next competition was a curious one. It was proposed that a certain number of Chinooks and Supernaturals should enter caves in which great fires had been kept burning, and see which side would sweat most freely under the influence of the heat. The Chinooks concealed ice about their persons, so once more they were victorious.

Then the Supernaturals made one last effort. " We will have a whale-catching contest," they said. " Our own Chief shall compete with the Chief of the Chinooks, and we will see which of them can first catch a whale." This did not suit Blue Jay at all. He thought that he was much more likely to be successful in such a contest than was the Chief, and he began to clamour and boast and make a great hubbub. His brother Robin, too, felt aggrieved that he had not had a chance to distinguish himself. But the Supernatural Chief's wife made short work of their complaints by taking Blue Jay under one arm and Robin under the other and bidding them keep quiet and let other people have a change to speak. Robin obeyed in sullen silence, but Blue Jay wriggled and struggled so that it was all the woman could do to keep him from getting away. As the party went down the beach to begin the contest, she whispered to her brother, " Four whales will pass you, but do not harpoon any until the fifth appears."

The young chief did as she told him, and when he saw the fifth whale, he struck his harpoon deep into the flesh, and brought it successfully ashore. The Supernatural Chief had made several attempts to strike the whales as they passed, but had failed each time ; so here was yet another victory for the Chinooks. When Blue Jay heard what had happened he struggled so violently that he fell from under the woman's arm and was drowned.

The Chinooks now said farewell, and prepared to return to their own land, and the Supernaturals saw them go with joy, for the visit had been very hurtful to their pride. The young chief said a sorrowful good-bye to his sister, who secretly gave him a magic rope. " Tie this to Robin's blanket," she said, " and it will preserve you in danger and give you a safe journey home." It was well indeed that she made him this present, for when the canoe was in mid-ocean the Supernatural people attempted to avenge their defeat by raising a great storm, which they hoped would overwhelm the canoe of their late visitors. But thanks to the magical rope, the Chinooks passed safely through and arrived home uninjured.

As for Blue Jay, he must have quickly come to life again after his disaster, for he appears as the hero of many other stories following this one of the visit of the Chinooks to the Supernaturals.

CHAPTER IV

MYTHS OF MEXICO AND PERU

" Is the dawn about to be ? "
" Yes," answered the old man.
Popol Vuh

THE mythology of Mexico and Peru differs widely from that of the Indians living in the north of the continent. Here in the South the early peoples who built up the myths had all the characteristics of those who live in a warm and enervating climate. They loved ease and luxury, dainty eating and drinking—everything that added to their bodily pleasures. They did not have the reverence for a purified, spiritual beauty that the Greeks had, and they lacked their heightened intellectual development. They were cannibals, and cannibals of a specially horrible kind—that is, they ate the flesh of their enemies, not in a wild and savage feast, the final act of a fierce struggle, but delicately prepared and served at luxurious banquets, for the gratification of appetite.

The religion of such a people was naturally little more than a system by which they could obtain from the gods the gifts which would satisfy their desires. The chief god of their worship was the Sun-god, known by different names among the different tribes, but pictured always as a deity who must be sustained by daily offerings of blood. Human sacrifices were offered to him, with strict ceremonial observances, at the feasts held in his honour. The Mexicans called the Sun-god Ihalnemohuani, which means, " He by Whom Men Live "; and they believed that in return for the offerings made to him he would take all those who were killed in battle to dwell with him and share his feasts.

The Mexicans had many gods, and human sacrifices were

The Book of Myths

necessary to the worship of each one of them. Many of them were Nature gods, as Tezcatlipoca, the Wind-god, Tlaloc, the god of rain and moisture.

There were a large number of food and drink gods, a group of maize gods being known as the Centotl, and a group of drink gods as the Pulque gods. When a man became drunk he was

TEPOXTECATL, A PULQUE GOD

said to be under the influence of the Pulque gods. They were worshipped under the form of a rabbit, which was considered to be the animal possessing the least sense. If a man wished to become only slightly drunk he worshipped one rabbit, and so on according to the degree he wished to reach ; the highest number being four hundred.

There were several gods of war, and several of feasting and merriment ; there was a god who gave success in card-playing, and a god of man-flaying, who was dressed in flayed human skins. The god of the highest nature seems to have been Quetzalcoatl.

The Twin Brothers

sometimes called the Man of the Sun, who was said to have left his home in order to teach man the arts of civilization.

Some of the most interesting and most pleasant of the stories of Mexican mythology are to be found in a book called *Popol Vuh*, which means ' The Collection of Written Leaves.' It was written by a Christianized native of Guatemala in the 17th century from records gathered among the tribes. The story of " The Twin Brothers," given here, comes from this source.[1] These gods were the grandsons of the Father and Mother gods, Xpiyococ and Xmucane, who helped Hurakan, the god of lightning, to create the earth.

The Twin Brothers

The people of Central America had a ball game, which they called *tlachtli*, that was played with great enthusiasm and enjoyment throughout the country. It was, as far as we can understand it, a sort of hockey, the object being to pass the ball through a small hole in a circular piece of stone. We are told that not only men, but even the gods themselves, delighted in this game.

There were once two brother gods named Hunhun-Apu and Vukub-Hunapu, who were very skilful players. One day during a game they came very near to the borders of Xibalba, or Hades, which was ruled over by two kings, Hun-Came and Vukub-Came. These two, when they saw how eagerly the brothers played, and how in the progress of the game they did not even shrink from approaching the dreary kingdom of Hades, thought that it might be possible to make them actually enter that kingdom and so put themselves into the power of its rulers. So they chose four owls to be their messengers and sent them to Hunhun-Apu with a challenge to a game of ball in Hades. The brothers hated the lords of the underworld as much as those lords hated them; but they could not resist the temptation to show their prowess before their enemies, so they accepted the challenge and the owl messengers led them down to the dark country of Xibalba.

[1] See *Myths of Mexico and Peru*, by Lewis Spence, M.A.

The Book of Myths

There they soon found out that the sending of the challenge was only a device to make them prisoners. Insults and indignities of every kind were heaped upon them, and finally they were killed. But before his death Hunhun-Apu had won the love of a princess of Xibalba, and had secretly married her. When her father heard of this he was furious and drove the princess from his kingdom. She came up to the earth above and sought out the mother of Hunhun-Apu, who was very kind to her and to the twin sons who were born to her, and whom she called Hun-Apu and Xbalanque; and they all lived together in the hut with Hunbatz and Hunchouen, the two sons of Hunhun-Apu and his former wife.

The twins grew up the naughtiest and most elfish children that can possibly be imagined, quite unlike their half-brothers, Hunbatz and Hunchouen. From morning until night there was no peace or quiet in their grandmother's house. They ran and shouted and tumbled and fought, played tricks on every one about them, and broke or destroyed almost everything they touched. At last their grandmother's patience was quite worn out.

" I will not have such bad, noisy boys in my house!" she cried. " Get you out, and find a living for yourselves as best you can in the woods "; and, to the great joy of Hunbatz and Hunchouen, she bundled them out of doors.

The twins were not at all troubled at being thus obliged to shift for themselves; it would be rather fun, they thought, to live in the woods and have no one to scold them. They were a little taken aback when by and by they grew hungry, and there was no dinner prepared for them; but there were plenty of animals in the woods, and they managed to catch and kill some of these. After a while they became such successful hunters that in all the villages and huts for miles around men spoke in praise of Hun-Apu and Xbalanque, lauding their skill and courage. This did not at all please Hunbatz and Hunchouen, who grew very jealous of their younger brothers.

" Horrid little creatures!" they said; " they think enough of themselves already, and what they will become if this goes on, goodness knows."

The Twin Brothers

They did their best to bring down the twins' pride. They tried every way they could think of to annoy and tease them, and were always on the watch to do them an injury ; and as they were the older and stronger, they managed to make Hun-Apu and Xbalanque very unhappy. At last the twins declared they would put up with it no longer.

" They are stronger than we are," said Hun-Apu, " but we have power over them, for our mother as well as our father was divine." So they determined to see what they could do by the exercise of the god-like power they had inherited.

" We will change them into apes," they said. " Foolish, spiteful creatures ! They are more like apes than men already."

So on the first opportunity they put strong spells on Hunbatz and Hunchouen, and turned them into the most hideous and uncouth apes that had ever been seen upon the earth. In this form they went home to their grandmother, who, when she understood that these chattering, grimacing creatures were her elder grandchildren, was in a terrible state of distress. She guessed at once that this was the work of the mischievous twins, and she went to them at once, and prayed them to allow their two half-brothers to take again the form of human beings.

" What can I do," she said, " with two such creatures in the house ? When they were boys they used to cheer me with the music of their flutes and with their songs ; now they can only make horrible noises which it is pain for me to hear."

" Well," answered the twins, " we will change them back again for your sake, although when we remember the way they have treated us, we think they have well deserved their punishment ; but we will do this on one condition only. We will bring them before you, and you must look on their antics and grimaces quite gravely. If you laugh, or as much as smile, they must remain as they are."

" I do not feel at all like laughing," replied the old woman. " I am more likely to weep."

So the twins brought in the two apes and they stood before their grandmother capering and grimacing in their uncouth fashion. She looked at them, and tried hard to keep her face serious and unmoved, but their contortions were so ridiculous, and they jabbered and mouthed and capered, each moment presenting a fresh picture of comic clumsiness, so that all her efforts were in vain, and she laughed long and loudly. In answer to her pleading the twins allowed her another and yet another trial, but each time the result was the same. She could not

HUNBATZ AND HUNCHOUEN TURNED INTO APES

restrain her laughter, and so Hunbatz and Hunchouen never regained their human form.

It would take too long to tell of all the tricks these mischievous twins played during their boyhood and youth. When they were nearly grown to men, they were set one day to clear a piece of ground that was covered with weeds and bushes, and make it ready for the planting of maize. They did not like hard work, so they laid a spell on their tools, which forthwith began to work by themselves.

Away went the twins for a day's hunting, and coming back at night they smeared their faces and hands with soil, and went

The Twin Brothers

home to their grandmother, groaning and complaining how tired they were, and boasting of the land they had cleared during the day. The old woman believed them, gave them a good supper, and praised them for their work ; but in the morning when she went to look, she found the ground covered with weeds and bushes, just as it had been before. She came back to the house in a rage, and scolded them loudly for coming to her with a false tale that had induced her to give them food and lodging.

The twins were very much surprised and went out to look for themselves. There in truth was the land they had left so clear and smooth the night before once more choked with weeds. This would never do ; and they set to work to find out who it was that had played such a trick upon them. Soon by their magic arts they discovered that the wild animals, not wishing the brothers to spend all their time in hunting, had replaced at night all that the magic tools had cleared away during the day.

" *Ha !* " said the twins, " we must see to this." So they got a large net and spread it over the ground. " If the creatures come again to-night," they said, " they will not find it so easy to get away again."

That night the animals stole to the field once more, and found themselves entangled in the folds of the great net. They struggled hard, and all managed to get away except the rat, though the deer and the rabbit left their tails behind, and have suffered from that loss ever since.

In the morning the brothers came to see what had happened. They saw the signs of the struggle, but found no creature on whom they could vent their anger save the poor trembling rat.

" Do not be afraid, little one," said Hun-Apu. " We will not hurt you. You shall go free, as the rest of them have gone "; and he disentangled the little rat and set him on the ground free to go where he would.

" Thank you, thank you ! " said the rat. " And now in return for your kindness I will tell you the story of your father and your uncle, that you may be warned, and escape the dread enemy by whose wiles they were destroyed."

Hun-Apu and Xbalanque listened while the rat told them how

their father and their uncle had been lured to their death by the lords of Hades, and they vowed to take terrible vengeance on these cruel and treacherous beings. The mention of the game of ball which their father had loved so greatly aroused their keenest interest, for their grandmother in their childhood had kept them as far as she could from all knowledge of the game, and since they had grown older they had cared for no other pastime than hunting. Now they thought they would like to try the sport that their father had loved.

"The clubs and balls of Hunhun-Apu are hidden away in your grandmother's hut," said the rat. "If you ask her for them she must give them to you."

The twins went home and demanded the clubs and balls that had belonged to their father. Sadly the old woman realized that the day she had so long dreaded was come, and that the gods had decreed that her grandsons should in their turn be drawn to the game that had destroyed their father. Sadly she gave them what they asked for, and from that hour Hun-Apu and Xbalanque lost their former delight in hunting and devoted themselves to the game of ball.

It was not long before news of this reached the lords of Hades. "Here," they thought, "is our chance to destroy the sons as we destroyed the father."

Once more messengers passed from the dark under-realm to challenge the divinities on earth; and in spite of their grandmother's entreaties and warnings, the brothers accepted the challenge. "Do not fear," they said; "the lords of Hades will not harm us. We shall return to you in triumph, having avenged our father. See, we will plant each a cane in the middle of the hut. Watch these, and while they remain straight and strong you will know that all is well with us; but if they dry up and fall it will be a sign that we are dead."

Shouting a cheerful good-bye to their mother and their grandmother, they set off on the dismal road that leads to Hades.

"Before we go any farther," said Hun-Apu, "let us consider how we can escape the snares which the rat told us were set for our father and uncle. The river of blood which they had

The Twin Brothers

to cross will not frighten us. Then there are the wooden images that our father took to be Hun-Came and Vukub-Came, and which he greeted, so that their followers made a jest of him, laughing loudly and rousing him to anger. They shall not make a jest of us, for we will send Xau, the deer, before us as a scout, and he shall prick them all with a hair from my leg, so that he will find out which are real men, and which are made of wood ; at the same time he can listen to their talk, and tell us which are really the two lords. When they ask us to sit in the seat of honour we will refuse courteously, knowing that it is in truth a red-hot stone ; and our spirits will not sink when we come into the dreadful House of Gloom, for we shall know that for those who are calm and brave it has no terrors."

All these things they did, to the very great disappointment of their enemies. Then came the game of ball, and the brothers, playing with easy, laughing confidence, gained a notable victory. More and more angry grew Hun-Came and Vukub-Came, so that they could no longer keep up the pretence of goodwill. They bade the brothers go to the royal garden and bring back four bouquets, and they secretly instructed the gardeners to allow no flower to be touched. The twins, convinced that some trick was intended, did not attempt to go themselves, but created a great army of ants which swarmed all over the garden and carried off the flowers.

"Take them away to the House of Lances," shouted the angry lords, " and shut them up securely."

The House of Lances was a terrible place, where demons armed with steel lances struck at the prisoners ; but Hun-Apu and Xbalanque defended themselves by their arts, and not one of the weapons so much as pierced their skin. They passed triumphantly through the hall, and bribed the owls who guarded the entrance to let them go free.

When the lords of Hades found out that their prisoners had escaped, they were in a fury of rage. They took the owls and slit their beaks in punishment. They pursued and seized Hun-Apu and Xbalanque and made them pass through all the tortures of that dreadful kingdom. One night the brothers were forced to spend in the House of Cold, another in the House of Tigers, and a third in the House of Fire; and from all they returned uninjured. Then their enemies shut them up in the horrible House of Bats, where hateful bat-like creatures with leathern wings and claws like swords made the air dark and fearful. Here the Ruler of the Bats swept down on Hun-Apu, and with cruel claws cut off his head. Hun-Apu fell lifeless to the ground, and Xbalanque, mad with rage and grief, made furious efforts to reach the loathsome creatures who hovered just beyond his reach, mocking his anguish. At that moment it chanced that a tortoise crawled along the floor, and by chance touched the bleeding neck of Hun-Apu. Immediately the creature became fixed to the place it touched, and rapidly changed into a new head, living and active, just like the one that had been cut off; and Hun-Apu sprang up, not a bit the worse for what had happened.

After this the lords of Hades gave up in despair their efforts to kill these wonder-working gods; and Hun-Apu and Xbalanque called in two sorcerers, by whose help they showed that they were immortal. Both the brothers lay down on biers and died; then the sorcerers ground their bones to powder, and cast the powder into the river. Five days later they made their appearance as creatures partly men and partly fish; the next day they came as ragged old men, and the next in their own proper form. Many other wonders they did, until the lords of Hades, amazed and crestfallen, felt that the power of which they had been so proud was as nothing compared to the power of these visitors from the upper world. At last their curiosity overcame their dignity, and they cried, "Let us too experience this marvel. Let us be put to death, and then restore our bodies that we may live, and remember what it was like to die."

The brothers saw that here was a chance of ridding themselves of the chief of their enemies. Silently they made a sign to two among the wondering crowd that stood about them. The two stepped forward, and the lords of Hades willingly submitted themselves to the death-stroke. Then Hun-Apu lifted his hand, and cried to the people, " Know all that we are gods from the world above, treacherously ensnared by these your lords, who now lie dead before you. We will not restore them to life. By their own will they died, and their doom is on their own heads. As for you, we will not destroy you, though your deeds have been foul and evil, worthy of death. But through all the future ages you shall be the servants of gods and men; you shall work for them, and the meanest and lowest tasks shall be yours. You shall have power no more over mortals, on the beasts alone shall your magic avail ought. You shall play no more the noble game of ball which you have tried to degrade. Thus the gods punish treachery."

Then Hun-Apu and Xbalanque returned to the upper world, and they set the soul of their father, Hunhun-Apu, and the soul of their uncle, Vukub-Hunapu, in the heavens, and they became the sun and moon, so that all men did them honour.

Quetzalcoatl

Long, long ago, hundreds of years before the people of Europe knew anything about the great land of America, a race of people called the Toltecs lived in the southern part of that country which we now call Mexico. They were ruled by Quetzalcoatl, the great god of the sun and the wind, who had left his home in the land of the Sunrise that he might teach the Toltecs and help them to become a happy and prosperous nation. He was an old man with a flowing white beard, and he wore a long, black robe fringed with white crosses. He was kind and wise, and while he reigned over them the Toltecs were very happy. Everything in the country prospered. The maize crops were more abundant than they had ever been before, the fruits were larger and more plentiful. It is even said that the cotton grew in all sorts of colours, richer and rarer than could be produced by any dyes. The hills and valleys were gay with flowers, and bright-coloured birds flitted through the air, filling the land with joyous song.

But the king-god Quetzalcoatl knew that if his people were to be really happy they must not spend their days in the idle

The Book of Myths

enjoyment of all this loveliness and plenty. They must work, and learn to take a pride in working as well as they possibly could. So he taught them many useful arts—painting and weaving and carving and working in metals. He taught them how to fashion the gold and silver and precious stones which were found in great abundance throughout the country into beautiful vessels and ornaments, and how to make marvellous many-tinted garments and hangings from the feathers of birds. Every one was eager to work, and because each man did his share there was plenty of leisure for all. No one was in want and no one was unhappy. It seemed as if, for these fortunate Toltecs, the Golden Age had really come.

The people of the neighbouring states, who were living almost like savages, were very jealous when they saw the prosperity of the Toltecs. The gods of these people were fierce and warlike, and they hated Quetzalcoatl because he was so unlike themselves. They plotted together to destroy the peace and good government which he had established.

Tezcatlipoca, the chief of these gods, disguised himself as a very old man and went to the palace of Quetzalcoatl.

" I desire to speak with your master, the King," he said to the page who admitted him.

" That you cannot do," replied the page, "for the King is at present ill, and can see no one."

" Nevertheless, go and take my message," said Tezcatlipoca, " and come back and tell me what he says."

The page soon returned, saying that the King would see his visitor, and Tezcatlipoca went in. He bowed low and respectfully before the god, and said that he had come to bring him a drug that would at once cure him of his illness.

" I have been expecting you for some days," answered Quetzalcoatl, " and I will take your medicine, for my illness troubles me exceedingly."

Then Tezcatlipoca poured out a cupful of his medicine, which was really nothing but the strong wine of the country. Quetzalcoatl tasted it, and liked it very much; he did not know what it was, for he never drank wine. After drinking the cupful he

Quetzalcoatl

declared that he already felt better, so that it was easy to induce him to drink cupful after cupful of this new, pleasant-tasting medicine. Very soon the wine had its effect, and he could no longer think clearly or act wisely, or take his usual place as the ruler of the country. Tezcatlipoca took care to keep him supplied with plenty of the tempting drink, so that he remained for some time in this state of intoxication.

This was Tezcatlipoca's opportunity, and he used it to the full. He set to work to bring upon the happy Toltecs every kind of misery that he could devise. He stirred up strife between them and their neighbours, and in many cunning ways he used his magic arts to lure large numbers of them to destruction. He brought plagues upon them, and disasters in which many lost their lives ; until at last, by his wicked devices, the once happy land was brought to a state even worse than that of its barbarous neighbours.

When Quetzalcoatl shook off the evil influence of the wine given to him by his enemy and came to his true self once more, the grief which he felt at seeing all his work undone made him resolve to leave the Toltecs and go back whence he had come. But first he determined to destroy what he could of the gifts he had given to the people. He burned the houses he had built, and changed the cacao-trees from which the Toltecs had obtained so much valuable food into useless mesquites. He buried his treasures of gold and silver in one of the deep valleys. All the bright-plumaged birds he commanded to follow him back to his own country ; and, full of anger and grief, he set out on his long journey, taking with him a train of pages, and musicians to lighten the way with their flute-playing. On the road, as he passed through the neighbouring states, he was met by some of the gods of the land. These gods were his enemies, and were glad to see him depart ; but before he went they hoped to gain from him some of his secrets.

" Why are you going away ? " asked one, " and whither are you bound ? "

" I am going back to my own country," Quetzalcoatl answered.

" But why ? " the other asked again.

The Book of Myths

" Because my father, the Sun, has called for me."

" Go then," replied the gods. " But first tell us some of the secrets, which are known to you alone, concerning the arts you practise; for we know there is no one who can paint and weave and work in metals as you can."

" I will tell you nothing," replied Quetzalcoatl. He took all the treasures he had brought with him and cast them into a fountain near by, which was called the Water of Precious Stones; and he went on his way, paying no heed to the entreaties of the disappointed gods.

As they journeyed on, the road grew ever harder and more dangerous, but Quetzalcoatl, his staff in his hand, pressed steadily forward; and his train, though they were weary and nearly exhausted, followed him. Only once did they stop to rest, and that was when an enchanter met Quetzalcoatl and gave him a cup of wine. The wine sent the god into a deep sleep, but in the morning he had recovered from its effects and was ready to set out once more.

That day was a terrible one for the wayfarers. At each step it grew colder and colder, and the poor pages, used to the sunny skies of their native land, felt their limbs gradually becoming benumbed and useless. At length Quetzalcoatl led the way through a narrow valley between a volcano and the Sierra Nevada, or Mountain of Snow. Here the cold was so intense that the pages one by one sank down and died. Quetzalcoatl mourned over them with many tears and sang wild songs of lamentation; then sadly he went on his way, still weeping bitterly.

He had now to cross a great mountain. He climbed up one side, then, when he had reached the summit, he slid down the opposite slope to the bottom. After this he soon reached the seashore, and there, awaiting him, was a raft. It was not made of timber, as most rafts are, but of serpents, twined together, with writhing bodies and lifted, hissing heads. On to this strange raft Quetzalcoatl stepped, and was borne away back to his own land.

The Mexicans believe that one day he will come again, and once more rule over his people and bring back to them the Golden

Quetzalcoatl

Age. When Cortes and his companions, in 1519, landed at Vera Cruz, which was the very place from which Quetzalcoatl was supposed to have departed centuries before, the people believed that here was their god returning to help them, and only slowly and reluctantly came to understand that he was a Spaniard, bent on conquest.

CHAPTER V

MYTHS OF THE EGYPTIANS

The Soul that rises within us, our life's Star,
Hath had elsewhere its setting
And cometh from afar.

WORDSWORTH

EGYPTIAN mythology is probably the oldest of all those known to us. Ages have gone by since it was evolved, and it has passed through many stages and undergone many alterations. The records of its early phases are scanty, and are drawn chiefly from inscriptions that have been discovered by modern explorers, and from books—most of them by Greek authors—written at a comparatively late date. It is difficult, therefore, to give any simple account of the Egyptian gods, especially as there are a great many of them ; we are told that eight hundred are mentioned in the earliest lists that have been discovered.

The ancient Egyptians were an agricultural people. They were ruled by a despotic king, and had a great and powerful nobility. The lowest class were slaves. The priests, also, were very powerful, and the gods were worshipped with very many and very strictly enforced ceremonial observances. This much we know : and we shall therefore expect to find that the gods are mainly personifications of such natural forces—the sun, the rain, the wind—as affect the welfare of the crops, and that they are held in extreme awe and their anger greatly dreaded.

There was in the myths of the ancient Egyptians no trace of the familiar, homely deity as he existed in those of the North-American Indians or the Norsemen. The gods of the Egyptians were remote and awe-inspiring, and had lost most of their human characteristics. The worship of the sun was the great feature of their religion. In addition to the great Sun-god Ra, chief and

Osiris and Isis

eldest of the deities, there were many others standing for the sun at different times and in different aspects; for example, Ptah was the rising, and Kepera the setting sun. There were also gods of the moon, the winds, and the waters; there were gods of the Nile, and a goddess of the First Cataract. The best-known of all the deities are perhaps Osiris, the god who judges the souls of the dead, and Isis, his wife. There were also gods with more mysterious titles, such as Amen-Ra, " That which is hidden," and I-em-hetep, " Come in peace." Many of the gods are represented as having the forms of animals—Bast, who stands for the fertilizing heat of the sun, was a lioness; and Hathor, the love-goddess, was a cow. More frequently they had the head of an animal and a human body—Anubis, who guides the dead in the underworld, had the head of a jackal; Thoth, the scribe of the gods, the head of an ibis. This is probably a relic of the totemism which existed in the early stages of the nation's development, but it adds to the strange and mysterious quality which is the great feature of Egyptian mythology.

Osiris and Isis

In the very early stages of its history, many thousand years before the birth of Christ, Egypt is said to have been ruled by a dynasty of gods. One of the first of these was Ra, the mighty Sun-god, who married Nut, goddess of the sky and the rain, and these two had a son whom they called Osiris. The future greatness of this son was magically proclaimed at his birth. A certain Egyptian named Pamyles was carrying water from the temple of Ra at Thebes when he heard a voice calling his name. " Go, Pamyles," it said, " and proclaim to all the world that the good and great King Osiris is born to-day." Pamyles obeyed the mysterious voice, and made known as widely as he could the message that had been given to him, so that it came at last to the ears of Ra. Ra saw that some power even above his own had spoken through the mouth of the wise Pamyles, and he decided that the man who had been chosen to make known the will of this power was the best person to train up the young

193

The Book of Myths

Osiris. So the child was given into the charge of Pamyles, who trained him in virtue and wisdom, so that when the time came for him to reign, he showed that he really was "the good and great King Osiris."

The Egyptians up to that time had lived as a barbarous nation. They knew nothing of the arts of peace or the true glories of honourable war. They did not till the ground or tend herds; they fought like savages, sometimes even eating the bodies of their conquered foes. Osiris taught them to dig and plough, to plant the vine, to live industriously and virtuously, and to worship the gods in a manner pleasing to those great beings. His people loved him so well that they delighted to please and serve him, and under his rule they became civilized, prosperous, and happy. The change that he wrought in his country was like the change from night to morning; it seemed as if a kindly wonder-working sun had shed its beams through the land.

Osiris married his beautiful and gentle sister Isis, the marriage of brother and sister being a common practice among the ancient Egyptians. Isis was tall and slender, and the movements of her supple figure made those who saw her think of corn-stalks in the wind. Her hair was the colour of the corn and her face had the brightness of a summer day. All about her spread sweet odours as of winds bearing the breath of flowers from fresh and fragrant places. Her ways were wise and tender, and she loved especially little children, the weak, the helpless, and the suffering. The Egyptians looked up to her as an all-powerful, all-loving mother, and worshipped her as a goddess. It was she, they said, who gave them the plentiful golden harvests, and satisfied their children with bread.

Isis helped her husband in everything that he did for the good of his people, and when he felt that a call had come to him to visit distant countries and bring the light to them also, she gladly undertook to do her best to carry on the good work while he was away.

This she did successfully, though Set, Osiris' brother, a cruel and wicked man, never rested in his cunning efforts to put himself in the place of the absent king. But the people loved

Osiris and Isis

Osiris and Isis, and were faithful to them in all things, so that Set, with rage and hatred in his heart, gave up his attempts.

He did not cease from his wickedness, however, but made a cunning plan to kill Osiris when he came back. He joined himself to others who were jealous of the great king—seventy-three in all—and together these evil men laid their plans. By cunning, secret means Set obtained the measurements of Osiris' body, and then he caused a chest to be made, curiously carved and richly ornamented, and of such a size that the king's body would fit into it exactly.

By this time Osiris had returned, and Set made a great feast of welcome in his honour.

" Do not go, my beloved," entreated Isis. " Set, your brother, is an evil man, who hates you and will work you harm."

But Osiris, having no guile or bitterness in his own heart, believed others to be as himself, and with words of confidence and cheer he tried to cast out the fear that troubled his wife; then, putting on his most splendid robes, he went in all trust and friendship to his brother's banquet.

Set and his chosen companions received Osiris with the honour that was his due, and all sat down, with high rejoicing, to the rich banquet that had been prepared. When it was over Set commanded that the chest he had had made should be brought into the hall, and when all had admired its beauty and rare workmanship, he proposed, as one who provides a sport for his guests, that each in turn should lie down in the chest, and that it should belong to him whose body fitted it with exactness. One after another the guests tried, but always it was a little too short, or too long, or too narrow, or too wide. But when Osiris laid down in it, it fitted him perfectly, and smiling in jesting triumph he was about to spring up and claim it, when the great lid fell with a crash upon him. He heard the eager, exultant voices of the men around him, and the sound of great nails being hammered in. Boiling lead was poured on, to make sure that no slight crack might allow air to reach the imprisoned king, and then the great chest was lifted on men's shoulders, and with joy in their wicked hearts, Set and his friends carried it out and set it adrift on the Nile.

Isis waited with an anxious heart for her husband's return, trying to believe that her terrible forebodings of evil were unfounded. But the triumphant Set, having got rid of his brother, made haste eagerly to seize upon the signs of royal power, and

ISIS AND THE CHILDREN

very soon the watching Isis knew that Osiris, the good and great king, was dead—slain by the treachery of those he trusted. The news pierced her loving heart like a sharp sword; but she knew there was still something she could do for her dear husband, for his soul would never rest in peace until his body was buried with the rites the gods commanded. So she got up, and cut off a lock of her bright hair, and put on a mourning garment, as it was the custom for widows to do among the Egyptians; and then she went out to try to find the chest in which lay the body of her husband.

Osiris and Isis

She travelled far, weary and hungry, and suffering many things, asking each person she met if he had seen such a chest as she sought ; but none could tell her anything about it.

At last, searching along the banks of the Nile, she saw some children at play, and of them she asked the same weary question : " Have you seen anywhere a chest, large and beautiful and richly adorned ? "

The children looked up into the sad, beautiful face of this stately lady and loved her, as all children loved Isis of the mother heart. " We saw men carry such a chest," they said. " It was heavy, and they bore it with labour, and as they came they talked to one another with loud and mocking words about a foe that they had slain. And they cast the chest on the waters of the Nile, just by this place, and hastily departed."

Then Isis thanked the children, and with hope in her heart she went on her way. But the chest had drifted far, and Isis searched for a long time without finding it.

Then Anubis, son of Osiris, came to help her, and the sacred birds worshipped by the Egyptians—the ibis, the bennu, and the falcon—pitying the distress of the heart-broken wife, at last told her where the chest could be found. It had drifted, they said, on to the shore of Byblos, and had rested on a tamarisk plant, which at once had grown with miraculous speed into a tree, enclosing the chest in its trunk. So tall and stately was the tree that all who passed by exclaimed at its beauty, and when the king of the country, Melcarthus, saw it, he commanded that it should be cut down, and set up as one of the pillars of his palace.

Isis listened, glad that she knew at last where the body of her husband rested, but grieving that it now seemed farther out of her reach than ever. But with a brave heart she set out for Byblos, and when she reached it she sat down by a well and waited. The people coming to draw water looked curiously at the stately, beautiful lady, but Isis remained still and silent until the queen's maidens came to draw water for their mistress. Then she rose and spoke kindly to them, and the sweet airs that always blew around her perfumed their long tresses and their garments, so that when they went back to the palace Queen

The Book of Myths

Astarte asked them whence had come the ravishing odour which she perceived with delight.

The maidens eagerly told of the lovely lady at the well, and the queen bade them go and bring the stranger to her ; and Isis came, calm and gracious and winning all hearts. Though she seemed only a poor wanderer, she was treated with much honour

ISIS LAYING THE BABE ON THE BURNING LOGS

in the palace, and Astarte begged her to stay and become nurse to one of the young princes.

To the motherly heart of Isis all children were dear, and she was glad to take this lowly office while she waited for the time when she might obtain what she had come to Byblos to seek. She stayed at the palace for many days and grew to love the pretty babe she tended. She fed him by giving him her finger to suck, and on this nourishment he grew strong, healthy, and beautiful. At night when the house was quiet Isis would build up a great fire upon the hearth, lift the babe from his bed, and lay him gently in the midst of the burning logs ; and then she would turn herself into a swallow and make a mournful song grieving for her dead husband.

The servants of the palace watched in awe the doings of this silent, majestic nurse who had come so strangely among them, and after a time whispers spread among them of strange things that were done in the little prince's chamber under cover of the night.

When Astarte heard these rumours she determined to find out the truth ; and so she hid herself in the apartment and saw Isis bar the door, pile logs on the fire, then gently lay the baby on that burning couch. But at that she could remain hidden no longer ; she darted from her place and snatched her child from what seemed to her a bed of death.

Then Isis spoke sorrowfully : " O Queen Astarte," she said, " you who love your child have done him a great wrong. Could you but have trusted him to my care in which each day you saw his strength and beauty increase I would have given to him the gift of immortality. But you have snatched him from me ; take him, then, for my work here is done, and it is time that I depart." [1]

Queen Astarte, with her babe in her arms, looked at the queenly figure of Isis and heard her lofty words, and a great awe of this woman who had been her child's nurse came over her. " Who are you ? " she cried. " Who can bestow on a mortal the gift of immortality ? "

Then Isis spoke, her voice low and sad: " I am Isis, the unhappy Queen of Egypt, wife of the murdered Osiris, and I seek my husband's body that I may bury it with the rites the gods command, that his tortured spirit may have rest. Help me, therefore, O sister queen, for the chest in which his murderers imprisoned him lies hid in the great pillar which holds up the roof of your palace."

As she spoke the thunder crashed and lightning played around her, so that Queen Astarte was terrified and sank to the ground, saying, " Take what thou wilt, O dread queen." Then Isis struck the tree, and it opened, and within was the chest made by the wicked Set.

[1] See the story of Demeter and Triptolemus, page 41.

The Book of Myths

When King Melcarthus heard what had happened he offered freely to Isis one of his ships, and in this the chest was taken back to Egypt. Once more in her own country she opened the chest, and the long-delayed funeral rites were performed; but even then her troubles were not over. She wished to tell her son Horus that her search had been successful, but she dared not leave her husband's body where it would fall into the hands of his enemies, and with much trouble she sought out a hiding-place for it in the depths of the forest. Even there the wicked Set discovered it, and in his rage he rent it in fourteen pieces, which he scattered throughout the country.

Isis, returning, found that her weary search must begin again, but with faithful, untiring love she sought long and patiently. She sailed down the Nile in a papyrus boat, and searched the country on either bank, and when she found one of the pieces of the cruelly torn body she buried it with honour, and raised a temple to mark the spot. She did not pause in her sad task till thirteen pieces had been thus buried. The fourteenth had been eaten by crocodiles. Then at Philoë she raised a magnificent temple in honour of Osiris, and to this for many ages afterward the faithful of Egypt made their pilgrimages.

Osiris now reigns as the King of the Underworld, where he judges the souls of the dead who are brought before him. Isis is still the loving mother of her people, making their land fertile, giving them the golden harvest, helping them in their troubles, and making winds of heaven bear freshness and healing over the world.

The Princess and the Demon

Long ago, in the days when Egypt was the greatest nation of the earth, there reigned over it a king whose name was Rameses. He was a mighty man of war, and conquered many of the countries that lay round about Egypt so that their rulers became his vassals and paid him tribute. Every year on the day appointed they journeyed to his city at the mouth of the Euphrates, to do him honour and present their offerings, and every year they came in greater numbers as fresh countries fell under his rule.

The Princess and the Demon

On one such day King Rameses sat on his throne and looked proudly upon the goodly show. Prince after prince, stately of carriage and in rich apparel, entered his presence, and bowed low before him; behind each came a train of dark-skinned, brightly clad slaves bearing tribute—gold and precious stones, sandal-wood and ivory, spices and oils, cloth of marvellous dye, rich silks, baskets filled with deep-hued fruits, and wine gleaming in crystal flasks—so that the chamber glowed with colour and sweet odours filled the air.

King Rameses noted each comer with a careful eye, strict to see that no due remained unpaid, and he spoke a gracious word to each vassal who rendered his homage and passed on. After a time came the Prince of Bekhten, ruler of a far-distant province; and then the king started up from his throne and took no more heed of the gorgeous procession passing slowly before him. For with the prince was his daughter, a maiden famed for her loveliness through all the land. She was tall and slender and of a grace passing men's imagination; her face was so beautiful that there could be found nothing in heaven or earth, no flower or star or glory of sky or sea to which it could be compared; so that looking on her men said, " Her beauty is the beauty of Amen-Ra, the great god of the sun."

To Rameses it seemed as if the sun had indeed entered his palace, and the first moment that he saw the maiden he loved her and desired her for his wife. The princess was willing, and her father rejoiced that such honour should be done her, and so with great pomp and splendour the two were married, and the princess became the Great Royal Wife. She was very happy with her husband, and he loved her more and more as the days went on; she filled her high place with a noble dignity, yet was kind and gentle to all, so that her people loved her well, and her beauty brought light and joy to the land.

In her far distant home the princess had left a little sister named Bent-reshy, who was very dear to her. Not long after the marriage a terrible thing happened to this little sister. A demon, very powerful and malignant, entered into her, and poor Bent-reshy became so ill that the prince her father feared she would die. The greatest physicians in the land were called, but none could do her any good, and prayers to the gods were unavailing. Then her father in his despair sent to the great King of Egypt, hoping that some aid might be obtained from that mighty kingdom.

Rameses and the Great Royal Wife were keeping the festival of the god Amen-Ra in his temple when the messenger arrived. Word was sent to them, and they came with haste. Then the messenger presented rich gifts, and said, bowing to the ground before the king: "This message sent my master, the Prince of Bekhten: The little sister of the Great Royal Wife lies ill, tormented of a demon. I pray thee therefore, O great king, to send a physician to heal her of her malady."

Then the king and his wife were very sad, and they consulted together as to how they could help Bent-reshy. All the wise men of the kingdom were assembled, and one of their number, named Tehuti-em-eb, was chosen, and he set off at once on the long journey to Bekhten.

A year and five months he travelled, making great speed, and at last reached the palace of the prince. But the demon was too strong for Tehuti-em-eb, and nothing that he could do was of any avail, though he used all his arts and laboured long. Then the Prince of Bekhten felt that his last hope was gone, and he covered his face and wept for his little daughter so tormented and soon to be lost to him for ever. But Tehuti-em-eb spoke words of hope.

" Be comforted, O Prince," he said, " for in the land of Egypt, in the temple of Khonsu, is a statue of the god Khonsu, Expeller of Demons. Ask yet once more of Rameses that he will send you this god, and then it may be that your daughter shall be made whole."

Then again were messengers sent to Egypt, while those who were left at home watched the little sister with fear in their hearts lest she should die before those messengers returned.

Now at Thebes, in the splendid temple which Rameses had built to the Moon-god Khonsu, there were two statues of the god,

The Princess and the Demon

one called Khonsu in Thebes and the other Khonsu, Expeller of Demons.

The messenger from the Prince of Bekhten arrived in Thebes during the month sacred to Khonsu, and he sought Rameses in the temple of the god. He bowed before the king and told his message; and the king turned to where stood the statue of

PROCESSION OF THE GOD KHONSU

Khonsu in Thebes in the likeness of a goodly youth, tall and handsome. "Is it your will, O great Khonsu, god of the moon, traveller of the sky, light in darkness," he cried, "that I send Khonsu the Demon Expeller to the far land of Bekhten that he may heal the little sister of the Great Royal Wife of her deadly sickness?"

The great god Khonsu bowed his bright head and spoke to the sorrowing king: "Send him, O Rameses, in faith, without doubt or anxiety, and my protection shall go with him, so that he shall quickly journey to Bekhten and look with power and healing on the little sister of the Great Royal Wife."

The Book of Myths

Then Rameses left the temple and hastily prepared a great train, with camels, and chariots richly ornamented, as for the journey of a king; and Khonsu, Expeller of Demons, went with the train toward Bekhten. When they drew near the city a great crowd came out to meet them, offering rich gifts and worshipping the great god Khonsu. " My daughter yet lives," said the prince, bowing low before him, " though at the point of death. Come at once, I pray, to her chamber, lest the demon, hearing of your approach, wax wrathful and rend her so that she die."

Then Khonsu the Demon Expeller came into the maiden's chamber, and as soon as he looked at her the demon came out and left her whole and well; and she sat up and embraced her father, so that he and his courtiers knew not what to do for joy. But those who stood near Khonsu heard a voice and words spoken, though they could see no one. " O Khonsu," said the voice, " thou art more powerful than I, and I am thy slave. If thou commandest that I go from hence I will go. But I pray thee ask of the Prince of Bekhten that he will make a holy day for me and a sacrifice. Then shall I go in peace."

Khonsu replied, " It shall be as thou hast asked."

Then Khonsu told the prince, and he appointed a day to be kept holy; and in the morning of that day the people came and offered first a sacrifice to Khonsu, Expeller of Demons, and then they offered a sacrifice to the demon; and the demon was satisfied, and departed from the land.

When he was gone there was great gladness, and Bent-reshy, smiling and happy, was once more the sunshine of her father's palace. But because her father loved her so dearly, a cloud of dread still hung over him, and he thought, " If Khonsu, Expeller of Demons, leaves my land, the demon may return, and once more torment Bent-reshy, or perchance may enter into other of my people so that sorrows shall come upon us."

So he would not let Khonsu go back, but kept him in Bekhten because of this fear. Three years passed and still the prince would not let the god return to his own place. Then one night he had a dream, and in his dream he stood in the temple before the shrine that he had made for Khonsu, Expeller of Demons,

The Legend of the Nile's Source

and suddenly the doors of the shrine burst open, and the beautiful god came out ; but as the prince looked, Khonsu changed into the form of a hawk and flew away toward Egypt.

Then the prince knew that the gods had sent him this dream in their displeasure to tell him that he could no longer keep Khonsu, Expeller of Demons, from his own place ; for the spirit of the god had taken flight, and only the outward form remained. The prince trembled, and resolved to make his peace with the gods. He sent back the statue of Khonsu next morning, with many rich presents, and such a train as was fitting for the journey of a king, and Khonsu came safely back to his own place. Once more his statue was set up in the temple at Thebes, and the rich gifts that the Prince of Bekhten had given him he gave to Khonsu in Thebes, keeping nothing for himself.

The Legend of the Nile's Source

The Nile is a great river, and Khnemu-Ra, the god of the Nile, is a great god, who from the beginning has been worshipped and has shown favour to the people of Egypt, so that they have flourished and increased. For from the Nile comes the food of the Egyptians ; every year the river spreads itself over the land with blessing, so that when it returns to its bed, the seeds that are sown bring forth great crops, and all the people are fed. But if the Nile will not spread itself, then there is no blessing on the land.

It happened in the eleventh year of the reign of Teheser that the Nile ceased to show favour to the Egyptians. It remained within its banks, nor spread itself with blessing, so that the crops were poor and the people complained. Yet the granaries were full with what remained of the last year's harvest, and none felt want ; all hoped for better things in the coming year. But again the Nile remained within its banks, and this went on for seven years, until there was no food left in the land. Thus in the eighteenth year of the reign of Teheser the famine was so sore that everywhere men, women, and little children were dying of hunger, while those who remained alive were so weak that scarcely could the strongest walk upright. And, worst of all, men's hearts became so hardened that they snatched from the hands of sick people and little children any morsel that these had obtained, and it seemed as if love and pity and courage had died out of the land as well as corn and grapes.

King Teheser was sorely grieved at the woes of his people, and he sought the help of the god I-em-hetep, son of Ptah, the great physician, who in former times had delivered the Egyptians from their troubles, but no answer came to his prayer. Then he said, " I-em-hetep will not answer because the matter is none of his ; it is to the god of the Nile that we must make supplication." So he sent to Mater, his governor in the southern provinces, to ask the name of the god of the Nile, and also where the river had its source.

Mater, journeying quickly, came to the king and bowed low before him, and said : " O king, in the region that thou hast given me to rule lies the wonderful island Elephantine. On it was built the first city that was ever known in the world, and out of it rises the sun. Within the island is a great cavern, which is in two parts, each shaped like the breast of a woman, and inside this cavern is the source of the Nile. At the proper season of the year the god Khnemu draws back the bolts of the door of the cavern, and the waters rush out to bless the land. But now the god draws not back the bolts. He sits in the temple of the gods which is built on the island of Elephantine, silent and motionless, because men have not made offerings to him of the good gifts he has given them, and have not remembered his name."

King Teheser when he heard this waited no longer, but rose up quickly and made his way to the temple of the gods ; and there he offered sacrifices and prayed to the god Khnemu that he would again unbolt the door that the waters might rush out and bless the land. Khnemu looked on him and saw the great anguish of his spirit and the love he had for his people, and he had pity on him, and said, " I am Khnemu, the Creator. My hands rest upon thee to protect thy person and make sound thy body. I am the Nile, who rises to give health to those who

Se-Osiris and the Sealed Letter

toil. I am the guide and director of all men, the Almighty, the father of the gods. Now I will have pity on you and on your land, and the Nile shall rise again as it has done in the times past ; for each year I will unbolt the door that the waters may rush forth and bless the land so that it shall be very fruitful and the people shall eat and be satisfied. This will I do because I have pity upon your misery, and the misery of your land. Yet remember, O king, how my shrine is broken down and no man has put his hand to build it up, although all around lie the stones that would make it whole."

Then King Teheser, his heart full of thankfulness, made answer : " O mighty Khnemu, Creator of all things, god of the Nile, who wilt give bread to my starving people. From henceforward your temple shall be honoured, and due offerings made, and I will make proclamation that all Egypt shall worship the good god Khnemu, and offer him thankofferings." So he bowed himself and went out, and he made a royal decree that the lands on each side of the Nile should be set apart for the support of the temple, that priests should be appointed to serve Khnemu, and that the land round about should pay a tax for their maintenance.

All these things he caused to be written on a rock, in remembrance of the great bounty of the god; and many thousands of years later, in the year 1890, this stone was found on the island of Sahul, and the story of the god of the Nile became known to the world.

Se-Osiris and the Sealed Letter

There was once a king in Egypt called Ousimares, and he had a son named Setne. This son was skilled in the learning of the Egyptians, and wise in all that concerned the ruling of the kingdom, and was his father's helper and adviser. He was married to a wife who was beautiful and kind; his only grief was that the gods had not granted him a son. But at last, in answer to the prayers of the princess, the god I-em-hetep gave them a son. There was great rejoicing in the royal palace over

The Book of Myths

his boy, who was named Se-Osiris. His father and mother loved him so dearly that they could scarcely bear him out of their sight. He grew very quickly, and learned with such marvellous speed that soon his teachers could do no more for him, for he was wiser than they were. When he was twelve

THE ETHIOPIAN BEFORE PHARAOH

years old he could read the magical books of Egypt better than any scribe or priest of Memphis.

It happened one day, about this time, that Ousimares sat in his Hall of Audience, with his princes and nobles about him, when a messenger came in and said, "There is come, O king, a rascally Ethiopian, who asks that he may have speech with the Pharaoh."

The king answered, "Let him be brought in"; and he came in and bowed before the Pharaoh and said:

"I have brought you, O king! a sealed letter, to try if any of your priests or magicians can read what is written therein without breaking the seal; and if they cannot I will go back to

Se-Osiris and the Sealed Letter

my country and tell my people how weak is the magic of the Egyptians; and they will make a mock of you and of your wise men."

The king was very angry and troubled, and sent at once for his son Setne; and Setne, too, when he came, was dismayed in his spirit because of the words of the Ethiopian. Yet he answered bravely, " Give me ten days, O my father, and I will see what I can do that we may not seem foolish in the eyes of these negroes, eaters of gum."

Ousimares turned to the Ethiopian and told him that in ten days an answer should be given him, and that meantime he should be lodged in the royal palace and entertained hospitably. Then the audience broke up, and the Pharaoh went away sadly and fasted till the next morning. Setne too was sad, for he did not know how to meet this challenge of the Ethiopian. How was it possible for a man to read a letter which was folded and sealed so that it was hidden from his eyes? He lay down on his couch, but he could not sleep. His wife came to him fearing he was sick, but he told her that his trouble was not one which she could help or understand; and Se-Osiris came, and to him his father made the same answer. The boy would not be satisfied, and still entreated that he might know the cause of his father's sadness; until at last Setne told him of the Ethiopian and his impudent message.

When Se-Osiris heard this he laughed out merrily. His father was puzzled, and said, " Why do you laugh, my son, when I tell you of that which has caused so much sadness to the Pharaoh and to me? "

Se-Osiris answered, " I laugh, my father, because you are troubled at such a trifle. Be comforted. I will read the letter of the Ethiopian."

Setne rose up hastily from his couch and looked in his son's face. " How shall I know, my son," he said, " that you can do this thing? "

" Go to the room where your writings are kept," answered Se-Osiris, " and take in your hand any one you choose; and I will read to you out of the writing that is in your hand."

Setne, greatly wondering, did according to the words of his son, and Se-Osiris read each writing without its being opened. In great joy Setne went to his father, the king, and told him of all Se-Osiris had done. At his words the king's heart was lightened, and the hearts of all those who stood near him ; and that night the king made a great feast in honour of his son, and of his son's son who would save Egypt from dishonour.

Next day the king sat once more in his Hall of Audience, and the Ethiopian was brought in, bearing the sealed letter in his hand. Se-Osiris came and stood beside him and charged him to say truly whether the words of the letter were indeed such as he, Se-Osiris, should say ; and he put a curse upon the Ethiopian if he should speak falsely. The negro was amazed to hear words like these from one so young, and he bowed low before him in fear. Then before the king and before Setne and before all the princes and nobles and captains and the Ethiopian messenger, Se-Osiris read in a clear voice, without halting or hesitation, the words of the sealed letter.

" It happened one day that the King of Nubia was taking his rest in the pleasure-kiosk of the god Amen-Ra, when he heard the voices of three Ethiopians and the words that they said. The first said that if Amen would keep him safe from the anger of the King of Egypt he could put a spell on the people of that country so that they should not see the moon for three days and three nights. The second said that if Amen would be gracious to him he would put a spell on the Pharaoh so that he should be magically brought to the land of the Negroes and there beaten publicly with five hundred stripes, and transported again to his own land, all in the space of six hours. And the third said that if Amen would preserve him he would send a blight upon the land of Egypt that should last for five years.

" The king hearing these words ordered the men to be brought before him ; and he asked, ' Which of you said that he would cause that the people of Egypt should not see the moon during three nights ? ' And they answered that it was Horus the son of Tirit (the sow). Again the king said, ' Which of you said that he has power to cause the King of Egypt to be brought

Se-Osiris and the Sealed Letter

hither ? ' And they answered that it was Horus the son of
Tnahsit (the negress).

"Again the king said, ' Which of you said that he would bring
a blight upon Egypt ? ' And they answered it was Horus the
son of Triphît (the princess). Then the king called Horus the
son of Tnahsit to him and said, ' If thou canst do as thou hast
boasted, and canst bring the King of Egypt here, rich rewards
shalt be thine'; and Horus bowed himself and went out to do
the king's will. He fashioned a litter and four bearers in wax,
and chanted magical spells over them, and breathed on them
so that life came into the bodies of the bearers. Then he bade
them make their way to Egypt and bring back its king."

When Se-Osiris had read thus he turned to the Ethiopian
and said, "The curse of Amen fall upon thee. These words
that I have read, are they not written in the letter thou holdest
in thy hand ? "

And the Ethiopian bowed low before him, saying, "They are
written there, my lord."

So Se-Osiris continued :

"All happened as Horus the son of Tnahsit had devised, and
five hundred strokes of the kowbosh were given to the Pharaoh
in the presence of the King of the Negroes ; and afterwards
he was carried back to Egypt. Next morning he woke in great
pain, with his body very sorely bruised. He lay thinking, and
much perplexed, for he could not at first remember what had
happened to him in the night. He called some of his courtiers
and asked them how it was that he found his body marked as
with heavy blows. When the courtiers heard his words they
were amazed and much troubled, for it seemed to them that
madness had fallen upon the Pharaoh. They spoke to him
soothing words, saying that the gods would comfort him. Then
suddenly the king remembered all that had happened, and he
told his courtiers how he had been transported to Ethiopia and
beaten in the presence of the King of the Negroes ; and he showed
them his bruised body. Then they all cried out in anger and
fear, and Pharaoh sent at once for his chief magician.

"The chief magician, as soon as he saw the king, knew that

this had been done by the magic of the Ethiops. Pharaoh bade him hasten and prepare his magic against the coming of evening lest once more the Ethiopians should accomplish their wicked will. So the chief magician made many incantations over the person of Pharaoh, and afterward he entered into a boat, taking with him many rich gifts, and journeyed to the temple where dwelt Thoth, the god to whom all learning was known, and who could teach men magic spells which could not be gainsaid. Long prayers he made to the god, offering gifts, and then he laid down in the temple and slept. While he slept a dream came to him, and Thoth, the great god, in the figure of a man huge in stature and with the head of a bird, sharp-beaked and bright-eyed, spoke to him, and taught him the magic spells by which he could prevail against the wiles of the Ethiopians.

" In the morning the magician remembered his dream, and made haste to write down the potent spell. Then, journeying back to Pharaoh, he found him safe and unmolested. The night came once more, and the Ethiopians again tried to transport the king to their country, but their magic was in vain ; and Pharaoh, waking in the morning, told his magicians all that had happened, and how the negroes had not been able to work him harm. Then the chief magician rejoiced, and prepared counter spells to avenge Pharaoh on his enemy. He made a litter and four bearers in wax, and put a spell upon them, and breathed life into them, and sent them to bring back the King of the Negroes, that he in his turn might receive five hundred blows upon his body."

Se-Osiris once more turned to the Ethiopian and asked him if this reading were true ; and the Ethiopian bowing low replied that the words of the letter were as those which had been spoken.

So again Se-Osiris went on :

" The spells of the chief magician, taught to him by the great god Thoth, were successful, and the King of the Negroes was beaten in Egypt with five hundred strokes and carried back to his own land ; and he awoke in the morning sorely bruised, and there was great consternation among his people. So he sent for Horus, son of Tnahsit, and commanded him to go to Egypt

Se-Osiris and the Sealed Letter

that he might find out how to bring to nought the spells of Pharaoh's chief magician. But nothing that the Ethiopians could do would avail against the spells taught by the great god Thoth, and three times was their king carried to Egypt and there sorely beaten. The king laid all this to the charge of Horus, son of Tnahsit, and threatened him with a slow and

"A GREAT FLAME SPRANG UP"

dreadful death if he could not keep him safe from the vengeance of Pharaoh.

"Then Horus, much dismayed and in fear of his life, went to his mother, telling her that he must go to Egypt and try what he could do there; and she, knowing the power of Pharaoh's chief magician, warned him that he would suffer defeat. Yet he said that he must go, and she promised that she would do all in her power to save him if he was overcome. He journeyed to Egypt, and coming to the Hall of Audience he cried out in a loud voice, 'Who is it among you who is putting spells upon me?'

The Book of Myths

Then Pharaoh's chief magician answered, 'Ha! Ethiopian, is it thou who workedst evil against Pharaoh?' Then Horus cried out in anger, and caused a great flame to rise in the midst of the hall, whereat Pharaoh and his nobles were startled and alarmed; but the chief magician caused a shower to fall and put out the flames.

"Then the Ethiopian brought about a great darkness, so that none could see the face of his neighbour; but this the chief magician quickly dispersed. And in the same manner every spell cast by the negro was brought to nought, and at last, owning himself vanquished, he begged for mercy, and promised that never again would he work magic against Egypt. The king commanded that he should be put in a boat and sent back to his own land; and so it was done to him."

So Se-Osiris finished the letter, and turning to the king, he said, "Know, O king, that this Ethiopian now before you is the re-incarnation of Horus, son of Tnahsit, returning now after five hundred years to trouble Egypt once more. But the gods, foreseeing that this would happen, have sent me, the re-incarnation of the chief magician, to protect the country and save Pharaoh from the magic of the Ethiopian."

As he said these words a great flame sprang up and consumed the negro as he stood in the hall, so that when they looked for him not a trace remained. But after, when they looked for Se-Osiris, he also had disappeared, and never again was he seen upon the earth.

Then Pharaoh and all his court gave honour and glory to Se-Osiris, the greatest of all the magicians. But Setne and his wife grieved for their only son, whom they had loved so much, and who had been taken from them.

CHAPTER VI

MYTHS OF THE BABYLONIANS

Thy chariot is as a voice of thunder.
To the lifting of thy hands is the shadow turned.
The spirits of the earth, the great gods, return to the winds.
Hymn to the Sun-god

BABYLONIAN mythology, like the Egyptian, had its beginnings in a past that is very far away. Inscriptions that have been discovered tell us of gods who were worshipped five thousand years before the birth of Christ. The earliest records of the Babylonian people show them as highly civilized, with a flourishing trade and many industries, and a strong love of wisdom, learning, and art. They were as a nation deeply religious, and regarded their gods with an awe far greater than that felt by the Greeks, or indeed by most of the other nations, and consequently these gods are imagined as of a higher and sterner nature, freer from human weaknesses, and not given to mixing familiarly in the affairs of men. In later times, when riches and luxury had corrupted the stern and eager spirit characteristic of the early race, their gods became corrupted too, and took on a softer, less pure, less unbending character. A great part of the history of the Babylonians is told in the Old Testament, and the chief of their later gods—Bel or Baal, Ishtar or Ashtaroth, Dagon, Asshur, Rimmon—are familiar to us through references made to them in the Bible story.

Tiawath and Merodach

In the beginning of time before the earth was made there existed nothing but a great deep of waters, vast and undivided and bottomless. Darkness and silence reigned around it and within, and there was no movement above or below. In the

215

The Book of Myths

depth of the abyss dwelt the great goddess Tiawath, in form like a monstrous dragon, and with her the god Kingu, her husband. Many ages passed, and then came a stirring of the waters, and out of them arose forms of light who made for themselves a place high above the abyss and called it heaven. These were the high gods, good and beautiful; first to come were Lahmu and Lahame; then, many years after, came Ansar and Kisar, and from these two were born Anu, god of the heavens, and Ea, god of the waters.

The mighty Tiawath in her dark home knew what was happening above her and was angry. Her husband and her son were angry too, for all three felt that the very existence of beings beautiful and good meant danger to all things foul and hideous. They prepared to make war upon the gods of heaven, and hate urged Tiawath on to tremendous efforts. With labour intense and unceasing she raised a force to fight against her enemies. By her power she called forth from the deep a host of hideous monsters, dragons more fearful than herself, with writhing scaly bodies, fierce claws, and hateful mouths where rows of cruel teeth gleamed horribly; huge serpents, with burning deadly poison dripping from their fangs; loathsome dogs, savage as fiends; creatures with forms so horrible and misshapen that none but the bravest dared even to look upon them. Each new creation surpassed the former in horror and deadliness, and Tiawath went on untiringly until company after company of these dread monsters stood before her. At their head she placed Kingu. " Only conquer these hated gods," she said, " and you shall rule over heaven and the deep and all things shall be in your hand."

Far above, in the region which their own brightness had made light and beautiful, the gods lived happily and at peace ; until one day Ea, god of the waters, discovered the preparations that Tiawath was making in the depths below his realm. Ea came quickly and told the news to his father Anar. The elder god rose in anger, and with stern and terrible words that sounded through all the spaces of the heavens he denounced Tiawath and threatened her with the vengeance of the gods. Then, growing calmer, he called to him his son Anu, and bade him

216

Tiawath and Merodach

descend to the realm of Tiawath, and explain to her that the gods
bore her no ill-will so long as she kept within her own borders,
and did not trouble their peace. " Speak good words to her,
my son," he said, " and it may be that she will give up her evil
designs."

Anu, obedient to his father, left the bright realm of heaven and
descended to the abyss, where the monster, horrible and foul,
had her dwelling. He began to speak fair words, but Tiawath
turned on him, her wicked lips twisted into a hideous grimace,
her cruel teeth gleaming, and snarled with a fierceness that it
chilled his blood to hear.

Anu fled in dismay, and returning to his father, confessed his
failure.

" Go you, Ea," then said Ansar, " and see if you can do better."
Ea descended to the monster's abode, but Tiawath put him to
flight as she had put to flight his brother.

" We will try no more," said Ansar, " to prevail with this
monster by fair words. We will choose out one of our number
who shall attack her with all the strength of the gods, and shall
destroy her utterly."

The gods met in solemn council, and Merodach, son of Ea,
was chosen as their champion, and they set about making him
ready for the combat. First, it was decreed and written that he
should be victorious. Then, with solemn rites, the gods bestowed
upon him the rule of the entire universe, laying down their own
power that it might pass to him and he might command all
things.

" Let us now," said Ansar, when all the ceremonies had been
duly performed, " test the power which we have bestowed upon
Merodach."

In the midst of the assembly was placed a garment, and Merodach said over it words of power, commanding it to disappear.
Immediately the garment vanished from their sight; until
Merodach spoke once more commanding it to return, and straightway it was again in the midst of them

By these signs the gods knew that their power had passed to
Merodach, and that he had become their head and ruler. Every

moment he increased in glory, in majesty, and in strength, and the other gods did homage to him. " May he pour out the soul of the keeper of evil, and may the wind carry her blood to secret places," they cried, bowing before him.

They fashioned for him a marvellous weapon, mighty to prevail against Tiawath. In his hand he took a club, death-dealing and terrible ; on his back he bore a mighty bow. He made a strong net to cast over his dread foe. Weapons more potent than these he made, winds and tempests, whirlwinds and storms, lightning and hurricanes. The gods prepared his chariot and harnessed to it fierce steeds, who stood impatient to be gone, tossing their heads and foaming at the mouth. He filled his body with swiftness and his countenance with majesty and terror. He put on his helmet which blazed fiercely in the eyes of the beholders. Then he mounted his chariot, and the gods of light and beauty sent after him high words of cheer as the noble steeds dashed headlong toward the abyss.

Soon he saw the monstrous Tiawath. She had risen to the surface of the water, and floated there, huge in bulk, armoured with gleaming scales, her hideous jaws open, showing her cruel teeth. Noisome flames issued from her eyes and nostrils, and from the depths of her great body came horrible noises, shrieks and hisses and mumblings. The monstrous army that she had fashioned was arrayed near her, creatures terrifying in their foulness. Yet Merodach was not dismayed, but faced them bravely. " Mother of evil," he cried to Tiawath, " rebel to the gods and disturber of their peace, Anu and Ea came to you in friendship, speaking good words, but you would not hear them ; now I come in wrath, an avenger who shall smite and slay you, that you trouble the gods of light no more."

Tiawath heard, and in her heart she trembled, for Merodach sat, clothed in light, and blazing in righteous anger. She called to her mind the dark magic that she knew, and she cast many spells, black and evil, on her adversary. But none of them had power over him or could harm his shining body ; and while yet her jaws were open, shrieking loud curses, a tempest sent by Merodach rushed in and held them wide apart, so that she could

Tiawath and Merodach

not close them; it entered into her body, and passed through all the coils and windings of its monstrous bulk, smiting it as with many spears. Merodach threw his net over her, holding her fast, while with a blow from his mighty club he took her life. Then he stood upon her body and cut out her evil heart. The monster army led by Kingu came crowding upon him, but he cast his net over them, killing many and capturing many. He bound Kingu and took from him the tablets of destiny that Tiawath had given him.

Then Merodach rested, watching how, in answer to the prayer of the gods of light, Tiawath's blood was being borne away to secret places by the north wind. From on high the gods watched and rejoiced, and prepared to welcome Merodach the conqueror with glory and triumph. But his work was not yet ended. He arose and stripped Tiawath of her scaly skin, and cut her body in two pieces. From one he made the earth, and from the other he made the firmament to be a covering for the heavens. He set lights in the firmament—Nibiru, the chief light which made the bright day, and Nannaru the moon, shining softly in the night-time; and to Nannaru he granted one day of rest in each month. He established constellations as stations for the great gods, and he set the bow and net with which he had overcome Tiawath as stars to shine for ever. He took the fierce winds that had served him in the fight and gave them a law, forbidding them to wander over the universe, and allotting to them a certain quarter from which they must blow. Then he returned to heaven, and the gods of light received him with honour and triumph, giving him glory and praise for the work that he had done.

Thus was Merodach established as ruler in the heavens, and lord of the earth, which he had created. Very beautiful was the earth, but it had no inhabitants; so when the gods besought Merodach to continue his wondrous works, the great god bethought him of this empty earth, and he said, " I will make creatures who shall have their dwelling upon it, who shall serve the gods and pay them homage." He took dust of the earth and mixed it with blood from his own body, and fashioned it in the form of man, and gave it the gift of life; and thus man in his nature

The Book of Myths

is of the earth, yet bears within him something of the divinity of the gods.

Because of these great deeds that he had done, Merodach was chosen by the Babylonians as the chief of their deities. He married Zarpanitum, the goddess who blesses the earth at seed-time; and he established his court in the heavens, bringing light and happiness to men, healing them of their sicknesses, and helping them in their troubles.

CHAPTER VII

MYTHS OF THE HINDUS

Recite ye this heroic song
In tranquil shades where sages throng;
Recite it where the good resort,
In lowly home and royal court.
Ramayana

HINDU mythology, like that of Egypt and of Babylonia, is of very ancient origin, but, unlike these, it is still living and forms the present religion of many thousands of people. It is an exceedingly mixed and complex religion, made up of parts taken from the religion of each of the many races which from time to time have invaded and settled in the land. Its traditions and laws are summed up in two great epic poems, the *Ramayana* (story of Rama) and the *Mahabharata* (story of the Indian people). All the Hindus know these two poems, and regard them with the same reverence as that which Christians feel for the Scriptures. Both poems are very long, and it will only be possible to give here one or two incidents from each; and in order that these may be understood it will be necessary first to state briefly some of the most important principles of the faith set forward in the two poems.

The Hindu believes that in the beginning a god named Brahma created the world; with him were associated two other gods, Vishnu and Siva. Brahma then proceeded to the creation of man. From his mouth he sent forth the eldest born, whom he called Brahma, who was to be the priest of the race; from his right arm came Kshatriyas, knight and warrior; from his thigh Vaishyas, trader and agriculturalist; from his foot Shudras, the labourer, and servant of the other three. Through all the ages these four divisions, or castes, as they are called, have persisted, and still to-day the line which separates one from the other

The Book of Myths

is as strictly marked as ever. Each of the three higher castes has its special laws and observances, and the standard of conduct is very high ; anyone who fails to keep the law in every particular loses his caste.

From time to time teachers have arisen in India who have tried to weaken this system of caste. The chief of these was Buddha, who lived about 500 B.C. He taught that actions, not birth, gave a man his place among his fellows :

> To cease from all sin,
> To get virtue,
> To cleanse one's own heart.
> This is the religion of the Buddhas.

Around the name of this new teacher various legends gathered. He was believed to have had many incarnations, that is, to have lived many lives on earth, each of them in a different body, and the stories of these were fully told. He gained a vast following, though he did not succeed in his attack on caste, and the Buddhist religion spread through India and to the neighbouring countries of China and Japan.

The Hindus have many other deities besides those connected with the religions of Brahma and Buddha, but none of these are very important. For the natives of India, as for other primitive races, the world was peopled with spirits, good and evil, who had their dwellings in mountains and woods and streams, and there are many references to these spirits in Hindu legends.

The Story of Rama

I. Rama's Banishment

Dasharatha, king of the great and beautiful city of Ayodhya, had four sons, Rama, Bharata, Lakshman, and Satrughna. All of them were handsome and brave, but Rama was the handsomest and the bravest. In his youth he did so many great deeds that his fame went throughout the land ; he was besides wise and courteous, learned in all the learning of his country, and skilled in riding and in the management of elephants and horses. He won his bride, Sita, daughter of King Janaka, by drawing a great bow which had been given to one of her ancestors by the gods, and which no other mortal was able to draw. Rama used such strength that he actually broke the bow in two pieces. His father loved and honoured this noble son so greatly that when he felt himself growing old, he decided that Rama, who was the son of his chief wife, should be solemnly proclaimed as heir-apparent and should take the government of the kingdom into his hands. Every one was pleased except the youngest of the king's wives, Kaikeyi, and she at once set about trying to defeat her husband's purpose. Long ago the king had promised to grant her any boon she might ask of him, and so far she had never claimed this promise. Now she induced him to renew it, with a solemn oath; and then she asked that Rama might be banished to the desert for fourteen years, and that her own son, Bharata, might reign in his stead.

Dasharatha heard her in astonishment and dismay. He was bound by his oath, but he could not believe that his queen really wished him to do these terrible things. He offered her anything she might ask if she would give up this plan against Rama; but Kaikeyi would not yield. The king's entreaties, his tears and his despair could not move her, and so at last, very sorrowfully, he was forced to bring this dreadful punishment on the son he loved. Rama was banished, and Bharata was proclaimed in his place.

An outcry of grief arose from the whole people. Bharata himself, when he heard what had been done, reproached his mother bitterly, and vowed that he would never take his brother's right, but would only hold the throne for him until his return. Rama took the blow quietly and without complaint, submitting to his father's will. His wife, Sita, and his brother, Lakshman, insisted on going with him into exile, in spite of all he could say to dissuade them, and the three sorrowfully prepared to leave the beautiful city for the unfriendly desert.

The morning came, and Rama, Lakshman, and Sita mounted the dazzling car of gold that Dasharatha had provided, on which was piled their weapons and armour and many rich gifts that the king had bestowed upon them, and drove away through the city streets. The people raised moving cries of grief, and many rushed after the car, wailing and lamenting loudly. But Rama drove very swiftly, and soon outdistanced his followers. For two days he drove, until he reached the boundary of his father's country, and, after bidding it a sad farewell, they went on more slowly until they reached the banks of the blessed Ganges, crystal clear and shining river. Here they dismounted, and Rama and Lakshman changed their royal garb for the dress of hermits; and they sent back the car and its driver to Ayodhya. Then they crossed the river, and on the farther bank they encamped that night under a tree.

For many months they wandered through the forest, stopping at each lonely hermitage that they passed, and spending a few days with the holy men who dwelt there. They had many adventures on the way, and slew many rakshasas—a race of demons ruled over by Ravana—and many evil beasts. At last they came to Panchavati by the river Godaveri, a fair and fruitful land; and here Lakshman built a spacious dwelling of bamboo, thatched with fragrant leaves. The three rested for a time, and lived happily and simply as the birds. Jatayu, a mighty vulture, came to visit them, and told them that Dasharatha was his well-loved friend; and he vowed friendship to Rama and Lakshman and Sita, and promised to protect Sita while the other two were out hunting.

But they were not long left in peace in their simple dwelling. They were attacked by a great army of rakshasas, fourteen thousand, " proud as lions, big of mouth, courageous, delighting in cruelty." Rama, seeing their approach, sent Sita and Lakshman to a secret cave and met the great army, standing stedfast and alone. All the gods and spirits of the air came to watch the battle. With his terrible bow Rama slew the fourteen thousand, and, last of all, slew in single combat their leader. The gods showered down great blossoms upon him as a sign of their pleasure in his victory. Sita and Lakshman came out from their cave and gave him praise and thanks; and once again the three lived in their spacious bamboo house in happiness and peace.

The Story of Rama

II. The Stealing of Sita

When the news of this combat came to Ravana, king of the rakshasas, he was furious, and swore that he would take dread vengeance on Rama. He called together his counsellors, and they, when they had considered the matter, decided that the best way to injure Rama was to carry off his wife Sita. So they set to work to devise a cunning plan by which this could be done. One of the rakshasas was transformed into a deer of marvellous beauty; its horns were like twin jewels, its ears like two blue lotus flowers; its sleek sides were soft as the petals of almond-blossoms; its back was starred with gold and silver, its hoofs as black as jet, its haunches slender, its lifted tail every colour of the rainbow. In this form he went down to the fair meadows on the banks of the Godaveri and roamed about, taking care that Sita could see him from her shady house. She sat there, beautiful in her bright-coloured robe, adorned with shining jewels. When she saw the deer, she cried out in delight, " See how beautiful it is; catch it for me, Rama, or kill it and bring it to me that I may view it more closely."

" Beware ! " cried Lakshman. " This is no common stag. It is a rakshasa, disguised, to draw you to destruction."

" All the more reason, then," answered Rama, " that I should slay it."

He took his bow and arrows and followed the deer, that led him on, appearing and disappearing, until they were a very long way from the bamboo house. But Rama was so skilful a huntsman that in spite of all the efforts of the rakshasa deer, he at last sent an arrow that pierced its breast and it fell moaning on the ground. Then, knowing he was about to die, the rakshasa took his own form once more, and as a last act of service to his master, Ravana, he called out, imitating exactly the voice of Rama, " Ah, Sita ! Ah, Lakshman ! " as if he were in dire need of help. Then Rama knew that he had been beguiled, and feared that some evil was planned to be done to Sita in his absence, and he hastened back with a great fear in his heart.

Sita and Lakshman had heard that piteous cry for help. " Go !

225

go!" cried Sita. "Rama is in danger. He is calling to you to aid him. Go! go!"

"Not so," replied Lakshman. "Rama is unconquerable, and this is some fresh device of the evil rakshasas to draw me from you."

"'Twas Rama's own voice," cried Sita. "Who should know it if not I? False friend and brother are you, who will not go to the help of one who has loved you and been true to you always."

"Rama charged me to guard you," answered Lakshman, "and I should indeed be faithless if I left you."

"No, no," sobbed Sita. "What harm could come to me? Ungrateful monster, will you leave your brother to die?"

Many more reproaches she heaped on him, until at last Lakshman left her to do her bidding, though he knew that this was against the will of Rama.

No sooner had he gone, than Ravana, who had taken the shape of a handsome youth, a Brahman, came to the door of the bamboo house. "The forest knew him, the very trees stayed still, the wind dropped, the Godaveri flowed more slowly for fear."

Sita, thinking that he was a holy man, hastened to give him food and drink. He sat down and began to talk to her, praising her beauty, and after a short time he asked her to be his wife, promising that she should live in a palace, and have servants and all things that she could desire. Sita was terribly alarmed, and reproached him for speaking in this way to the wife of Rama. Then a fury came upon Ravana, and he took again his own shape, hideous and terrifying, with ten faces and twenty arms. He seized the fair Sita by the hair and dragged her into his golden car, which could go very swiftly through the air, without noise, or wings, or wheels. "Rama, my husband!" shrieked Sita, in terror. "Lakshman! brother! Oh, why did I send you from me!" But no answer came, and she cried to the trees and flowers, the river and the birds: "Oh, tell my husband that the wicked Ravana has stolen me away!"

The car rose steadily, and Sita saw that every moment was taking her farther from the earth, whence help might come. They rose above a tall tree, whereon sat the vulture Jatayu,

The Story of Rama

asleep. " Jatayu ! " called Sita, and at once he awoke and came to her aid. First he spoke mildly to Ravana, begging him to set Sita free ; but Ravana would not listen. With his red eyes blazing he sprang upon the vulture, and there in mid-air a fierce fight began. Ravana shot many arrows at Jatayu, and threw sharp-pointed spears, so that the bird's body was half hidden by the weapons that pierced it. Jatayu with his feet broke two great bows of Ravana's, and then, with a last effort of his failing strength, he attacked the golden car, so that it fell to the earth. But Ravana sprang up, seized the weary Jatayu and cut off his wings ; and the vulture fell down, all but lifeless. Sita sprang from the car and flung her arms round her friend's body, but Ravana roughly dragged her away, and once more set his car in motion, so that it rose quickly and flew like a strong-winged bird across the sky.

Then there was a great mourning in the land that Sita had left behind. Trees and flowers drooped in sorrow, the birds sang no more, the young deer went sadly ; the mountains lifted up protesting heads to heaven, while their tears ran down in waterfalls ; and the sun was darkened.

But Sita, still trusting that Rama would save her, looked round, even while the savage grip of Ravana bruised her tender flesh, for someone who would bear a message to her husband. As the car passed the summit of a mighty mountain she saw five great monkeys sitting there ; and stealthily taking off the veil of glowing colours that enfolded her bright head as sunset clouds enfold the glory of the sun, she let it drop among them. It was well that she did so, for very soon the car left the land and crossed a wide sea where no creature could be seen who might take news to Rama.

On the other side of this sea was Lanka, the great city of the rakshasas. Here Ravana brought his car to earth, and carried Sita off to his palace, where he shut her up in an inner room, with guards to watch over her ; and he set spies by the seashore, lest Rama should come that way to seek his wife. Then after a while he went to Sita, and once more prayed her to become his wife, tempting her with promises of riches and splen-

227

dour that should be hers. Sita answered as she had answered before, hiding her face, and sobbing in the anguish of her spirit. Then Ravana turned from pleading to anger, and called to the attendants he had set to guard the captive, women rakshasas ugly and hateful. He bade them, by means subtle or violent, so to torture her that her proud spirit should be broken.

SITA LETS HER VEIL FALL AMONG THE MONKEYS

Thus the beautiful and tender Sita was left to the savage crew, who surrounded her as fierce hounds crowd round the stricken doe in the forest. Yet her spirit was unsubdued, and each day she returned to the fierce king of the rakshasas the same answer; and she awaited with patience and confidence the time when Rama, her husband, should deliver her from this shameful captivity.

III. The Search for Sita

When Rama reached the bamboo house by the Godaveri and found that Sita was not there, sorrow and anger came upon him. Bitterly he reproached Lakshman for leaving her, and Lakshman owned his fault in meekness. Together they searched the neighbourhood of the house, until they found Jatayu, lying at the point of death. The vulture with his last breath told what had befallen Sita; then his head sank down, and he died. Rama mourned for him sorely. "Ah, Lakshman!" he said, "this kingly bird dwelt here in contentment for many years, and now is dead because of me; he has given up his life in trying to rescue Sita. Behold, among the animals of every rank there are heroes even amongst birds. I am more sorry for this vulture who has died for me than even for Sita's loss."

They burnt the body of Jatayu with due observances and rites, and then they set out to search for Sita. They had not gone far when they met a rakshasa, horrible to look at, and him they fought and mortally wounded. The rakshasa rejoiced when he knew himself near to death, and said, "I thank you, noble Rama, that in slaying me you have given me back my true and honourable form; for I was cursed by a hermit, and only by death can the curse be removed." They burnt his body on a pyre, and from it he arose, no longer ugly and evil, but as a noble youth, strong and handsome. As he mounted heavenward he told them of the five monkeys whom Sita had seen sitting on the mountain, and counselled Rama to seek their aid.

So the two journeyed onward until they came to this mountain, and there were the five monkeys, still sitting, sad and silent. The chief of them was named Sugriva. He had been the King of the Monkeys until his brother, Vali, had driven him into exile. When he saw Rama and Lakshman coming he feared that they had been sent by Vali to work him ill; so he fled away, and sent one of his followers, named Hanuman, to speak to the strangers. They told him why they had come, and he in turn told them of Sugriva's troubles, and, each trusting the other, they followed Hanuman, who called Sugriva forth, assuring him there was nothing to fear. Rama and Sugriva talked together and made a compact, walking sunwise round a fire that Hanuman had kindled. Sugriva showed Rama the veil that

Sita had thrown down, and told him of the direction in which Ravana had carried her. "If you will help me to win back my throne from Vali," he said, "I will bring great hosts of monkeys to fight for you, and we will attack the city of the rakshasas and bring your wife back in triumph."

Rama agreed, and immediately they set out for the city where Vali had established himself. The usurper could not stand before the might of Rama, and quickly he was driven from his throne, and forced to flee away. But by that time the rainy season had set in and they could do nothing for four months; and the delay grieved Rama sorely, for he feared that Sita was suffering horrible things, and might even be dead before he could reach her. But when the sky became clear, and the rivers and streams returned to their beds, Sugriva sent out messengers to summon the monkey host. They came in hundreds and thousands and millions, all the monkeys in the world, to follow where Sugriva should lead them.

The King of the Monkeys humbly offered all this host for Rama's service, making him their leader; but Rama besought Sugriva to take command, since he best understood this matter.

The first thing to do was to find out where Sita was hidden. Companies of monkeys were sent to search throughout the world, in all known lands, inhabited by men or by demons, but after a month all came back sad and dejected, for they could not find the city of the rakshasas. No one knew what to do next, until an old, old vulture, brother of Jatayu, who dwelt in a cave close by, came out, hearing his brother's name spoken, and asked for news of him. When the story was told, he said, "I saw Ravana carrying a maiden over the sea, and they travelled for more than a hundred leagues. Do you, then, cross the sea to bring her back, for I know that she is in the city of Lanka."

Then the monkey host marched down to the sea, but when they saw its great expanse they despaired of ever crossing it; for though they could make great bounds, some twenty leagues, some fifty, and some even a hundred, yet none could leap to the farther shore of this sea, and have strength for the return.

The Story of Rama

Then one of the monkeys called on Hanuman. "Hanuman, son of the Wind-god, our hopes rest on you. Remember how when you were yet a child you thought the sun in the sky was a fruit and sprang easily three thousand leagues toward it; prove thyself now a hero, and help us in our distress."

Then Hanuman roused himself and prepared for a mighty

HANUMAN'S LEAP

leap. He rushed up the mountain, so that it shook through all its caves, and stood on the top, praying to the Wind-god to bear him safely across. His body grew larger and shone like a flame, his hair bristled, and his voice was as the thunder. He gave a great spring, and right over the sea he flew, past rakshasas who tried to stop him, until he landed on a mountain on the opposite shore close to the place where stood the city of Lanka, and there he took again the shape that was usual to him.

From the mountain Hanuman saw the golden walls of the city

and the roofs of the high buildings. He waited until the sun went down, and then, making himself smaller and smaller until he was the size of a cat, he crept into the city and took his way to the palace of Ravana. The moon was full, and by its light he saw the moat and towers of the great palace and the dwellers within it. He sprang from court to court, searching in every chamber for Sita, but could not find her. When he had been through the whole palace he returned to the city wall and sat there, weary and cast down. He thought of what would happen if he returned without discovering Sita—the grief of Rama and Lakshman, the disappointment of Sugriva and his army. He imagined the wailing that would greet his news, the cries of sorrow and despair; and he said to himself, " I will find her, or I will die in the search. Better that than to return and see the broken hearts of my friends."

Then Hanuman prayed to all the gods of the Hindus, and fixed his mind intently on the object of his quest; and it seemed to him that he walked in the Asoka wood beyond the walls of the city, and that there he met Sita. At once he sprang up and hastened to the beautiful forest. The air was fresh and delightful, bright flowers glowed among the fair greenness of trees and grass, and woodland creatures darted hither and thither in happy security. Soon Hanuman came to a pavilion, wonderfully built, with golden pavements and silver walls. Round about it was a garden, and in the garden an Asoka tree which exceeded in beauty all those that grew around. Hanuman sprang up this tree and looked far out in the forest. He saw a round palace of crystal set on marble pillars; its stairs were coral and its floors of burning gold. Within the palace he saw a prisoner. She was lying, weak and wretched, on a miserable couch, moaning in her pain. Soiled garments covered her wasted figure, and around her were her guards, horrible she-rakshasas cruel and pitiless.

" This must be Sita," thought Hanuman, and his heart swelled with anger as he saw that beautiful lady, like a white dove among fierce vultures. Then, as he looked, he saw a splendid train proceeding through the forest. Ravana, followed by many women, gorgeously clad, came to visit his captive. When Sita saw him horror and dread overwhelmed her. She hid her face and sobbed in anguish. To all Ravana's pleadings she answered as she had answered before, that Rama was her husband, and she would have no other. Then Ravana grew angry and threatened her.

" Two months more I will give you," he said, " and then if you will not submit you shall be tortured and slain."

So he returned with his train of wives, and Sita in her misery crept to the foot of the Asoka tree and lay there, weeping. Hanuman's heart was glad when he saw her come, but he knew that he must use caution lest the rakshasas should hear him when he spoke to her. In low tones as he sat in the tree he recited the deeds of Rama, glorifying him, and Sita looked up and saw the monkey sitting there. Then he came softly down, and spoke to her in tones of humility and supplication. At first Sita feared that this was but another device of the rakshasas and that the monkey was an enemy in disguise. But when Hanuman showed her the signet ring that Rama had given him, joy took possession of her, and she thought herself already saved. Hanuman besought her to let him carry her away over the sea, but she would not. " Go you and bring Rama quickly," she said, " he alone shall save me "; and she gave him a jewel from her hair as a token to Rama, and told him, moreover, things known only to her husband and herself to prove to Rama that it was indeed Sita with whom Hanuman had talked.

So Hanuman left Sita beneath the Asoka tree, but he thought as he went, " Now that I have succeeded in the errand on which I came I will work the rakshasas all the harm that is in my power before I depart." Then he flew round the Asoka trees working destruction among them, and in the pavilion. The rakshasas who guarded Sita were afraid, and sent word to Ravana, who despatched a servant who was mighty at shooting with the bow to kill the offending monkey. But although wounded, Hanuman hurled a bolt which put an end to the servant's life. Then a whole host came against him, and a terrible battle was fought. Hanuman killed many of the rakshasas, but none of them could injure him, until a brother of Ravana loosed at him a Brahman shaft. This shaft had power which could not be gainsaid, and Hanuman, when he felt himself stricken, knew that he must submit. He fell to earth, and allowed the rakshasas to bind him as closely as they could with cords and bark, without resistance. For he knew, the cunning monkey, that if other bonds were added, the Brahman shaft would lose its power, and he trusted to his own skill to rid him of these other bonds. Besides, he thought that it would be well that he should be brought before Ravana and speak to him face to face.

His captors dragged him before their king, and there he told his story. He told of the monkeys' alliance with Rama and of all that had followed it, and advised Ravana to give up Sita lest a great vengeance should fall upon him. In rage Ravana started up and commanded that Hanuman should be slain; but his counsellors reminded him that as the monkey came as an envoy, his person was sacred.

"Set fire to his tail, then," commanded Ravana. So they fetched cotton soaked in oil and tied it round the monkey's tail and put a light to it. Hanuman bore the pain with fortitude, and quietly allowed the rakshasas to lead him in triumph through the streets of the city. All the time his keen, bright eyes were watching each winding of the way, each strong place, each opening, so that when he came again with the hosts of Sugriva he might be able to lead them aright.

Soon Sita, in the Asoka wood, heard by the shouts and clamour of the crowd that the monkey had been taken, and that Ravana had commanded them to set fire to his tail. Then she prayed earnestly to Fire, and begged him to be merciful to Hanuman; and at that moment the monkey's sire, the Wind, blew between the flame and his tail, so that while the fire still burnt, the tail was cold.

When Hanuman perceived that his pain had ceased, he gave thanks to Rama and Sita, whose power, so he believed, had delivered him. Great strength and courage came to him, so that he snapped his bonds and rose high in the air. Through Lanka he rushed, and with the fire at the end of his tail he set fire to one after another of the city's buildings, Ravana's palace,

and the palace of the princes, so that they were burnt with all
their treasures. Nearly half the city he burnt in this way,
before he came down to the sea, and put out the fire of his tail
in its waters. ‑ As he did so a horrible idea came to him. "Sup-
pose," he thought, that Sita has been burnt in the fires that I
have kindled." Swift as the wind, he flew back to the Asoka
tree, and there he found Sita unhurt. Quickly he renewed his
promise to rescue her, and started on his return journey across
the sea.

On the other side the monkey hosts were anxiously awaiting
him, and when they saw him coming they crowded down to
the shore and welcomed him with great joy. They brought him
to Rama, and there he told his story; and when Rama saw the
jewel that Sita had sent he wept with mingled grief and gladness.
He gave great praise to Hanuman and embraced him, calling
him brother; and Sugriva also praised and thanked the heroic
monkey.

IV. *Adam's Bridge*

As soon as Hanuman had left Lanka, Ravana hastily called
a council. He knew that it would not be long before the hosts
of Rama and Sugriva attacked the city, and he wished to make
some plan for meeting them. His generals boastfully declared
that the conquest of such a foe would be easy; but Vibhishana,
Ravana's younger brother, pointed out to him that ever since
Sita had been brought to Lanka misfortunes had fallen upon the
city, and evil omens had distressed the people.

" Give back Sita to Rama," he said, " for if you do not, greater
evils than these shall fall upon us."

Ravana, in a fury, vowed that not the gods themselves should
make him restore Sita; and he spoke so roughly and insultingly
to his brother that Vibhishana in his turn became very angry.

" I will suffer no more such words from you," he said; and
at once he called to his four personal followers, and they flew
across the sea to where Rama and Sugriva were marshalling
their host of monkeys for the march to the seashore. All were

smitten with a great surprise when they found by his words to Rama that he wished to ally himself with the enemies of his brother. Sugriva put no faith in him, but feared treachery, and was for slaying all five of the rakshasas. But Rama, always trustful because there was no guile in his own heart, made an alliance with Vibhishana and promised to set him on his brother's throne when Ravana should be defeated.

RAMA DRAWING THE GREAT BOW

The march was continued, and soon the seashore was reached. But how could the great host cross the watery expanse which stretched between them and the place which held Sita in captivity? "Do you, Rama," advised Vibhishana, "seek aid from Ocean, that he may help you to build a bridge."

So for three days and three nights Rama lay on a couch of grass, and fixed his thoughts intently on Ocean; but no answer came. Then Rama rose in anger, and took his bow, and loosed deadly arrows at Ocean, so that great storms arose distressing all the creatures of sea and sky. But still Ocean neither showed himself nor spoke; and then Rama took a Brahman arrow blessed with a Brahman charm, fitted it to his bow, and drew. A great darkness fell all around and the storm raged still more terribly. Ocean arose, richly dressed and decked with jewels, and with many mighty rivers in his train; and he spoke fairly to Rama, trying to appease his anger, and promised that he would help him to build a bridge, whereby the host could cross.

"Be it so," replied Rama; "but my bow, being bent, must send out the Brahman arrow. Where in your domain will you that it shall fall?"

"Over there, toward the north," answered Ocean, "is a region in which dwell evil spirits, rebellious to my rule. Let it fall there."

So Rama sent the arrow into the midst of that place, and it dried up and became a desert; but Rama blessed it, and at once it grew fruitful.

"Now," said Ocean, "I will tell you that there is one among your

THE BUILDING OF THE BRIDGE

host who is able to build this bridge with the help that I shall give him; and that one is Nala, whose father built the great city of the rakshasas." And having said this Ocean withdrew and hid himself once more beneath the waves.

Nala came forward and spoke to Rama.

"It is true," he said, "I can build the bridge with Ocean's help."

"Do so then," said Rama. "I give you command over the monkey host that they shall all do according to your bidding."

So Nala directed the monkeys that they should go to the forest and bring trees, and to the seashore and bring rocks ; and they obeyed him with eagerness, for the heart of each one was on fire to cross the sea.

A noise and bustle arose which drowned the roaring of the waters ; the monkeys darted hither and thither, bearing incredible loads. They climbed steep cliffs and hurled down huge masses of rock ; they brought palms and pomegranates, coco-nut and sweet Asoka trees, and purple and red and yellow blossoming trees. On the first day the bridge stretched out from the land for fourteen leagues, and by the fifth day it was finished—" broad and elegant and firm, like a line of parting of the hair on Ocean's head."

Then the great host poured across it with shouting and triumph, and the battle began.

(The story goes on to tell how, after desperate fighting, Ravana was killed, Lanka taken, and Sita restored to her husband. Dasharatha having died, Rama by the direction of the gods returned to Ayodhya, where he was received with great joy by the people and by Bharata, who at once restored to him the crown ; and Rama reigned long and happily over his father's kingdom. The full story may be read in *Myths of the Hindus and Buddhists*, by Sister Nivedita and Dr Ananda Coomaraswamy.)

Drona and the Princes

There was once in India two families of cousins, the Pandavas and the Kurus. They were princes, and, the fathers of both families being dead, they were brought up by their grandfather, Bhishma. Bhishma is one of the most noted heroes of Indian legendary history. He is the model knight—brave, chivalrous, wise, and kind—and in his youth he did many noble and marvel-

Drona and the Princes

lous deeds. In his old age he strove to bring up his grandchildren in true knightly fashion, teaching them to love virtue and knowledge, and to be just in all their dealings. When they were old enough to learn the arts of war, Bhishma sought anxiously for a teacher, but could find none to satisfy him, and so for some time he was their only instructor.

One day the boys were playing at ball in the forest outside the city, when one of them, throwing carelessly, sent the ball into an old well. They tried every means they could think of to get it back, but none availed, and their sport was stopped for the want of this ball. They were loth to give it up altogether, and go home, and they lingered, talking together, and trying to think how they could recover it. As they talked they noticed a man, thin and dark and in the habit of a Brahman or holy pilgrim, sitting on the grass near by them. At once they ran to him and told him their trouble. "Oh, Brahman, can you help us to get back our ball? All our game is stopped because it has fallen into the well, and we cannot reach it."

The Brahman raised his head and looked at them with a kindly smile on his dark face.

"What!" he said, "you are princes, and you have not learnt to shoot well enough to help yourselves in a little matter like this? See, I will throw this ring into the well after the ball. Now, if you will promise to give me my dinner—for I have travelled far, and am very hungry—I will take a few blades of grass, and with them I will recover both your ball and the ring."

"Give you your dinner!" cried the boys, "why, you shall feast sumptuously, and we will give you such presents that you will no longer be poor, if you will only do as you say."

"Very well, then," answered the Brahman, and he stooped and picked a handful of the long, coarse grass that grew all around. "Now see! By my magic I can make these blades of grass as potent as any weapon."

He held a single blade in his thin, brown fingers, while the boys crowded round him. Then with a quick, deft turn of his hand he sent it swift and straight down into the well. The boys bent over the edge and looked eagerly down. There it was, the soft, green blade. Its point had entered the ball, and it was standing out like a needle stuck into a cushion. Still they did not quite see how this feat, wonderful as it was, could help them to recover their ball. The Brahman took another blade and threw it ; and lo ! it pierced the top of the first blade, and stood upright and unbending. The young princes exclaimed in amazement, and as blade after blade was thrown and the curious chain grew longer and longer, their excitement rose, and they shouted aloud. At length the Brahman put the last blade of the chain into the hand of the eldest prince.

"Draw up now," he said ; and the prince, pulling at the chain, found it firm and strong. Up came the ball, but the boys scarcely noticed their recovered treasure in their astonishment and delight at the wonderful feat performed by this stranger.

"Now the ring!" they cried. "Let us see you bring up the ring."

So the Brahman fitted an arrow to his bow, and, taking careful aim, he shot it down the well ; and up it came again with the ring upon it.

"See!" he said, and handed them the ring. The boys were wild with delight. They poured out question after question, asking the Brahman how it was done, and could he teach them to do the same. The stranger answered them with kindly words, and smiled, pleased with their boyish enthusiasm. Soon they remembered that they had promised him a dinner if he would restore their ball, but this they felt was an altogether ridiculous reward for a man who could work such marvels.

"What reward can we give you ? " they cried. "Come with us now to the lord Bhishma. He will give you whatever you may ask."

The smiling face of the Brahman grew grave. "Go and tell Bhishma, the royal grandsire, that Drona is here," he said ; and he sat down on a stone by the wayside, and bent his head on his hands, giving himself up once more to his thoughts.

The lads rushed off, eager to tell the royal grandsire all about the wonderful stranger. Bhishma listened very attentively to the tale of the excited boys. Could this Brahman, he wondered,

Drona and the Princes

be the teacher he had been looking for? He knew something of Drona, whose father had been a very learned sage and great teacher, to whose dwelling in the mountains many pupils had flocked. Drona himself was noted for his learning and his simple life, which had gained for him, it was said, divine gifts of understanding and knowledge.

"Go bring the Brahman to me," said Bhishma; and the princes, who longed to see more of the wonderful man, trooped joyfully off.

"You are to come to the royal grandsire," they cried; and Drona rose and came into Bhishma's presence. He told his story—how he had married, and a son had been born to him, and for this son's sake he had left the home where he had lived in poverty, and had tried to win a position for himself by the help of some of the friends he had known in boyhood in his father's home. But instead of kindly help he had met only with coldness and scorn, and now there was nothing before him but to hold some humble position that would keep him from want.

"Come then to my household," said Bhishma. "Teach the young princes to shoot, as you only can teach them. No reward shall be too great for you if you do this, and whatever we give you we shall still remain your debtor."

So Drona came to live in the palace, and he taught the young princes the use of arms. They practised diligently, and one vied with another in shooting with the bow and throwing the dart. Princes and nobles from the country round came begging that they might share Drona's instructions, and every day his fame grew greater and spread more widely.

Of all his pupils Drona loved best Arjuna, the third of the Pandavas. None showed such devotion to the master as he did, and none practised so constantly and so earnestly shooting with the bow. One day, Drona, wishing to test his pupils, set up an artificial bird on the top of a tree. Then he ordered them to take their bows and stand ready to shoot at the head of the bird. "I will take you one by one," he said, "and see whose aim is the truest."

The young princes looked carefully to their bows, and each

chose the best arrow in his quiver, for each one longed to excel and gain the praise of the admired master.

"Come to me, first, Yudhishthira," commanded Drona; and the eldest of the Pandavas stepped forward. "Now take your bow, and be ready to shoot when I give the word. Do you see that bird on the top of the tree?"

"I do," answered Yudhishthira.

"Tell me exactly what you see," went on Drona. "Is it myself, your brothers, or the bird?"

Yudhishthira fixed his eyes stedfastly and said, "I see you, and my brothers, the tree, and the bird."

Three times Drona asked the same question, and three times the prince gave the same reply. "Stand on one side," said Drona, sighing deeply.

One by one he called up his pupils, and asked of each the question he had asked of Yudhishthira. All of them—Pandavas, Kurus, and nobles—gave the same answer: "I see you, and my fellow-pupils, the tree, and the bird."

Drona's disappointment grew deeper as he ordered one after another to stand aside, and marked their look of bewilderment and shame. At last there was only one left untried, and that was Arjuna.

"Come now, Arjuna," said Drona, and a smile drove the disappointed look from his face, for he thought, "He, the best of all my pupils, will not fail me." "Stand forward and tell me what you see."

"I see the bird, and that alone," answered Arjuna.

"Describe the bird to me," ordered Drona.

"I cannot describe the whole bird," replied Arjuna, "for I see only the head."

"Shoot then," said the master.

The arrow flew, and the bird's head disappeared.

"That is what it means to shoot," said Drona. "Learn, then, my pupils, that he who would hit the mark must first see the mark, which means to see that only."

By lessons such as these Drona trained the princes, till they all, but especially Arjuna, gained the skill in arms which filled all beholders with astonishment in the days to come.

Shiva and Uma

The great god Shiva sat on a sacred mountain of the Himalayas
sunk in profound thought. His body was smeared with ashes,
and his hair and his long green beard were matted and unkempt.
A tiger skin was bound about his loins, and over his shoulders
was drawn the shaggy undressed pelt of a lion. Still and silent

SHIVA

he sat, hour after hour, day after day. Around him rose a fair
forest, the tops of its tall trees shining in the sun ; in its depths
were unnumbered flowers, bright and beautiful, and brilliant
flitting birds, and bees that hummed in ceaseless activity. The
scent of sandal-wood was in the air; shadowy shapes of wood-
nymphs glanced from tree to tree, faintly visible in the radiant
sunlight ; music came, with glorious waves of sound. But the
great god Shiva saw nothing, heard nothing ; his mind was firmly
set in thought ; all his activity was turned inward ; he was cut off
from the scene around him by the intensity of his inward vision.

243

The Book of Myths

Then above all the sweet woodland noises there was heard another sound at which the woodland nymphs stayed their dance, and stretched forward their heads, listening intently. The birds rested on the wing, the bees ceased humming, and hovered in the shining air. Everything listened, save Shiva. It was the sound of footsteps—footsteps that came light and swift and joyous up the mountain slope. In another moment a maiden came in sight—a maiden so lovely that though her robe was stained and ragged the brightness of her beauty gave a new glory to the sunlit mountains. This was Uma, the wife of Shiva, daughter of the great mountain, Himalaya. In her arms she bore a jar of sacred water. Behind her came her sister and a train of ghostly attendants, moving noiseless, unheard, and but dimly seen.

When Uma saw her husband she smiled happily and came swiftly toward him. But he neither spoke nor moved. He did not see her as she stood beside him in her glorious loveliness. Then she came behind him and lightly placed her two white hands before his eyes.

Instantly the radiant sunlight paled, the air grew chill, everywhere was an awful stillness. Nymphs, birds, and insects hid themselves, shuddering in fear ; it seemed as if the whole earth were sinking into a deathly swoon.

But only for an instant. There came a blaze of light, fierce and scorching so that every corner of the earth was lit with its glare. On Shiva's forehead a third eye had appeared, that shone with consuming brightness. Its fierce rays touched the forest trees so that they shrivelled into blackened stumps, while deer and antelopes came rushing frantically from among them. It leaped from one mountain peak to another, and the great heights were consumed, with all their treasures of plants and gems. North and south, east and west it travelled, till all the world was ablaze ; and the sky seemed ablaze too as it reflected that awful light.

Uma, dismayed at the mischief she had wrought, clasped her hands and implored her lord to have pity on the fair world, and not consume it utterly. Then Shiva, roused from his inward

Shiva and Uma

thought, turned a look of loving-kindness upon the blazing, tortured earth. The flames sank, and a cool freshness came into the air. In a moment a peaceful earth lay beneath a radiant sun. The mountains rose proudly, the trees stood cool and green against a blue sky, and all living creatures were glad.

"Tell me, I pray you, O my lord," Uma implored humbly, "why this thing has happened. Wherefore sprang the third eye on your forehead?"

Her husband answered, "Sinless lady, when the light of my eyes was hidden, the world, of necessity, grew dark. To give it light, I created at once the third eye, but its fierce energy went beyond what I had intended, so that the world was consumed; and then, for the love of you, O my wife, I subdued the light, and restored the earth, so that it was once more moist and green."

CHAPTER VIII

MYTHS OF THE JAPANESE

In stones there are spirits,
In the waters is a voice heard :
The winds sweep across the firmament !
B. H. CHAMBERLAIN, *The Death Stone*

THE religion of the original inhabitants of Japan was a combination of Nature-worship and Shintoism, which means the worship of the dead. Their chief deity was Amer-terasu, the great Sun-goddess ; and there were also Thunder and Lightning gods, a god of the Sea, who was called the Dragon King, a Moon-god, a Wind-god, and many other personifications of the forces of Nature. Mountains and trees, flowers and animals were also worshipped, for the Japanese have always had an intense love of natural beauty. Besides these, every hero or noted man was after his death raised to the position of a god, and every Japanese worshipped his own ancestors. Later on in their history, when the religion of Buddha was introduced from China, they adopted most of the Buddhist myths and legends ; so that, finally, the mythology of Japan had to do with a vast number of gods not forming a definite hierarchy or family, like those of the Greeks and the Norsemen, but each having his own separate history and significance.

The influence of the Japanese love of beauty is seen in almost every part of the mythology. It is not beauty of a grand classic style, such as the Greeks worshipped, but a beauty of pure bright colour, graceful form, perfection of detail, exquisite finish. Everything in Japanese art is small and dainty and complete, and the legends have the same characteristics.

Jizo, the Children's God

Jizo, the Children's God

One of the best-loved of all the Japanese deities is Jizo, the god of the children. The Japanese people believe that when little children die they go to the "Dry Bed of the River of Souls." It is a grey, sunless land, and the children, looking around, can see nothing but shadowy heights rising against a pale sky, and dim valleys. No soft green grass or bright flowers grow in this dreary place, and the bare feet of the poor little ghosts tread the hard stones that line the river-bed. They remember their fathers and mothers and brothers and sisters left behind on the bright, warm earth, and they cry bitterly, heartbrokenly, as living children never cry, however great their grief. Then it is that Jizo comes to comfort them. His beautiful face is so loving and tender that when he smiles on the lonely little spirit children it seems to each one that he sees once more the dear face of his mother, and feels the touch of his father's kindly hand. Jizo is both father and mother to these forlorn little beings, so early called to make the great journey from life to death. He comforts, too, the mothers who are left behind; they know that their lost darlings have a friend who will love them and care for them.

Day by day these little ghostly children play around the great god Jizo, who looks down on them with smiles. His shining robes make a bright spot in that dreary land, and the children gather round him, piling up the stones of the river into little towers, which stand for prayers—one for father, one for mother, one for each of the friends they have left behind in the happy land of home.

This does not please the *oni*—the ugly, red-eyed spirits of evil —for the prayers are charms hindering them in their wicked work. They hover round, watching their opportunity, and sometimes they manage to overturn the towers and speak taunting words to the little helpless spirits. Then the children in their fright run to Jizo, and he hides them in the wide sleeves of his robe and drives away the hateful oni with his sacred staff.

There is a cave in Japan which is called the Ancient Cavern

and far within its depths is an image of the god Jizo. Here in the night-time the ghosts of the children gather, creeping softly from the Dry Bed of the River of Souls over the sea to the cavern. They gather the stones and build their little towers, offering their prayers to the gentle god. In the morning the footprints of their little ghostly feet can be seen all over the sand of the cavern, but the children have vanished ; for the dead may not look upon the sun.

There was once a poor Japanese woman who gained her living by rearing silkworms and gathering their silk. One day when she went to the temple to worship the gods she saw an image of Jizo, and as she looked at it she fancied that the god seemed cold. She went home and made a cap which she thought might be some comfort to this kind deity whom she loved. "I am poor," she said, as, returning to the temple, she placed the cap on the head of the image, "and I can only give you this cap which is a little thing and no fit gift to offer to a god. But my heart is full of love, and if I could I would clothe your entire body in the richest of clothing."

Some time after this the woman died. For three days her body remained warm, and so her friends would not allow her to be buried. They were very glad of this when, on the third day, she opened her eyes and rose from her bed as well and strong as she had ever been during her life.

She took up her old work and lived poorly and industriously as before, but she never forgot the wonderful experiences of those three days when her soul had been parted from her body. It had appeared, she said, before the great Lord and Judge of the Dead, Emma-O. The great god had looked angrily on her, and accused her of breaking the law of Buddha by killing silkworms for her living.

"Take her away," commanded Emma-O, "and throw her into the great vessel that is filled with fiery, molten metal."

The order was obeyed, and for a moment the woman suffered most terrible agony, and cried out in her anguish. Then suddenly the metal became cool and pleasant to the touch and all the pain ceased ; and the woman, looking up, saw Jizo, calm and

The Crystal Buddha

beautiful, with a loving smile on his face. He took her hand, and spoke comforting words, telling her that her sorrow was now to be changed to joy. He led her before the terrible Emma-O, and pleaded for her, telling how, through love and reverence toward the gods, she had offered out of her poverty a cap to the image in the temple. So earnestly did he plead that Emma-O relented ; and the woman, in great joy, left the dread hall of judgment, and came back to her own bright land.

The Crystal Buddha

Long, long ago there lived in Japan a maiden named Kohaku Jo, who was so beautiful and so good that she outshone all the other maidens in the country as a star outshines a candle. Her father, Kamatari, was a great State Minister, and he loved her dearly, and treasured her as something beyond measure rare and precious.

" My daughter shall mate with no common man," he often thought. " She is a fit bride for a king, so lovely is she, and so winning. Some day I shall see her reigning as queen of her husband's kingdom, and then I shall be content." He would not listen to one among the throng of suitors who came pleading to him for Kohaku's hand ; and she, not thinking of marriage, lived happily with him in his palace, the delight of his eyes, and the joy of the whole household.

The fame of this fair daughter of Kamatari spread through all the land, and reached at last the Emperor of the neighbouring country of China. As he listened to her praises it seemed to him that he saw her before him, and that her face was the face he had seen whenever he had thought of the lady whom he should love. He longed that her bright beauty might shine on his lonely palace and make it glad. Day and night the sweet face was before him ; and at last he sent for his ambassadors and heralds, and said to them, " Prepare now a train of my servants, and array it richly ; then go into Japan, to the palace of Kamatari, the great Minister, and say to him that Koso, Emperor of China, asks of him the hand of his daughter, Kohaku

Jo, that she may be his wife, and sit with him on the throne of the great country of China. Take gifts with you, precious and acceptable to the maiden and her father ; and say also that, according to the custom of the country, it shall be granted to my bride to choose three of the choicest treasures of her husband's kingdom to be sent back to her own land."

So it happened that one day Kamatari heard a great noise and commotion in the courtyard of his palace, and when he looked forth he saw that a long and stately train of men had entered its gates. They were dressed in the Chinese fashion, and at their head was borne a banner of yellow worked with a silken dragon. Kamatari gave orders that all things should be prepared to receive these guests, and he welcomed them with the pomp and ceremony that befitted the ambassadors of the mighty Chinese Emperor. When they had told their errand he was glad, and answered with courteous words, promising to give his daughter to the Emperor for his bride. Then the embassy retired, to rest in the chambers that had been prepared for them, and Kamatari bade a servant go find his daughter, and tell her her father would speak with her.

Presently she came, entering his room like a bright gleam from the golden sun. She bowed before him, and then sat down on the white mat at his feet, patiently awaiting his pleasure.

" Kohaku, my little daughter," said Kamatari, " to-day great honour has been done to you and to your father. The Emperor of China has sent ambassadors to ask your hand in marriage, and I have granted his request. You will be the bride of a king, my Kohaku, and one who is young and wise and good, and you will sit with him on his throne as I have seen you sit in my dreams."

Poor Kohaku's heart sank within her, and tears filled her eyes. She did not want to go away from her father and her own dear land to marry this strange king of a strange country. But she knew that what her father had done was according to the law and custom of Japan, and she knew, too, that he sought only her happiness ; so she rose and stood before him, her head bowed, and said, " I will do according to your will, my dear father."

The Crystal Buddha

Kamatari himself was sad at the thought of parting with his much-loved daughter. Yet he knew that the day must come, and he rejoiced in the thought of the destiny that awaited her. He told her many tales of the wonders and riches of this far-distant China. "Three of its choicest treasures you will be permitted to choose," he said, "that you may send them back to your home in Japan, to keep your memory fresh in the hearts of your own people."

Kohaku was silent for a moment, and her eyes were bright and thoughtful. Then she said, " I pray you, my father, that I may send these treasures to the temple of Kofukuji, where I have found blessing ever since I was borne thither as a small babe." And Kamatari answered that it should be so.

From among the maidens who had been her companions since her childhood she chose those who were to go with her to her new home, and the others who were to be left grieved sorely at the thought of the parting. Not many days were allowed her to make her farewells, for the ambassadors were eager to depart ; but before the last day came Kohaku paid a visit to the temple at Kofukuji, and at the sacred shrine she prayed for protection on her journey, and promised that the three choicest treasures she could find in China should be sent there for a thank-offering.

Then, very sad, although she tried to keep a brave heart, Kohaku set out with the ambassadors. The winds were favourable, and the ship passed swiftly over the sea. To the poor Japanese maiden the journey seemed all too short, for she dreaded the meeting with the Emperor. But when she saw his kind, handsome face, she lost her fear, and began to think that she might be very happy with him in this far-away land. As for the Emperor, his first glimpse of Kohaku changed the shadowy love that he had felt for the maiden of his dreams into a real and deep devotion to this timid, trembling girl, so fair and sweet, who had left her home and her friends to come to him. He tried in every way he could think of to please her and make her happy. He made his palace into a home of perfect and glowing beauty ; one so lovely, he said, must live among lovely things.

The Book of Myths

The very flowers in his garden, the trees, and the blue waters of the lake seemed to know that they had a fair new mistress, and to shine with a rare brilliance. Kohaku loved to wander in this garden; and that her dainty feet might not touch the ground as she walked, the Emperor called his gardeners and his goldsmiths and bade them make a path for their royal mistress.

THE TREASURES OF THE KINGDOM ARE DISPLAYED TO KOHAKU

"It is to be such a path," he said, "as has never been seen before. You must first carve many lotus flowers from silver and from gold, and these you must place so that the Empress may step from one to another, and her lovely feet not be soiled."

Thus Kohaku lived surrounded by beauty and by the loving care of her royal husband; and each day she grew happier, so that in her new home as in her old she became the light of the dwelling and the joy of all within it. But she did not forget Japan, and her father, and her childhood's friends; and she did not forget the promise she had made in the temple of Kofukuji.

The Crystal Buddha

One day she told the Emperor of this promise, and he joyfully ordered the most precious treasures of his kingdom to be brought and set before her that she might choose the three she most desired. From all parts of his Empire his servants brought in rare and lovely objects, until Kohaku was dazzled with the glory of the array. Wherever she looked she saw pure and glowing colour and exquisite form. How could she choose when everything was so beautiful? She set her mind on the temple at home, and tried to think what gifts would be the most acceptable and the most worthy; and at last she decided on a musical instrument that, if struck, would go on playing for ever; a box made of inkstone, containing a supply of Indian ink that could never be exhausted; and a crystal that shone like a star, shedding brightness and glory all around. Whoever gazed into this crystal saw, no matter from which side he looked, an image of the great Buddha riding on a white elephant, and he who gazed had peace in his heart for evermore.

The thought of giving these treasures to the temple at home made Kohaku's heart beat fast for joy, and she was all impatience to see them sent off. A skilled and faithful seaman, Admiral Banko, was appointed to convey the treasures, and the young Empress herself gave them into his charge, bidding him guard them with care, as sacred things. The ship set sail, and all went well until the coast of Japan was actually in sight. Then suddenly a great tempest arose. The ship staggered before the mighty winds that threw themselves upon it, shrieking like beasts who fall savagely upon their prey; the waves rose like mountains and broke like the shattering of great rocks; thunder crashed and lightning made a fiery path across the heavens. The brave Admiral did not fear for himself, but he grieved lest he should not be able to carry out the charge that had been laid upon him, for every moment he expected that his ship would be destroyed in the fury of the storm.

Then, as suddenly as it had arisen, the storm died. The sun shone, the black clouds disappeared, and in its place gleamed a sky of purest blue; the sea beneath was stirred only by the graceful, dancing motion of the sparkling waves. The ship steadied itself and sailed on, swift and straight, like a white bird. At once the Admiral rushed to see whether his treasures were safe. The musical instrument was there, and the inkstone box, but the crystal had disappeared.

Despair took possession of the Admiral. He felt himself an untrustworthy servant who had failed in the task that he had been set to do. He knew that the magic crystal was the choicest treasure of the kingdom, and he felt guilty of its loss, though he knew not how he could have kept it more safely. He almost decided to take his own life ; then he thought that it was his duty to live, and try if by some means he could recover the jewel ; so he made all speed, and very soon landed safely in a Japanese harbour.

At once he made his way to Kamatari, and told him what had happened. Kamatari was too wise to blame the Admiral, for he saw at once that the crystal had not been stolen by mortal hands.

" It is the Dragon King of the Sea," he said. " He raised the storm, and while it was raging he entered your ship, unseen and unheard, and carried off the jewel. It is, doubtless, now hidden in the sea, and we will try every means in our power to recover it."

He went down among the fishermen whom he saw on the seashore, and told them that he would give a great reward to the man who should restore to him the crystal. The fishermen eagerly set off and rowed out to sea, and let down their nets ; but though they worked hard, and searched the sea for many miles, they were at last obliged to return, having found no trace of what they sought.

Kamatari and the Admiral knew not what to do next, and were talking sadly together, when a poor woman, a shell-gatherer, with a baby in her arms, came up and bowed low before the great Minister of State.

" O my lord ! " she said, " if you permit me, I will go and search for the crystal. I have a stout heart, though I am frail of body, and I have a longing to succeed so great that it will give me strength. For the reward, O great one, I pray that you will take the babe who lies in my arms and bring him up as a

The Crystal Buddha

samurai,[1] that he may not be poor and ignorant as are these fishermen."

Her word touched the kind heart of Kamatari. He thought of his own daughter, and the love he bore her, and how, that she might be a queen, he had suffered the grief of parting, and sent her over the seas ; and he felt that this poor shell-gatherer loved her son in the same way, and was willing to suffer that he might receive good gifts. He solemnly promised that if she restored the crystal he would care for her son and bring him up as his mother desired. So the brave woman took off her outer garment, and tied a strong rope round her waist, giving the end of it into the hands of the fishermen. Then she took a knife and stuck it in this rope girdle, and without hesitation she plunged into the sea.

Down and down she went, past dark rocks and darting fishes, until she saw before her the enormous palace of the Sea King, standing upon the gleaming, golden sand. It was built of coral and ornamented with bunches of many-coloured seaweed, and from it shone a dazzling light. The woman swam nearer to find out whence came that shining glory. On the topmost pinnacle she saw the crystal Buddha she had come to seek ; but on every side of it were coiled fearful dragons, guarding the treasure. Their eyes were closed and they seemed to be asleep, so she swam softly toward the pinnacle, praying earnestly to the gods that she might be able to seize the crystal before the dragons awoke. With heart fast beating she put out her hand, snatched the jewel from its place, and sped away through the water. But on the instant the dragons awoke and came rushing after her with horrid noises, their great tails lashing the water, their hideous claws grasping after their prey. The poor woman thought only of the jewel that she held clasped in her hand. How could she keep it safe ? She took out her knife and cut a deep gash in her left breast ; then she thrust the crystal Buddha inside, and pressed the torn flesh down upon it. The pain was horrible ; it seemed to the woman that her life was going from her in great throbs of agony. But the blood that streamed

[1] A samurai was a military retainer; he was held in high respect.

The Book of Myths

from her wound was, in fact, her salvation, for dragons hate blood, and flee from it in fear; so that when these creatures came to the reddened water that surrounded the woman, with horrible shrieks they turned and swam swiftly back.

Then the woman was glad, for she knew that her task was accomplished; but her strength was ebbing fast, and she feared that she should not reach the shore alive. With a great effort she jerked the rope sharply; then her eyes closed, and she was only dimly conscious that she was being drawn through the water, slowly and gently at first, and then more swiftly as the straining eyes of the fishermen discerned her figure beneath the waves, and marked how limply it hung upon the supporting rope.

They laid her on the sand, and Kamatari bent over her, his face pale with fear, for her countenance was deathly white and blood streamed from a wound in her breast. "Alas!" sighed Kamatari, "she has given her life and given it in vain," for there was no sign of the crystal Buddha in her hands or about her clothing. The woman, though she was very near to death, heard his words. She lifted her feeble hands, drew the crystal from its hiding-place in her flesh, and dropped it into Kamatari's hand, where it glowed with pure splendour, not soiled or marred in any way. Then she opened her eyes and smiled at Kamatari a happy smile that told of a spirit full of love and peace. "Remember your promise," she murmured, and then lay back on the sand and died.

Kamatari and all those around felt their hearts strongly moved by the deed of this brave and simple woman, who had given up her life for love of her little son. Kamatari took the baby home to his palace, and there he was brought up with the same care and tenderness that had been given to the beloved Kohaku. As soon as the boy was old enough to understand, he was told the story of his brave mother, and taught to hold her memory in reverence. He grew up brave and good and handsome, and became a noble samurai. When Kamatari died he took his place as Minister of State, and gained great fame for his wisdom. On the shore, at the place where his mother had died, he built a beautiful temple in her honour, and to this day

The White Hare of Inaba

pilgrims come from all over the country and make their offerings in this temple, remembering the love and heroism of the poor shell-gatherer.

The White Hare of Inaba

The people of Japan believe that certain animals, particularly the fox, the cat, the badger, and the hare, have to some degree magical powers, and are able to influence the lives of men. The hare, they say, lives in the moon, and spends his time there in grinding in a pestle and mortar the drugs which are used to make the Elixir of Life. He often visits the earth, and he lives to a very great age. When he has lived for five hundred years his fur turns white, and then all good Buddhists should regard him with reverence.

The legend of the white hare of Inaba is a very old one, and well known throughout Japan. Long ago, the legend says, there was a king of the country who had eighty-one sons. Eighty of these princes were haughty and overbearing, and so jealous of each other that they were constantly quarrelling. Each thought that he was the one who ought to inherit his father's kingdom, and each wanted to marry the beautiful princess of Yakami, in Inaba, who did not want to marry any of them.

The one remaining brother was good and kind, and would have been friends with all the others if they would have let him; but though they quarrelled among themselves, they all united in hating him, and there were so many of them that he had no chance against them. They jeered at him and persecuted him in all sorts of petty ways, giving him always the hard and unpleasant things to do when they allowed him to take part in any of their expeditions and adventures. But he went on quietly doing his best and taking no notice of their ill-treatment, for he hated quarrelling, and was quite content to spend a large part of his time alone in the woods and mountains, among the animals and the birds that he loved.

At length the eighty princes decided to settle the question of who was to marry the princess by going to Inaba in a body and

The Book of Myths

asking her to make her choice. Each felt sure that he would be the favoured one, and as they travelled they quarrelled dreadfully, and said many hard words to one another. The eighty-first prince, who had come only that he might help to carry the baggage of the others, walked by himself, and to be out of the way of their loud voices and rough behaviour he fell some distance behind.

When the princes reached Cape Keta they stopped for a short time to rest, and one of them saw a white hare lying on the ground, shivering and miserable because he had lost all his fur and was quite bare. This was just the sort of thing to please these unloving and cruel brothers. It seemed to them quite a splendid joke. "*Ha, ha!*" they cried, "look at him!" The poor hare tried to shrink away, but they called to him and said, "Do you want your fur to grow again? Very well, then, run down and dip yourself in the sea, and then make haste to the top of a mountain where the wind may blow freely upon you." Then they went on their way laughing, enjoying the thought of the trick they had played upon the unfortunate animal.

The hare really thought that the brothers had pitied him, and had given him good advice. He ran as fast as he could to the sea and bathed himself in its waters. Then streaming with wet and very cold, he rushed up to the top of the nearest mountain. The keen wind blew upon him and pierced his unprotected body like a sharp sword. It dried up the water, but left the skin cracked and smarting so that the poor creature cried aloud in his pain. He knew now that the princes had played a cruel trick upon him, and he lay down upon the mountainside, moaning in shame and anger.

As he lay he saw a figure carrying a heavy bag come slowly along the path toward him. This was the kind prince, and when he saw the poor hare he stopped. "You are in pain," he said gently. "Your skin is bare and sore, and you are cold. How does it happen that you are in such a plight?"

The hare looked up when he heard the kind voice, and he knew at once that this was really a friend, who would not mock him as the other princes had done.

The White Hare of Inaba

"I will tell you first," he said, "how I lost my fur. I was on the island yonder, and I wished to go to Cape Keta, so I set to work to devise a means of crossing the sea. There are many crocodiles in the waters round about here, and I called out to them, 'I am trying to count how many crocodiles there are in the sea, and how many hares on the land; will you help

THE HARE AND THE BRIDGE OF CROCODILES

me?' They were very willing to do this, so they arranged themselves in a line, stretching from the island across to this point. Then I stepped from the back of one to the back of the next, counting each one as I passed. When I reached the shore I turned round and mocked at them. 'Do you think I wanted to count you, you foolish creatures?' I said. 'I don't care how many of you there are, or how many hares live on the land. I wanted a bridge to pass over from the island, and you have made one for me.' They were very angry at this, and the crocodile nearest to me lifted his head and snapped at my

beautiful white fur and tore it off so that I became as bare as
you see me." And again the hare laid his head on the ground
and wept.

"You played a horrid trick upon the crocodiles," said the
prince rather sternly. "I do not wonder they were angry, and
I think you quite deserved your punishment. Still, I am sorry
for you and will help you if I can. But is that all the story?"

The hare hung his head at the reproof, which was so gently
spoken that it made him feel, not angry, but very sad. "While
I was still lamenting the loss of my hair," he went on, "eighty
princes passed by. They told me that if I bathed in the water
of the sea and then ran to the top of a mountain and dried
myself in the wind my fur would come back to me. I believed
that they told me truth, and I ran joyfully to do as they said.
Alas! as you see, it has only made my sufferings worse than
before."

"Go now," said the prince, "bathe in fresh water and wash
the salt from your skin. Then take ripe sedges, scatter their
pollen on the ground, and afterward roll in it. You will find
that the sore places on your body will be healed, and that a
beautiful new coat of fur will grow upon you."

The hare went down to the river, scarcely knowing whether
he was being tricked again, but trusting the kind face of this
solitary prince. He bathed in the stream, scattered the pollen
dust and rolled in it; and behold, fur grew upon his back once
more, and he was covered with a beautiful, thick, white coat.

Delighted, he bounded back to where the prince still stood upon
the headland. "Thank you, thank you many times," he cried;
"and now in return for your kindness I will tell you of the good
fortune that is coming to you. You will marry the princess, and in
time you will sit upon your father's throne and reign over the land."

The prince could not believe that such good fortune would
ever be his. He loved the princess, but he had never dared to
hope that she would prefer him before his brothers. But when
he reached Inaba he found that the princess had refused every
one of them, and they were preparing, in very bad tempers,
to return home. If it had not been for the hare's words the

The Moon Maiden

modest prince would not have ventured to hope that he might succeed where his brothers had failed; but the thought of the good fortune that had been promised to him gave him courage. He presented himself before the princess and boldly asked for her hand; and he was delighted to find that she loved him dearly, and for his sake had rejected his brothers. They were married, with great rejoicings, and so the first part of the hare's prophecy came true. The second part came true also when the prince's father died, and left his throne to the one among his many sons who was kind and gentle as well as brave.

The Moon Maiden

Once on a time, in the spring of the year, a fisherman named Hairukoo, sat down on the seashore to rest. He looked round and saw the blue sea sparkling in the sunlight, and the tall pine-trees that made a dark background to the shining sand, and he said to himself that the world was very fair. Then, close to him, hanging on a tree, he saw an object so beautiful and so rare that he thought no more of the lovely scene before him but only of this one treasure. It was a robe made of pure white feathers, wonderfully fashioned, and soft to the touch as a swan's breast. He was just about to lift it from the tree when he saw a maiden dressed in a thin white garment coming toward him from the sea.

"The robe is mine," she said. "Give it to me, kind fisherman." She was a lovely maiden, and her voice was so sweet that Hairukoo found even more pleasure in looking at her and listening to her words than in handling the robe of feathers.

"Not so," he said. "I have found it, and I cannot possibly part with a thing so wonderful. It must be placed among the treasures of Japan."

The maiden clasped her hands imploringly, and cried, "But without it I cannot fly, and I shall never get back to my home in the heavens. Give it to me, kind fisherman, I pray you."

Hairukoo could not make up his mind to part with the wonderful robe, and he hardened his heart to resist her pleadings.

The Book of Myths

" No," he said, " I will not give it to you. I found it, and it is mine."

" O, give it to me!" cried the maiden. "I cannot stay on earth for ever. I long to return to my bright home in the heavens. Of what use is it to you ? It cannot help you to fly. But for me it means happiness and peace. Without it I cannot see again the fair Moon country that I love."

THE MOON MAIDEN DANCES TO THE FISHERMAN

For a long time Hairukoo persisted in his refusal, but at last he began to feel sorry for the poor Moon Maiden, and relented a little.

" I will give it to you," he said, " if you will dance here on the sands before me."

At once the maiden's face brightened. " I will dance for you gladly," she said. " I will dance the wonderful dance which in my home I dance with my sisters, and which makes the Palace of the Moon turn round, so that even men may see it. But I cannot dance without my robe of feathers."

The Moon Maiden

"I will not give it to you until you have danced," said Hairukoo. "If I do you will fly away up to the blue skies and I shall never see you dance at all."

The Moon Maiden grew very angry. "On earth it may well be that you break your promises," she said; "but among those who dwell in the realms of heaven falsehood is unknown."

The fisherman was ashamed, and handed the robe to the maiden without another word. She put it on, and drew from under it a musical instrument which gave forth the most delightful sounds. Then the maiden in a clear, sweet voice sang of the wonderful things that were to be seen in the Palace of the Moon, where thirty kings were throned in state. Fifteen of them wore white robes, and while they reigned the moon shone down upon the people of the earth; fifteen were robed in black, and under them the moon waned, until it was seen no more. While the maiden sang she danced also, her robe of feathers gleaming softly as it waved to and fro with the graceful movements of her body. Then last of all she sang of Japan, and blessed the country, promising that the gods would grant it fruitfulness and beauty.

Then her song became a chant in a language that sounded strangely in Hairukoo's ears, her feet left the golden sand, and her white robe of feathers bore her up and up, above the tops of the tall pine trees, and over the mountain. Still her song, so marvellously sweet, floated down to the wondering fisherman, who watched her as, like a lovely white bird, she mounted into the blue heavens until at last she disappeared from his sight, for she had passed into her own country and reached the Palace of the Moon.

CHAPTER IX

MYTHS OF THE CHINESE

Who made Heaven and earth ?
Who made insects ?
Who made men ?
I who speak don't know.
Miao Creation Legends

THE Chinese people have few myths, and not many of those are well known outside the mainland. Very little has been discovered concerning the beginnings of their mythology ; we do not know whether they evolved it themselves, or whether they borrowed its substance from other nations—perhaps from India. They believed that everything in Nature was inhabited by its particular spirit, and they went farther in this belief than most peoples, giving a spirit to stone and wood and iron, and even to articles of furniture and ordinary household objects. These spirits, they held, had once inhabited the bodies of men who had lived and died upon the earth, the ancestors of its present inhabitants. Their religion thus became a system of ancestor-worship, and this lasted for many ages, until Buddhism was introduced from India, and to a large extent drove out the earlier form of worship.

The Chinese led a secluded life for centuries, carefully shutting themselves off from intercourse with other peoples; thus their myths were not enriched by influences from other sources or cultures, remaining as simple tales. They have not formed a real part of the life of the country, loved and cherished, told and retold, by the finest minds of the nation, with fresh beauties added in each telling.

So literal are the mind and imagination of the Chinese person,

The Divine Archer

that when he thinks of the spirit world he tends to think of it as an exact reproduction of his own country, divided into the same number of provinces, ruled in the same way, so that of the multitude of State officials employed in China each has its spiritual counterpart in the other world. This conception produces such curious myths as that of " Mr Redcoat."

The Divine Archer

More than two thousand years before the birth of Christ an Emperor named Yao reigned over China. One day he was walking in the streets of his chief city when he saw a man carrying a bow and arrows, and round the bow was bound a strip of bright red cloth. The Emperor could not help noticing the man, for he was taller and finer looking than most of the Chinese warriors, and had an air of great distinction, though he was poorly clothed. When he saw the Emperor looking at him the man came up and prostrated himself.

" Pardon, O Celestial Highness," he said. " I am an archer, and I have come from the mountains where since my youth I have lived as a hermit. Now I wish to offer you my services, for I am skilled in the use of the bow, and can besides travel through the air on the wings of the wind."

" We will test your skill," said the Emperor. " Shoot now an arrow at the pine that grows on top of yonder mountain."

The archer bent his bow, and sent an arrow swift and true to the mark ; then he leapt upon a passing breeze, and mounting upward, drew out the arrow and returned with it to the Emperor.

" It is good," said Yao, delighted. " You shall enter my service, and you shall be called Shen I, the Divine Archer."

Not long after this time many terrible calamities fell upon the land. Ten suns appeared in the heavens and burnt up all the crops ; fierce winds overthrew the trees of the forests and the houses of the towns, while the rivers rose above their banks and covered great tracts of the country. Monsters appeared upon the earth, a great man-devouring serpent a thousand feet long, and huge boars, savage and of enormous strength. The

The Book of Myths

Emperor could do nothing to relieve the woes of his unhappy country, but he thought of Shen I whose powers were beyond the powers of mortals. He sent for him, and said, " All this misery is the work of demons who for some reason that I know not are troubling the land. Go then, take three hundred of my bravest warriors and destroy these demons that we may be at peace."

Shen I was glad to be sent on such a service, and determined to do his very best. He decided that he would first capture the winds which were rushing all over the country and doing terrible damage. He flew to the top of a high mountain, and looking down he saw at the base a curious monster. It had the appearance of a great white and yellow sack, and as he watched he saw it draw in a deep breath, and swell out to an enormous size. Then it blew from its mouth, and fierce winds rushed out shrieking over the land, while the monster shrank to a shrivelled heap. This it did again and again, so that Shen I knew that he had found the cause of the fierce tempests that had troubled them. He fitted an arrow to his bow and shot at the sack, and at once a fierce dragon rushed out and hid itself in a deep mountain cave. Shen I hastened to the entrance of the cave and sent an arrow into its depths, whereupon the dragon appeared with a drawn sword.

" Hence ! " he cried, " and do not dare to attack Fei Lun, the great God of the Winds."

Shen I's answer to this was to shoot another arrow which wounded the monster in the knee so that he fell to the ground ; and finding himself helpless before the archer, he threw down his sword and begged for mercy, vowing that he would from henceforward live in friendship with his conqueror. Shen I bound him with strict oaths that he dare not break, and then left him in order to perform the next part of his task.

He resolved now to find out what was causing the appearance of the nine suns, and he led his soldiers to the banks of a river whence could be seen a large expanse of sky. He saw in the distance three mountains standing side by side, and on the top of each he saw three marvellous birds, who were continually blowing out fire, which blazed with such fierce heat as almost

The Divine Archer

to shrivel the earth. At once he sent nine arrows, which pierced the birds one after another. The fierce light faded into a red glow, and gradually died away. Shen I then sent his men to the tops of each of the mountains, and there they found nine red stones, with an arrow fixed in each.

This second adventure having been swiftly accomplished,

THE WHITE RIVER MAIDEN RIDES BACK TO SHEN I

Shen I turned his attention to the floods that were covering great tracts of the land. He shot an arrow into the waters, which began to retreat with all speed and gather themselves up into the bed of the river. In the midst of the foaming, rushing torrent he saw a man clothed in white, and a maiden with him, and after them came twelve servants; all were riding on white horses. Shen I shot an arrow at the man and pierced his left eye, and he shot another into the hair of the maiden; immediately the whole company dashed off as fast as their horses would carry them. But the maiden soon drew rein, turned her steed, and came toward Shen I with the arrow still in her hair, which was of the palest gold.

"I thank you, courteous stranger," she said, "that you so guided the flight of your swift arrow that it did not take my life. I am Heng O, the younger sister of Ho Po, the Spirit of the Waters, and if you will I will be your bride."

Shen I looked on the maiden as she stood before him, tall and slender in her shimmering white robe; her face was fair and pale, and her voice sweet as the sound of running water. He bowed before her, well pleased so take her for his wife, and they went together to the Emperor. Yao praised Shen I, and gave his consent to the marriage, and made a great wedding feast for the archer who had served him so faithfully.

For a short time Shen I lived quietly with his wife, but soon the Emperor called upon him to finish the work that he had begun. This was but a small matter to the Divine Archer. An arrow in the left eye put an end to the great serpent, and then Shen I set cunning traps for the boars, by means of which they were all slain. Yao was delighted that his country was now free from the troubles that had oppressed it, and he bestowed on Shen I the title of Marquis Pacifier of the country.

Soon after this the Emperor called upon the archer to serve him once more. It happened that one of the daughters of Hsi Wang Mu, the Goddess of the Western Air, wished to visit her mother in her palace on the topmost height of the Kiun Lun Mountains. This daughter mounted on a dragon and flew through the air toward the palace, leaving behind her a streak of golden light to mark her passage.

The Emperor Yao saw this streak of light, and marvelled; so he called Shen I and asked him what it could be. Shen I at once mounted into the air, reached the path of light, and was carried upon it to the mountain. Here he found in front of him a great door, guarded by a horrible monster. As soon as the monster saw Shen I he made a hideous clamour, and called together a great company of huge birds, bidding them fall upon Shen I and slay him; but with one of his marvellous arrows the archer put the whole company to flight. Then, suddenly,

The Divine Archer

the door in the mountain opened, and a lady with ten attendants came out. This was Chin Mu, the daughter of the Goddess of the Western Air. Shen I bowed before her, and told her of the errand on which he had been sent, and she explained to him what had caused the streak of light that had been seen upon earth. Then she invited him to enter her house, and she bade her servants set food before him and attend to all his wants. Shen I, when he saw that she was well disposed toward him, found courage to make a request.

" I have heard," he said, " that you possess the pills of immortality. I beg you to give me one or two."

" That will I do," replied Chin Mu, " if you will build for me a palace near this mountain."

Shen I agreed, and at once set to work. He chose for the site a height called White Jade Tortoise Mountain, and he summoned all the mountain spirits to help him. In a fortnight the work was completed. Precious and sweet-smelling woods were used for the framework of the palace, the walls were of jade, the roof of glass, the steps of agate. Chin Mu was well pleased, and willingly bestowed the reward that she had promised.

" Receive this pill," she said. " It will give to whoever swallows it immortality and the power to fly through the air for any distance. But remember that a year's preparation is necessary in order that its full benefits may be received."

Shen I gave her many thanks and returned to the palace of the Emperor, to whom he told all his adventures. He hid the pill under a rafter in his house, and at once began the course of diet and exercise which should enable him, in a year's time, to receive immortality.

Almost immediately after his return the Emperor sent him out upon another adventure. This time he was bidden to vanquish a man called Chisel-tooth, who lived in a cave, and was known throughout the country for his evil deeds. With one arrow Shen I broke the long projecting tooth from which the man received his name, with another he killed him, and turned homeward, bearing the broken tooth as a trophy.

Heng O, left alone in the house, noticed that a most delicious odour was spreading itself through all the rooms. She looked round, trying to discover whence it came, and saw a beam of pure white light which she traced to its source in a timber under the roof. It shone clearly and stedfastly through the day and the night, and Heng O watched it in wonder. At last, urged

by her curiosity, she brought a ladder, set it up against the rafters, and mounted it. There, lying on a wooden ledge, she saw a small, round white object which was sending out a beam of purest light. She took it in her hand, admiring its soft glow, and then, impelled by some strange power that she could not resist, she put it in her mouth and swallowed it. At once she felt through all her body a wonderful lightness; she seemed to be no longer standing on the firm earth, but floating freely in space.

HENG O SEES THE BEAM OF PURE LIGHT

"I believe I could fly," she said, and stretched out her arms toward the open window. At that moment she heard sounds in the house, as if someone had just entered, and immediately after she heard her husband's voice. He came straight toward the place where she was standing, for he was anxious to assure himself that the pill of immortality was still where he had left it. Before he even greeted his wife, he put out his hand and felt along the ledge, and, of course, found nothing.

"O my wife," he said, "a terrible thing has happened. I left in this place a treasure beyond price, and it has vanished. Can you tell me anything about it?"

Heng O was in terror when she heard these words, and knew that she had swallowed the treasure for which her husband

The Divine Archer

sought. Scarcely knowing what she did, and thinking of nothing but how to escape his anger, she spread out her arms once more. Instantly she rose into the air, and found that she was able to fly easily and swiftly. She darted out of the open window and made her way onward and upward, thinking every moment that she heard her husband behind her. Shen I, indeed, had seized his bow and arrows, mounted a current of air, and started in pursuit of his wife ; but before he had gone far a strong gust of wind met him, whirled him round as it might whirl a dead leaf, and at last brought him to the ground. He started up again and looked around him, but could see not one dark speck anywhere against the blue sky. His wife had vanished.

Heng O continued her terrified flight until she came to an immense crystal globe, and on this she rested. There was nothing growing on the globe except cinnamon trees, and it was very cold. The icy air made her cough, and as she coughed the covering of the pill she had swallowed was sent out from her mouth. At once it changed into a pure white rabbit, and ran away among the cinnamon trees.

Poor Heng O felt very lonely and unhappy, far away from her home and her friends, alone in this frozen world, without food or shelter, but she determined to make the best of it ; so she drank some dew, ate some cinnamon, and lay down to rest.

Meanwhile Shen I had been caught again by the hurricane and carried up into a very high mountain. On the top of this mountain stood a wonderful, cloud-built palace. Its walls looked as if they had been made out of a piece of the bright blue summer sky ; its domed roof, which seemed to touch and pierce the heavens, shone with the glowing tints of sunset. Here lived Mu Kung, King of the Immortals, and husband of the Goddess of the Western Air. Shen I boldly entered the palace, and found himself in the presence of this great monarch. The king received him very kindly, and Shen I told him all about Heng O and the pill of immortality.

" Be comforted," said the king, " soon your labours will be over, and you will become an Immortal. As for your wife, do not blame her. She did only what fate decreed beforehand that she should do. She is now an Immortal, living in the Moon. To you I will give the Palace of the Sun, as a reward for the service you did in destroying the nine false suns that troubled your country."

Then Mu Kung called aloud, and a servant came at his summons. "Bring me here," commanded the king, "a red Chinese sarsaparilla cake and a lunar talisman."

In a moment the servant returned, bearing these things on a dish that looked like a silver star.

"Eat this," said the king, giving the cake to Shen I. "By its power you will be protected from the heat of the sun, and live in comfort in the midst of its fiercest rays. And this," taking up a small, flat stone that shone with a greenish glow, "will enable you to visit your wife in the Palace of the Moon; but though you may pass to her, she will never be able to come to you."

Shen I thanked the king for his gifts, and then he ate the cake, and put the talisman inside his robe.

"One thing more," said Mu Kung; "you do not yet know the laws which govern the sun's rising and setting, and so you must take with you the bird of the golden plumage, who by his notes will tell you the times when the sun must give to the earth morning, noon, and night."

"And where can I find this bird?" asked Shen I.

"You must take the charm which I will give you to Peach Blossom Hill, far away to the east, where lives the Dawn," answered the king. "From there you will see, in the middle of the Eastern Ocean, an enormous tree, several thousand feet high. It is called the fusang tree, and on its branches the bird of the golden plumage used to sit, and watch until the sun took its morning bath. Then it would give a cry, so loud and shrill that it shook the heavens and woke up all the people upon earth. So piercing was it that I ordered that it be put in a cage on Peach Blossom Hill, and since then it has called less shrilly."

Shen I took the charm and journeyed on to Peach Blossom Hill, where he was given the bird. "This bird," he was told, "lays eggs which hatch out nestlings with red combs, who answer him every morning when he starts crowing. He is usually called the cock of heaven, and the cocks below which crow morning and evening are his descendants."

Shen I mounted the bird of the golden plumage and rode swiftly toward the sun. Because of the sarsaparilla cake that he had eaten, the heat did not cause him any discomfort, and for some time he lived in perfect happiness and content. Then one day he thought of his wife, Heng O, and felt a great longing to see her. He took out his talisman, mounted a ray of sunlight, and flew to the Moon. When he saw the huge, frozen-looking globe, and the cinnamon trees standing alone on its bleak slopes, he thought what a desolate place was this, and how dreary a home for his wife. At first he could see no sign of her, but searching farther, he came upon her sitting sad and lonely in a grove of cinnamon trees. When she saw him she started up in affright, and would have fled from his anger. But Shen I spoke gently, trying to calm her terrors.

" Do not fear, my wife," he said. " I am not come here in anger. I am no longer an inhabitant of earth, and all that is past is forgotten."

He would fain have taken her back with him to his bright home in the sun, but that could not be ; so he set to work to build a palace where she might dwell. He fashioned it of cinnamon trees with diamonds and amethysts and rubies and emeralds wrought into the structure, and he called it the Palace of Great Cold. Then he returned to the sun and built there a palace for himself which he called the Palace of the Lonely Park ; and so he became Lord of the Sun, while Heng O was Lady of the Moon.

On the fifteenth day of each moon Shen I visits Heng O in her palace, and that is why at this time the moon shines with special brilliance.

Kuei Hsing and Mr Redcoat

One of the most widely worshipped of the Chinese gods is Wen Chang, the God of Literature. He presides over all the schools and colleges of the kingdom, and is always invoked

The Book of Myths

by those who wish to pass examinations. There are also two secondary gods of literature, Kuei Hsing and Chu I, and in the temples dedicated to Wen Chang, two smaller altars, one in honour of each of these gods, are placed on either side of the great altar.

The story that tells how Kuei Hsing became a god says that he was once a scholar, very clever and learned, but with an ugly, even a repulsive face. Every year an examination was held in the chief city of China, and the candidate who took the highest place was presented by the Emperor himself with a golden rose. On one occasion this prize was won by Kuei Hsing, but when he presented himself to receive it, the Emperor exclaimed in horror at the sight of his face, and refused to give the rose to a student of such unpleasing appearance.

Driven to despair by this terrible public slight, the poor prize-winner rushed away and threw himself into the sea. After he had disappeared beneath the waves, a sea-monster rose to the surface bearing him on his back. Kuei ascended to heaven, became a god, and was worshipped by scholars. In time he took his place as a lesser god of literature, and was represented as a very small man with the face of a demon, and holding a writing-brush in his hand. Even to-day it is common in China to hear people say of a candidate who has been placed first in an examination, " He stands alone on the sea-monster's head."

Chu I, or "Mr Redcoat," as he is more often called, is said to have been a native of China, who refused to marry a princess and live in the Crystal Palace, preferring a life of hard study which would enable him at last to become a Minister of the Empire. The legend concerning him, which is familiar to all students throughout China, has led to his being regarded as the god to whom examination candidates whose knowledge of their subject is somewhat scanty may make their prayer. An examiner, it is said, was one day marking the essays written by candidates at a recent examination. He came to one that was of such poor quality that at once he set it aside as a failure. Before he could take up another paper from the pile at his side the rejected essay was in some mysterious manner placed once more before him. At the same time he was startled by seeing

Kuei Hsing and Mr Redcoat

the figure of an old man, with white hair and beard, and wearing a long red garment standing beside him. The old man looked at the essay, nodded his head slowly and gravely, then looked at the examiner. It was clear that he wished it to be understood that the essay must be allowed to pass. The examiner could not doubt that this was a being from the spirit world, and he was so struck by the fact that such a being should take the trouble to interfere on the student's behalf, that it seemed to him he could do no less than grant the degree to a person so favoured. In China now, when a candidate is known to have but a poor chance of passing an examination, his friends comfort him by saying: " Who knows ? perhaps Mr Redcoat will nod his head."

CHAPTER X

MYTHS OF THE AUSTRALIANS

It was Time's morning;
Earth there was none,
No lofty Heaven;
Only a deep profound.

A T the time this book was written, not much was known about the religious beliefs of the native Australians and they were considered a primitive people.

In the first place, they were extremely superstitious ; they feared the magic of their 'medicine men' so greatly that if a native thought that one of these dread men having decreed his death had performed certain rites he would lose all hope and would very soon die.

The Aborigine, as the native is called, invented only crude and simple weapons ; he made no pottery ; he devised no methods of communicating with others at a distance save by the message-stick, rudely notched, and fire signals. His dwelling was never more than a mere shelter made from the bark and boughs of trees roughly arranged, and his art was limited to crude representations of familiar objects carved on rocks and trees and shells, and simple drawings and decorations with charcoal, clay, and ochre upon the walls of caves.

Nevertheless, although these men did not build temples or make images of gods, we have learned that they believed in another life, in Bullimah, the abode of the blest, or in Eleänbah Wondah, the abode of the wicked, and had visions of a Being who corresponds to the Christian ideal of a universal Father, and there is no doubt that the Australian Aborigine is possessed of an intelligence and a moral sense which link him with the rest of the great human family.

The Gifts of Byamee

It would be strange if it were not so, for the Australian native has descended from one of the highest races. Unfortunately for him, he became isolated in the great forests and spaces of Australia, and for countless centuries had no intercourse with his fellow man, otherwise we may be certain that this most ancient of all the peoples would have developed to a higher stage.

Fortunately, quite a number of native stories have been collected, and these reveal that the Aborigine had a mind which reached beyond his earthly home. They also show that while like other child-men he wondered at and often dreaded the things he did not understand, he tried to explain many of them, as did the ancient Greeks and all other child-men.

The Aborigine deemed that he was a part of nature, akin to everything around him, and life and death were shared with his brothers the birds, the animals, the stars, the trees, and all else that had their being in his wonder world of the Never, Never. From his beliefs sprung myths and legends which will take their place with those others which the world cannot afford to forget.

The Gifts of Byamee

Byamee was a mighty medicine man, and after his days on earth had been finished he returned to his own place, which is called Bullimah, or the abode of the blest. Here he sits for ever on a crystal rock which towers high above the clouds on the Oobi Oobi mountain ; his head and shoulders are as they appeared on earth, but the lower parts of his body form the top of the crystal mountain.

While Byamee trod the earth the plains and the hills were aglow with bright flowers that grew everywhere, but these did not spring up again, but faded and died, when the great Creator went away. The earth became parched and bare as though a drought had settled upon it, and as the years passed the golden time of flowers would have become forgotten but for the stories of the tribe which kept its memory green.

As there were no flowers, the only bees in the land lived in three trees which were sacred to Byamee, for they had been

277

marked by his hand and might therefore not be touched by men. The children cried for honey, but search as they would the women always returned with empty baskets, for the wirreenuns, their wise men, forbade them to gather the stores from the sacred trees.

Now, when the great Spirit who in all places is ever watchful for Byamee saw that the people did not touch the trees of his lord, much as they hungered for the sweet honey, he told Byamee of their obedience, and Byamee was pleased and commanded that a sweet food such as the children would love should spring from the Bibbil, or box-tree.

Ere long white spots appeared on the leaves of these trees, and from them flowed a syrup which hardened on the branches or fell in small lumps on the ground beneath. The children eagerly ate this food and the hearts of all were glad.

But although the tribe was grateful for this gift they never ceased to long for the flowers of which the stories told them, and seeing this the wirreenuns said among themselves : " We will go and seek the good Byamee. Surely he will grant the people's prayer and make the earth beautiful as when he dwelt among men."

They decided to keep the object of their journey secret, and one day they set out to the far away Oobi Oobi mountain. As they drew near, the great rock looked dark and forbidding; on every side were frowning walls that no human foot could scale. However, when they had almost lost hope they saw the steps which the spirits had cut in the rock to make a path for Byamee when he visited the earth, and with stout hearts they set their feet upon this mountain ladder. Up and up they mounted, and the staircase seemed unending. Three days they climbed, ever seeing high above them the same steep rocky walls, but toward the end of the fourth day they came out, well-nigh spent, upon a terrace on which a clear spring gurgled into a rocky basin. With grateful hearts they drank of this stream ; straightway their thirst was satisfied and their weariness was forgotten.

Close by was a circle of boulders, and the wise men walked

The Gifts of Byamee

into this and looked around. There was nothing to be seen, but suddenly a voice broke the great stillness. " This," it said, " is the place where men may learn of the wisdom of Byamee. What seeketh ye ? "

It was the voice of the All-seeing Spirit, and the wirreenuns told of the sorrows of the tribe that the earth should be bare and desolate, and how they had come to beseech Byamee to send again the flowers that he had taken away.

When they had spoken, the wise men were caught up as by a whirlwind and transported to a great garden where flowers bloomed in beauty and abundance such as they had never imagined. The sight was too much for them, and they burst into tears. But a moment later they were stooping low and eagerly plucking all the bright blooms that their hands could hold. Then, they had hardly straightened themselves from this joyous task than they were whisked through the sky again to the rock whence they had been transported.

Once more they heard the heavenly voice: " Tell the people that the flowers you carry shall be theirs for ever. The East Wind shall make them flourish on every tree and shrub. Never shall they cease to spring from the earth. Sometimes only a few will blossom, but when the East Wind does not bring the showers, and the blossoms are few, and there is little honey, then the Bibbil trees shall yield sweetness that the children may be fed. Take back these promises to the people; they shall never fail."

The voice ceased, and the wise men turned and went back with awed but grateful hearts. After some days they came safely to the place where the people awaited them, not knowing whether their wise men would return. The wirreenuns were greeted with shouts of welcome, and they were quickly surrounded by an excited throng of men and women who gazed with wonder and admiration upon the sweetly perfumed flowers. When they were told of the promises of Byamee they were wellnigh mad with delight.

When all had looked their fill upon the lovely blossoms, fresh as when they had been gathered in the heavenly fields, the wise men took them and flung them on this side and on that. They fell on the trees and the hills and the plains, and wherever they fell, flowers like unto them have sprung up ever since.

And this place is still called by the natives Ghirraween, which means 'the place of flowers.' The bees of Byamee cause the East Wind to bring refreshing rain down the mountain of Oobi

EMU

Oobi, but sometimes a drought will parch the land, and then the blackfellows wait hopefully for the change which they know must come, " For," say they, " the promise of the good Byamee will not be broken ; the flowers and the green grasses will come again."

How the Sun was Made

Long ages ago, before men lived on the earth and only giant birds and beasts roamed over the plains and through the forests,

How the Sun was Made

there was no sun, so that the world was in darkness save for the light of the moon and the stars at night.

On one of these sunless days Dinewan, the emu, and Bralgäh, the crane, were quarrelling. During the dispute Bralgäh rushed to the nest of Dinewan, and taking one of her great eggs she hurled it high into the sky where, falling with great force upon a heap of dry branches, it broke, and the yolk was scattered over the pile of kindling.

In a moment a flame leapt up, and very soon the heap of branches was a mass of fire, the glow from which lighted up the face of the world, so that all living creatures looked up in fear at the awesome sight.

The dwellers in the heavens also gazed with wonder at the great light, and a good spirit noted how beautiful the earth looked in the ruddy glow, and determined henceforth to make a fire every day. So he bade the lesser spirits, his servants, collect every night a huge pile of wood and set this alight at daybreak.

At first this fire burns slowly and it does not give out much heat, but

THE COOKOOBURRAH, OR
LAUGHING JACKASS

some hours later, toward midday, when the heart of the great pile is well alight, the heat is very fierce. As the day draws near to its close the wood is gradually consumed, and by sunset only the embers remain. These soon die out or are covered up by the clouds to be kept for lighting the fire on the morrow.

When it is nearly time for the fire to be lighted the spirits send the morning star as a warning to all on earth to be ready to greet the great light.

Some, however, sleep soundly and do not see the starry messenger, and so the spirits decided to send also a herald who would make a great noise. But who could they choose? As they were

The Book of Myths

debating among themselves suddenly the evening air bore to their ears the harsh cry of the laughing jackass.

"We will ask him to be our herald," they said. " If he will not, then we will no longer make the great fire, and the days will be dark on earth even as they used to be."

But the cookooburrah is a good-natured bird, and he readily promised to lend his aid. " The earth shall not lose the warm light that the people love," said he, and so it is that as the morning star grows dim his laughter tells the heedless ones that another day is dawning.

Parents forbid their children to imitate the laughing cry of the cookooburrah lest he be offended   A child who disobeys finds that an extra tooth grows above his eye-tooth.   This punishment is from the good spirits, who know that if their herald should refuse to utter his warning call the light of the world will cease to shine, men will die, and darkness will again take possession of the land.

PRONOUNCING LIST OF NAMES

KEY TO THE PRONUNCIATIONS

$\ddot{a}$ as in father.		$\bar{o}$ as in low.	
$\bar{a}$,, late.		$\bar{u}$,, duty.	
$\bar{e}$,, see.		g ,, go.	
$\bar{\imath}$,, high.		$\dot{g}$,, gem.	

Ægir, *ē'-gir*
Æsir, *ē'-sir*
Alcmene, *alc-mē'-nē*
Algonquin, *al-gon'-kin*
Alphæus, *al-fē'-us*
Amen-Ra, *a-men-rä'*
Amer-terasu, *a-mer'-ter'-a-soo*
Angur-boda, *än'-gur-bō'-da*
Ansar, *an'-sar*
Antæus, *an-tē'-us*
Anu, *ä'-noo*
Anubis, *a-nū'-bis*
Aphrodite, *af-ro-dī'-te*
Apisirahts, *a-pis'-i-rahts*
Apollo, *a-pol'-o*
Arachne, *a-rak'-ne*
Arethusa, *a-re-thū'-sa*
Arjuna, *är'-ju-na*
Artemis, *ar'-te-mis*
Asgard, *as'-gard*
Ashtaroth, *ash'-ta-roth*
Asshur, *ash'-ur*
Astarte, *as-tar'-tē*
Ate, *a'te*
Athene, *a-thē'-ne*
Augean, *o-ġē'-an*
Aurora, *o-rōr'-a*

Ayodhya, *a-yodh'-yä*

Baal, *bä'-al*
Balder, *bäl'-der*
Bast, *bast*
Bekhten, *bekh'-ten*
Bent-reshy, *bent'-resh-y*
Bharata, *bha'-ra-ta*
Bhishma, *bhish'-ma*
Bifröst, *bē'-frost*
Bilskirnir, *bil'-skir-nir*
Bragi, *Bra'-ġē*
Brahma, *brah'-ma*
Bralgäh, *bral'-gah*
Buddha, *bood'-a*
Bullimah, *boo'-li-mah*
Byamee, *bī-ä'-mē*

Caduceus, *ca-dū'-si-us*
Calliope, *ca-lī'-o-pē*
Centaur, *sen'-tor*
Centotl, *sen-totl'*
Cerberus, *ser'-ber-us*
Cherokees, *cher-o-kēs'*
Chin Mu, *chin'-moo'*
Chiron, *kī'-ron*
Clymene, *clim'-e-nē*
Cortes, *cor'-tēs*

283

The Book of Myths

Cyane, *sī'-a-nē*
Cybele, *sib'-e-lē*
Cyclopes, *sī-clō'-pēs*
Cycnus, *sik'-nus*
Cyllene, *sī'-lē'-nē*

Dag, *däg*
Dagon, *dā'-gon*
Danaus, *dan'-ā-us*
Dasharatha, *da-sha-ra'-tha*
Demeter, *dē-mē'-ter*
Diana, *dī-an'-a*
Dinewan, *din'-e-wan*
Dionysus, *dī-on-ī'-sus*
Draupnir, *drowp'-nir*
Drona, *dro'-na*
Dvalin, *dvä'-lin*

Eira, *ī'-ra*
Eleänbah Wondah, *el-e-ān'-bah won'-dah*
Eleusis, *el-ū'-sĭs*
Elli, *el'-lē*
Emma-Ō, *em'-ma-ō*
Epimetheus, *ep-i-mē'-thūs*
Eros, *ē'-ros*
Euphrates, *ū-frā'-tēs*
Europa, *ū-ro'-pa*
Eurydice, *ū-rid'-i-sē*
Eurystheus, *ū-ris'-thūs*

Fensalir, *fen'-sä-lir*
Frey, *frī*
Freya, *frī'-ya*
Frigga, *frig'-a*
Fulla, *ful'-a*

Geirrod, *gīr'-od*
Ghirraween, *gir'-ra-wēn*
Giallar, *gyäl'-ar*
Gioll, *gyol*

Gleipnir, *glīp'-nir*
Glooskap, *gloos'-kap*
Gna, *gnä*
Godaveri, *god-ä'-ver-ē*
Gordius, *gor'-di-us*
Grimnir, *grim'-nir*
Gullin-bursti, *gul'-in-burs-tē*
Gungnir, *gung'-nir*
Gunlod, *goon'-lod*

Hades, *hā'-dēs*
Hairukoo, *hīr'-oo-koo*
Halfdane, *half'-dane*
Hanuman, *ha'-noo-man*
Hathor, *hä'-thor*
Heimdall, *hīm-däl*
Hephæstus, *he-fes'-tus*
Hera, *hē'-ra*
Hercules, *her'-cū-lēs*
Hermes, *her'-mēs*
Hesperides, *hes-per'-i-dēs*
Hesperus, *hes'-per-us*
Hiawatha, *he-awä'-tha*
Hlidskialf, *hlids'-kyalf*
Hodur, *hō'-dur*
Hœnir, *hē'-nir*
Horus, *hōr'-us*
Hraesvelgr, *hrä-svelgr'*
Hrauding, *hrow'-ding*
Hsi Wang Mu, *hsi'-wang'-moo'*
Hugin, *hoo'-gin*
Hun-Apu, *hoon-a'-poo*
Hunbatz, *hoon'-batz*
Hun-Came, *hoon-ca'-me*
Hunchouen, *hoon-chow'-en*
Hunhun-Apu, *hoon-hoon-a'-poo*
Hymen, *hī'-men*
Hymir, *hē'-mir*

Idavold, *ē-da'-vold*
Idun, *ē'-doon*

Pronouncing List of Names

I-em-hetep, *i-em-hā'-tep*
Ifing, *ē'-fing*
Inachus, *in'-a-kus*
Indaba, *in-dä'-ba*
Io, *ī'-o*
Ionian, *i-ō'-ni-an*
Iörmungandr, *yer'-mun-gandr*
Ipalnemohuani, *i-pal-nem-oh-u-äni*
Ishtar, *ish'-tär*
Isis, *ī'-sis*
Ixion, *ix-ī'-on*

Janaka, *jan'-a-ka*
Jatayu, *ja-ta'-yu*
Jizō, *jiz'-ō*
Jötunheim, *ye'-toon-hīm*
Jötuns, *ye'-toons*

Kaikeyi, *kī'-ke-yē*
Kamatari, *kä-mä-tä -rī*
Kari, *kär'-ē*
Kepera, *ke-per'-a*
Kewawqu, *kē-wōk'*
Khnemu-Ra, *khnem-oo-ra'*
Khonsu, *khon'-soo*
Kisar, *ki'-sar*
Kiun Lun, *kyoon'-loon'*
Kofukuji, *kof-oo-koo'-ji*
Kohaku Jo, *koh-ä-koo'-jo'*
Kokomikis, *ko-ko'-mi-kis*
Kshatriyas, *kshat'-ri-yas*
Kuei Hsing, *kwū'-hsing'*
Kurus, *koo'-roos*
Kvasir, *kvä'-sir*

Lahmu, *lah'-mu*
Lakshman, *laksh'-man*
Lofn, *lōfn*
Logi, *lō-gē*
Loki, *lōkē*

Lorride, *lor'-rē-de*
Lybia, *lib'-i-a*

Mahabharata, *ma-hä-bhä'-ra-ta*
Maia, *mā'-ya*
Malsum, *mal'-sum*
Manitou, *man'-i-tu*
Mater, *mä'-ter*
Medecolin, *me'-de-col-in*
Melcarthus, *mel-car'-thus*
Merodach, *mer'-o-dak*
Midas, *mī'-das*
Midgard, *mid'-gärd*
Miölnir, *myel'-nir*
Mu Kung, *moo'-koong'*
Munin, *moon'-in*
Muspelheim, *mus'-pel-hīm*
Mycenæ, *mī-sē'-ne*

Nala, *na'-la*
Naunaru, *nan -a-roo*
Nereus, *nē-rūs*
Nibiru, *ni'-ri-boo*
Niflheim, *nifl'-hīm*
Nut, *noot*

Oceanus, *o-sē'-an-us*
Odin, *ō'-din*
Olympus, *o-lim'-pus*
Orion, *o-ri'-on*
Orpheus, *or'-fūs*
Osiris, *o-sīr'-is*
Ousimares, *ous-i-mar'-es*

Pactolus, *pac-tōl'-us*
Pamola, *pam'-ō-la*
Pamyles, *pam-ī'-les*
Panchavati, *pan-chä'-va-tē'*
Pandavas, *pän'-da-vas*
Peleus, *pē'-leus*
Penelope, *pen-el'-o-pē*
Persephone, *per-sef'-on-ē*

The Book of Myths

Phaeton, *fā'-e-ton*
Phœbus, *fē'-bus*
Phrygia, *fri'-oi-a*
Pleiades, *plī'-a-dēs*
Pluto, *ploo'-tō*
Poseidon, *po-sīd'-on*
Priam, *pri'-am*
Prometheus, *pro-mē'-thūs*
Ptah, *ptä*
Pulque, *pul'-ke*
Pygmies, *pig'-mēs*

Quetzalcoatl, *ket-säl'-ko-ätl*

Ra, *rä*
Ragnarok, *rag'-na-rok*
Rakshasas, *räk'-sha-sas*
Rama, *rä'-ma*
Rameses, *ram'-e-sēs*
Ran, *rän*
Ravana, *rä'-va-na*
Roskva, *ros'-kva*

Satrughna, *sa-trugh'-na*
Senecas, *sen'-e-cas*
Se-Osiris, *sā-o-sīr'-is*
Setne, *set'-ne*
Shiva, *shiv'-a*
Shudras, *shoo'-dras*
Sigyn, *sē'-gen*
Silenus, *sī-lē'-nus*
Sirius, *sir'-i-us*
Sisyphus, *sis'-i-fus*
Sita, *sē'-tä*
Siva, *sē'-va*
Skadi, *skä'-dē*
Skidbladnir, *skid-bläd'-nir*
Skirnir, *skēr'-nir*
Skrymir, *skrim'-ir*
Sleipnir, *slīp'-nir*
Sudri, *soo'-drē*

Sugriva, *soo'-grē-va*
Sulmoneus, *sool-mōn'-ūs*
Swart-alfa-heim, *swärt-alf'-a-hīm*
Syrinx, *sir'-inks*

Tantalus, *tan'-ta-lus*
Teheser, *te-hā'-ser*
Tezcatlipoca, *tes-cät'-li-pō-ka*
Thetis, *thet'-is*
Thialfi, *the-älf'-ē*
Thiassi, *the-äs'-sē*
Thok, *thok*
Thoth, *thoth*
Thrud, *throod*
Tiawath, *tī'-a-wōth*
Titans, *tī'-tans*
Tlaloc, *tlä-lōk'*
Tmolus, *tmō'-lus*
Tnahsit, *tnah'-sit*
Toltecs, *tol'-tecs*
Törmungandr, *ter'-mun-gandr*
Triphît, *trip-hēt'*
Triptolemus, *trip-tol'-e-mus*

Uller, *ool'-er*
Uma, *oo'-mä*
Utgard-Loki, *oot'-gard-lō'-kē*

Vaishyas, *vīsh'-yas*
Vakub-Hunapu, *voo-koob-hoon'-a-poo*
Vala, *vä'-la*
Valaskialf, *vä'-la-skyalf*
Valhalla, *val-hal'-a*
Vali, *vä-li*
Valykrs, *val'-kirs*
Vanas, *van'-as*
Vasud, *vä'-sood*
Venus, *vē'-nus*
Vibhishana, *vi-bhis-ha'-na*
Vida, *vē'-da*

Pronouncing List of Names

Vishnu, *vĭsh'-nu*
Vukub-Came, *voo-koob'-Cä'-me*

Wasis, *wä'-sis*
Wirreenuns, *wi'-rē-noons*

Xbalanque, *ex'-ba-lank'-e*
Xibalba, *ex-i-bal'-ba*

Yakami, *ya-kä-mi*
Yudhishthira, *yoo'-dhi-shthīra*

Zarpanitum, *zar'-pa-ni'-tum*
Zephyrus, *zef'-i-rus*
Zeus, *zūs*
Zodiac, *zō'-di-ac*